P9-CRO-772

THE WINE LOVER DINES

A Selection of Fine Recipes to Match the Wines of the World

Tony Aspler · Jacques Marie

Prentice-Hall Canada Inc., Scarborough, Ontario

Canadian Cataloguing in Publication Data

Aspler, Tony, 1939–
The wine lover dines

Includes index.
ISBN 0-13-960519-3

1. Wine and wine making. 2. Food –
Sensory evaluation. I. Marie, Jacques. II. Title.

TP548.A86 1986 641.2′2 C86-094442-5

Prentice-Hall Inc., Englewood Cliffs, *New Jersey*
Prentice-Hall International Inc., *London*
Prentice-Hall of Australia, Pty., Ltd., *Sydney*
Prentice-Hall of India Pvt., Ltd., *New Delhi*
Prentice-Hall of Japan Inc., *Tokyo*
Prentice-Hall of Southeast Asia (Pte.) Ltd., *Singapore*
Editora Prentice-Hall do Brasil Ltda., *Rio de Janeiro*
Prentice-Hall Hispanoamericana, S.A., *Mexico*
Whitehall Books Ltd., Wellington, *New Zealand*

ISBN 0-13-960519-3

Coordinating Editor: Sharyn Rosart
Production Editor: Shelley Tanaka
Design: Gail Ferreira-Ng-A-Kien, Janet Eidt
Illustrations: Suzanne Boehler
Manufacturing Buyer: Don Blair
Cover Photograph: Video Photo Enterprises. Kitchen courtesy of the Lippiats.
Composition: Attic Typesetting Inc.

Printed and bound in Canada by Alger Press

1 2 3 4 5 6 AP 91 90 89 88 87 86

Contents

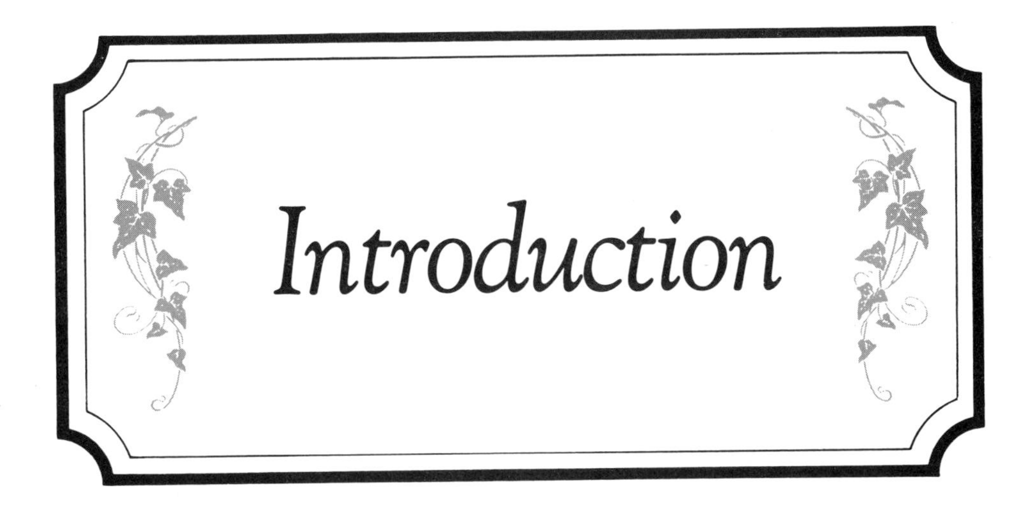

Introduction

Master chef Jacques Marie was born in Normandy where eating and drinking have been raised to the level of art. I was brought up in England, where it is not polite to inquire too deeply about the dish in front of you. On the other hand, the British are great wine lovers and acknowledged connoisseurs because they don't grow their own. Instead, they import everyone else's. (Actually, they do make wine in England, but not enough of quality to cause their neighbors across the channel to pale at their presses.)

Jacques and I decided to collaborate on a book that brought together our mutual experience of cooking and dining around the world. We realized that there are thousands of cookbooks on the market and almost as many wine books, but none that seriously addresses the problem of choosing the right wine for the right dish. *The Wine Lover Dines* is a ready reference book that takes a comprehensive look at the wines of the world in terms of the dishes of the world—a book that explains why a specific wine style goes with a certain dish.

In order to help you select a wine to accompany a dish, we have explained just how the human palate experiences taste. We have broken down the major wines of the world into categories, and in a series of easy-to-read charts, we have designated styles of wine for meat, fish, poultry, game, and so on. The wine style has been chosen not only for a named cut of meat or fish, but for the way you intend to cook it, whether it be fried, grilled, braised in a cream sauce or in its own juice. We have also prepared charts for soups, cheeses, desserts, and nuts.

In addition, we have suggested specific wines to accompany the most popular classic dishes of the world. And since we believe that wine is meant to be consumed with food, we have chosen recipes from wine-producing areas around the world to set off the wines of that region. As it is not always possible to find the exact bottle we refer to in your cellar or local store, we also offer a series of alternative, complementary choices from other wine-growing regions.

If France is represented by more recipes than any other country, that's because Jacques' heritage is showing. Coming from Normandy, he believes that the French know more about food than anyone else. My predilection for Italy is reflected in the wine selections.

The Wine Lover Dines is not a cookbook in the accepted sense. It is a guide to a total dining experience. We have chosen a variety of recipes from around the world as vehicles for experimentation in wine diplomacy—the art of creating food and wine alliances.

Don't look for *cuisine minceur* here: the recipes chosen are rich in the classical tradition. And generally these are not dishes that can be thrown together at the end of a business day. Some of them are intricate; a few involve ingredients unavailable in the average supermarket. But they are well worth the effort and time. You and your guests will appreciate the end result—especially if you pull off a diplomatic coup.

Bon appetit and cheers!

Tony Aspler and Jacques Marie

THE WINE LOVER DINES

THE MARRIAGE OF FOOD AND WINE

"I am tempted to believe that smell and taste are in fact but one single composite sense whose laboratory is the mouth and its chimney the nose."

—Brillat-Savarin

The Miracle of Taste

Food, at its best, is art. Any chef worth his salt tries to compose a dish using different tastes, in the same way that an artist uses colors. Wine served with food adds an extra dimension of color, texture, flavor and temperature. Like a seasoning, it can enhance the taste of a dish when thoughtfully applied.

Successful marriages have harmony and balance even when both partners might be completely opposite in character (say, Stilton with port or pâté de foie gras with Gewürztraminer), and there is nothing quite as sensual as a beautifully prepared dish accompanied by a glass of wine that sets it off to perfection.

But, unromantic as it may sound, our appreciation of the gustatory experience is largely based on chemistry. There are three general principles that determine how we taste:

- Taste and smell are inextricably bound together. (Remember how you took unpleasant medicine as a child by holding your nose?)
- We can only taste a substance if it can dissolve in water (saliva).
- A healthy person can differentiate among about five thousand smells, although these are thought to be varying combinations of four basic types: fragrant, burnt, acid and rancid.

Smell and taste are highly subjective perceptions, as is the vocabulary to describe them. Our ears and eyes pick up sound and light waves that can be measured, but there is no method to qualify a smell or a taste, except for the individual reaction to it.

SMELL

When we salivate over the smell of freshly baked bread or the bouquet of a 1953 Château Cheval Blanc, we are responding to nerve impulses transmitted to the brain from two small clusters of sensory hairs at the top of the nose chamber. These tiny sensors are reacting to the fragrances found in the substances. In the case of wine, the acids, alcohol, ether and aldehydes combine to produce the bouquet which is carried to the nose by its evaporating esters.

Our olfactory perception—our ability to smell—is biologically linked to our brain, our saliva glands and our facial and neck muscles. Just as our eyes and ears pass information to our brain cells which store that data in memory banks, so the nose passes on sensory data which can, with training, become one's personal bouquet bank. In fact, your nose can tell you seventy percent of what you want to know about a wine.

Our sense of smell, while not as developed as that of lower animals, can detect odors from a minute amount of a particular substance—as little as approximately four hundred molecules. But to taste the same substance, we would need 25,000 times as many molecules.

TASTE

When we rhapsodize over the flavor of bouillabaisse or baklava, we are reacting to messages delivered to our brain from the hair-like endings of taste buds on our tongues. Just as with smell, the taste buds are linked to the saliva and gastric glands, as well as to various facial and stomach muscles. The human tongue is like a sensory keyboard. If certain keys are touched, they will flash a signal upstairs which identifies the sensation as a taste.

THE SSBS FACTOR

While the human nose can distinguish some five thousand aromas and flavors, our tongue is only able to identify four basic tastes: salt, sweet, bitter and sour. Any of these four primary tastes can be experienced on all parts of the tongue, but there are specific areas that respond with greater sensitivity to these tastes. We experience the sweet taste of sugar on the tip of the tongue, saltiness on the tip and front sides, sourness along the sides at the back of the tongue and bitterness across the palate at the back of our mouths. And the tongue is not the only sensor in the mouth: the mucous membranes of the inside cheeks and throat, the lower lips and the roof of the mouth also react to such stimulation.

But not everyone responds in the same way, because we all have different numbers of papillae or taste buds. Babies and children have more taste buds than adults, and as we age the number decreases, especially after age forty-five. The average adult has a few thousand taste buds, and each is made up of forty to sixty cells which cluster together at different levels on our tongue. These individual sensory cells are constantly being regenerated, since they live only for about ten days. In addition, one's age, sex, state of health, mood, character, environment and even the time of day will determine the intensity of response to the taste of a given substance.

Our perception of the four basic taste sensations—salt, sweet, bitter and sour—is not simultaneous. For example, because the papillae that register bitterness are deeply embedded at the back of the tongue, a bitter taste is generally an aftertaste. A bitter taste is slow to develop, yet it seems to stay in the mouth for a long time. The effects of saltiness or sweetness occur immediately, because those papillae are on the surface of the tongue, at its tip and sides. The sensation of sweetness comes in a rush, reaches its peak in a couple of seconds and fades quickly away. The sensations of saltiness and sourness on the other hand, are also instantaneous, though they are more even and persistent.

The SSBS Factor is present in wine. When we sip a glass of wine most of the time we are able to perceive sweetness and sourness, occasionally bitterness and less often saltiness. But the SSBS Factor is especially important when it comes to the marriage of food and wine. If the wine is compatible with the dish, then the union is harmonious; if it is out of balance, then one partner dominates. Ultimately, your own palate is the judge. In matters of choosing the right wine for the dish you have prepared or ordered, you are the marriage-maker. There are, however, certain chemical reactions that occur when different foods and wines come into contact with one another; an understanding of these will help you to narrow down your choice and avoid the culinary equivalent of marital dissension.

SALTINESS

The Greeks used to preserve their wine by adding sea water to it. As late as the beginning of this century, Mediterranean wine makers preferred salt to sulphur dioxide as an anti-oxidant—one gram of salt was added to each liter to kill harmful bacteria in the wine.

Today, thank heaven, it is a rare wine that bullies the taste buds into sending a salty signal back to the brain. But for those occasional bottles that do, it becomes a significant element at the dinner table. The salinity of a dish will increase the secretion and density of the saliva in the mouth, and this will alter your overall response to a wine. And the presence of salt in wine changes the acidic reaction in the mouth.

The impression of saltiness can be given by a wine that has been over-treated with sodium-ion exchange or with calcium sulphate. Some mineral salts picked up by grapes through the roots in the soil may exhibit the same taste. Yet saltiness need not be detrimental. A wine that you find less pleasurable when drunk by itself may well complement certain dishes by the very fact of its residual salinity. For instance, Manzanilla, the Spanish sherry aged by the sea, picks up a salt character from the offshore winds at Sanlucar de Barrameda. The crisp, salt character of this fortified wine goes very well with fresh shrimp or salted nuts.

SWEETNESS

The sensation of sweetness is perceived mainly on the tip of the tongue, on the inner lips and the lower gums. The mouth responds immediately by secreting a thick saliva.

A wine will appear sweet to our palate because of its fruit sugars and alcohols (which are merely converted sugars). Of the many sweet compounds in wine the two most important are glucose and fructose (which is twice as sweet as glucose).

The alcohols in a wine buttress the sensation of sweetness, while tannins—a bitter taste—diminish it.

Glycerol, that colorless substance that sticks to the glass and runs down it as tears, is present in all wines. It is particularly heavy in sweet wines like port and Sauternes, but although it tastes sweet it is not a sugar.

A wine may contain less sugar and yet taste sweeter than another wine rated with a higher sugar content. It all depends on balancing acidity. Sweet wines have a richness of texture that can match rich foods. Delicately sweet foods like biscuits or pears need light sweet wines such as Asti Spumante, while heavier desserts with cream and butter require a wine of greater substance, such as Barsac.

BITTERNESS

The sensation of bitterness is identified along a crescent-shaped area at the back of the tongue. It is more of a feeling than a taste—like the effect of cold, strong tea on the tongue, cheeks and gums. That sensation of astringency or bitterness in wine comes from elements such as tannins (vegetable substances), polyphenols, as well as certain salts, acids and alcohols.

Tannins are present in the grapes themselves (try biting into a grape pip or stalk and experience the woody, bitter taste) and are also introduced into wines during the vinification process (when the fermenting must comes into contact with wood vats) and later while maturing in casks. Red wines, because they are fermented in contact with the skins, have a higher concentration of tannin than white wines.

The effect of excessive tannin on your palate diminishes a wine's vinosity—its generous character—by contracting the glands that secrete saliva. Tannin also hardens the surface of the tongue and mucous membranes, inhibiting the perception of other flavors.

From such a description it might appear that tannin is an enemy of fine wine. Far from it. The natural grape tannin and the tannins from the wood give red wines their potential for long life (if such other elements as grape sugars, acids and alcohol are in balance). Tannins contribute to the complexity of the bouquet and give a red wine structure. To make wines that will last for fifty years, vintners used to crush their grapes on the stalk, introducing quantities of tannin into the fermenting must. Today, the demands of the marketplace call for table-ready wines, and most wine makers will destem the grapes before they are crushed, to cut down the amount of tannin in the finished product.

The interaction of wine's hundreds of elements will soften tannin over years of bottle aging, although some wines that are heavy in tannin and lack the necessary balancing fruit and acidity may never evolve into a drinkable old wine.

By their very nature, white wines that are fermented and aged in stainless steel vats as opposed to wooden casks will have less tannin than reds that are macerated on the skins. But white wines can also be bitter because of the youthfulness of the vines, which can impart a "green" taste to the wine.

A small amount of bitterness in wines can have its place—a young red Bordeaux with evident tannin or an Amarone (Italian for bitter), for instance, can be a perfect match for a strongly flavored casserole or a spicy vegetable dish like ratatouille.

SOURNESS

If we identify saltiness on the edges of our tongue, we perceive the sensation of sourness in two parallel zones slightly more toward the center. This particular taste irritates the gums and inner cheeks, triggering an abundant secretion of thin saliva.

The sensation of sourness that we experience in wine comes from the acids it contains. Tartaric, malic and citric acids are all present in the grapes before fermentation. Succinic, lactic and acetic acids are produced during the alcoholic fermentation.

Each of these acids has its own distinctive flavor: tartaric has a very hard taste; malic tastes like green apples; and citric tastes like fresh lemons. Succinic acid is very intense and contributes to the building of vinosity—the essential quality of a wine—acting like sodium glutamate on food, as an enhancer. Lactic acid tastes of buttermilk; and acetic acid is vinegary. There are many other acids present in wine in tiny amounts, which all contribute to the complexity of flavor, but the above six are the main ones.

Of all the elements in wine, acidity is the most important when it comes to matching wine with food. When consumed by itself, a wine high in acidity may appear astringent and aggressive; but when served with complementary dishes, the wine will enhance their flavors and heighten the enjoyment of them. The combination of a high acid wine with a salty food, for instance (such as oysters with Chablis, sardines with Vinho Verde) is one of the simplest and most elegant partnerships; both elements play off each other to heighten the taste sensation of each.

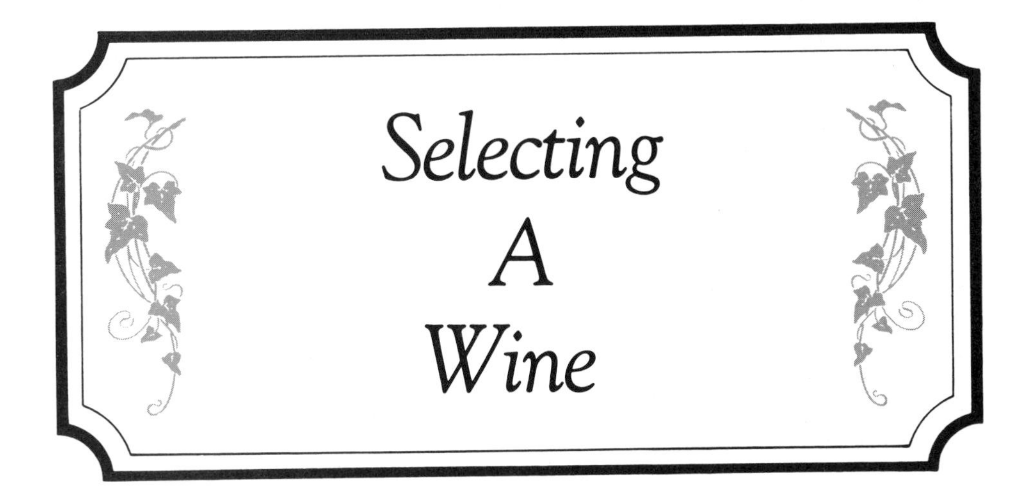

Selecting A Wine

What is it about wine that makes it such a felicitous partner for food? Apart from the aesthetic pleasure we derive from the sight of a glass of ruby-red claret or a golden Burgundy with hints of green, wine makes food taste better. As we have noted, in order for us to receive taste sensations all substances have to be transformed into solutions before our taste buds can respond. Wine speeds up this process.

Our palates are very sensitive, and they can tire and dull when subjected to the same taste over the period of a meal. Frequent sips of wine refresh and revive the palate and restore the acuity of our taste buds. This is especially true for fatty foods like duck and goose. A fine red Burgundy will cut through the greasiness that builds up on our tongues and clean the palate. By the same token, the acid in white wines cuts through the oiliness of fish or the saltiness of oysters and shrimp.

The principles for matching food and wine have been worked out by experience over the centuries to the point where they have taken on the authority of commandments handed down from Mount Sinai. Your table will not be struck by lightning if you don't follow them, but like all such homilies they do reflect the wisdom of accepted practice.

Everyone has heard the old cliche of "red wine with meat, white wine with fish." This injunction is rather like saying, "Never leave home without an umbrella." You know it's prudent but sometimes you just don't feel like carrying an umbrella, especially when the sun is blazing.

There is a good reason for not putting most red wines with some fish (the oiliness will make the wine taste steely), or certain whites with red meat (the wines taste thin and acidic). But there are dishes, such as salmon poached in red wine, that suggest you break the rules. And a fine white Burgundy can go beautifully with fillet steak and Béarnaise sauce.

The rules, then, are for the unadventurous. Ultimately, the choice is yours, but there are some common-sense principles that will enhance the enjoyment of your choice of wines.

1. DRY WINES BEFORE SWEET WINES Sweetness in a wine tends to dull the palate, whereas acidity refreshes it. A dry wine after a sweeter one will taste sharp and unpleasant.

2. CHILLED WINES BEFORE ROOM-TEMPERATURE WINES A wine that has spent time in the ice bucket or refrigerator will anesthetize the palate. This is a variant on the next principle, since whites are chilled and nearly all reds are served at room temperature. The exception, of course, is a white dessert wine after the red wine with cheese (unless you want to serve a Sancerre with the chèvre—but we're getting down to personal preferences here).

3. WHITE WINES BEFORE RED WINES Red wines have more body and in most cases more complexity than whites. If you taste a white after a red, it will seem thin and highly acidic. Again, the exception is sweet white dessert wines.

4. YOUNGER WINES BEFORE OLDER WINES Older wines exhibit more bouquet and complex flavors than younger wines. Work up to the best wine of the evening. If you serve it first, the following wines will suffer by comparison.

5. LIGHT-BODIED WINES BEFORE FULL-BODIED WINES Drinking a Beaujolais after a Côtes-du-Rhône or a Mosel Riesling after an Australian Chardonnay is rather like having your consommé after the pheasant pâté en croute.

6. WINES OF THE SAME REGION If you're serving a range of wines, try to select them from the same area. This way your guests can compare vintages or estates. Red Burgundy and Bordeaux on the same table don't really work together, but if you want that combination, drink the Bordeaux first.

7. MATCH THE WEIGHT OF THE WINE WITH THE WEIGHT OF THE FOOD Not literally, but you wouldn't put a ninety-five-pound weakling in the ring with a Sumo wrestler. By the same analogy, don't serve Frascati with lobster Newburg or Beaujolais with chicken curry. In other words, don't let the wine overpower the dish or vice versa. Avoid heavy whites with delicate fish, or light reds with richly spiced stews and casseroles.

8. LIGHT WINES AT LUNCH, FULLER-BODIED AT DINNER Don't serve powerful reds and luscious dessert wines at lunch. They're too heavy to enjoy. Save them for dinner. Choose lighter wines in keeping with the luncheon menu, particularly whites and rosés.

9. AVOID WINTER WINES IN SUMMER There are no such things as winter wines, but the idea is not to waste fine red Burgundies and Bordeaux on a hot summer night. Tepid wine in the heat kills your enjoyment of them.

10. AVOID MORGANATIC MARRIAGES Even in fun, don't serve Château Margaux 1953 with frankfurters and beans (otherwise the authors will be around to reclaim this book!). And don't bring out your fine wines for patio barbecues.

11. SELECT YOUR WINES TO BALANCE EACH OTHER You plan your menu to ensure that the dishes complement each other, that you don't have too many rich sauces or a delicately flavored dish following a highly spiced one. Think of your wines in the same way.

12. A FINE WINE DESERVES A FINE GLASS Don't serve good wines in plastic mugs, polystyrene cups, pewter tankards or the tinted glasses in the wrought-iron stand your aunty brought back from Benidorm. Part of the pleasure of a fine wine is to see its true color.

WINE SELECTION

When it comes to wine selection, start with your main course. Once you have chosen the wine for it, then work backwards.

If you only want to serve one wine throughout the meal, make sure that it will complement your starter course as well as the main dish and the cheese to follow. The most versatile wines in terms of matching the greatest variety of dishes are dry Champagne, dry German Riesling, white Burgundy or a dry rosé.

If you are ordering in a restaurant and four people all want different main dishes ranging from fish to poultry to game, the best bet is a white Burgundy.

WINE'S ENEMIES

There are certain tastes and smells that are inimical to wine and should be avoided.

BANANAS Boring fruit. Cook them in rum and butter, but avoid wine.

CHOCOLATE Sweet and bland. Reduces sweet wines to flabbiness.

CITRUS FRUITS Too acid. Will kill wine.

COFFEE Powerful, bitter flavor, too much for any wine, especially black coffee with sugar. Try a digestif like Cognac or a liqueur.

CURRY POWDER Use it sparingly and you can match it with a powerful Loire white or Traminer, but when used in curry, opt for beer.

EGGS Alkaline and difficult to match, although the Burgundians cook eggs in red wine; a cheese soufflé with red Bordeaux works nicely.

PICKLES Too acid and spiced.

SMOKED FISH OR MEAT Again, too overpowering and spicy. There are exceptions—smoked salmon and Gewürztraminer, for example.

VINEGAR The acidity in vinegar kills any sweetness a wine might have. If you must use vinegar (such as in a salad dressing), use a little wine vinegar, or supplement the vinegar with a little wine.

Wine Service from Cellar to Glass

If you are fortunate enough to have a cellar that keeps your wine at a consistent 13° to 15°C, you will want it to reach room temperature before serving. (Room temperature in centrally heated homes is invariably higher than red wines should be served; 20°C is ideal for full-bodied reds.)

Red wines should be brought to this temperature by standing upright in the dining-room several hours before the meal. Older wines, which have thrown a sediment, should spend twenty-four hours upright to allow the particles to settle on the base for effective decanting when opened. When uncorked, without agitating the bottle, pour the wine gently in one prolonged motion into a clean, dry decanter. Use a candle flame to watch the wine pass through the neck of the bottle. When the lees (sediment) begin to move up the neck, stop pouring. (If you're parsimonious like us, you can strain the lees through muslin or coffee filters into another receptacle to get that last precious glass!)

Decanting serves two purposes: it separates the wine from the sediment so that it looks bright and crystal clear, and it also introduces air into the wine, which activates the esters that carry the bouquet. Merely pulling the cork from the bottle and leaving it for a couple of hours does not aereate the wine. Only decanting does the job. (If you prefer to have the dusty, cellar-stained bottle on the table, you can always rinse it out and pour the wine back in.)

Most wines will benefit from being opened three to six hours before serving, except for venerable old bottles (twenty years or more) which should be enjoyed when the cork has been pulled. Young wines benefit from exposure to air and fine wines will open up more gracefully if allowed a few hours' breathing time.

It is our experience that the best Italian, Spanish and Portuguese reds require lengthy airing (six hours or more) to reach their peak; red Bordeaux and the Cabernet Sauvignon wines generally also need two to three hours.

WINE TEMPERATURES

There are no hard and fast rules when it comes to the exact temperature a wine should be served at—all of those wine thermometers and temperature bracelets are virtually useless, unless you want to see if you've worked up a fever trying to decide if your Beaujolais Nouveau is cool enough!

Very few of us have the kind of cellars that used to be the final resting places for the great wines of Europe—a slightly humid underground cave with an unvarying coolness of around 12°C all year round. If you visit the Bordeaux chateaux, for example, you will see the ideal cellars containing bottles that have been lying undisturbed for fifty years or more.

Today we keep our wines on a kitchen shelf, a rack in the closet of an apartment bedroom, under the stairs or—if we're lucky—in a walled-off area of the basement. It is all but impossible to maintain a constant 12 degrees. While this is the ideal storing temperature, ten degrees higher is not going to ruin your wines as long as there are no dramatic fluctuations.

In the great houses of England during the nineteenth and early twentieth centuries, the butler would bring up a claret from the cellar in the morning and stand it on the sideboard in the dining-room to reach room temperature for dinner. But room temperature in a drafty English manor is very different from that of an apartment in Manhattan or a bungalow in Sydney.

What, then, is the proper temperature for wine?

White wines should be served chilled, but no wine should be served so cold that it frosts the glass. First of all, you cannot taste or smell it. Second, you cannot appreciate its color.

In general terms, the sweeter the wine—still or sparkling—the colder it should be. Sweeter wines such as Sauternes should be served colder than dry Chardonnays or Sauvignon Blanc. Placing the bottle in a bucket half filled with water and ice cubes for thirty minutes is the most efficient way of bringing down the temperature of a wine. This ensures that the entire surface of the bottle will be subjected to the same temperature. For drier wines, twenty minutes is sufficient. (If the wine gets too cold, remove it from the bucket and let it stand on the table.)

The act of chilling brings down sweetness and allows the non-volatile acidity to express itself. (Volatile acids are diminished by cooling.)

If you have to decant an old Sauternes or any white wine that has precipitated its tartrates, it is prudent to chill the decanter into which you will pour the wine. (Incidentally, these tartrates are harmless. Composed of potassium bitartrate, they have no taste at all. You should not send a wine back that exhibits tartrates. They are, in a perverse kind of way, a mark of quality, even though they might look unsightly at the bottom of the bottle.)

Red wines should be served no warmer than 20°C (which is lower than most people keep their thermostat). A few degrees less is recommended for very mature fine wines.

An overly warm red wine that is lukewarm on the palate will seem flat and flabby, but if the wine is young and shows a lot of tannin and acidity, a degree or two over the 20° limit will mask its harshness.

Light reds, like Beaujolais, Chinon, Bardolino and Valpolicella, can be lightly chilled; in fact, they display their fruitiness better this way.

Sparkling wines should always be chilled. There's nothing worse than a glass of tepid Champagne. Chilling also activates the bubbles. (A warm glass of Champagne will explode with foam when the bottle is opened, but it will go quite flat very soon.)

Rosé wines should be treated like dry whites. **Sherries** and **Madeiras** should be served lightly chilled if dry and just below room temperature (15°C to 18°C) if mature and sweet. **Port,** if white, should be chilled or served on ice as an aperitif. Tawny port can also be served cool, while vintage port should be served at the same temperature as claret or Burgundy.

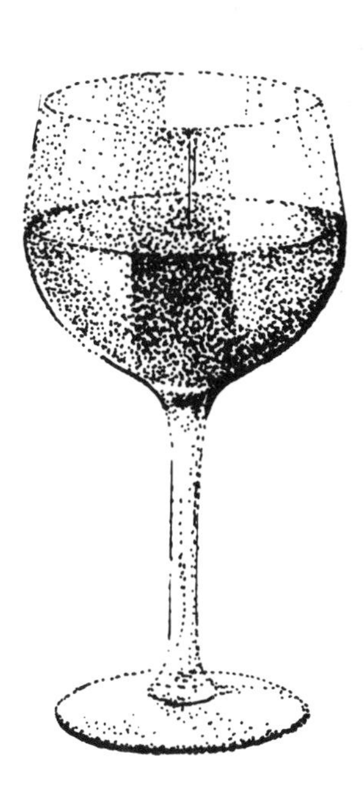

Cooking with Wine

If food were only sustenance, we might as well take it in pill form. Why not ensure that mealtimes are a pleasure by bringing out and enhancing the fresh flavors of the food we cook?

Nothing lifts a dish out of the commonplace and gives it style and flair than the addition of wine to the cooking pot or pan. Wine can add as much to a dish as herbs and spices. Judiciously applied, it can make a cook look like a chef.

The use of wine is central to the classical French and Italian as well as the country culinary traditions. Remove it from the kitchen and you reduce the sumptuous gastronomic palette of colors to monochrome. The smell of the evaporating spirit mingling with the other kitchen aromas is the best aperitif of all, setting the gastric juices flowing. But as in all things, excess is worse than nothing at all. Too much wine in a dish can be as unappealing as a wine glass accidentally toppled into your spaghetti.

A good table wine is a product of Nature, the result of the fermentation of sun-ripened grapes. Wine contains trace amounts of all thirteen minerals needed to support human life as well as several vitamins. It is healthier for you than most urban drinking water.

When you cook with wine, you are not consuming alcohol. The alcohols in wine are very volatile, and they evaporate at temperatures well below the boiling point of water. No cook worth his or her salt would add raw wine to a sauce without cooking it (the alcohol will spoil the taste and the winey flavor will predominate). If you want to be doubly sure that the alcohol has been evaporated, you can bring the wine to a quick boil before adding it to the food, but this is not really necessary. (When the alcohol is evaporated off in the cooking process, the caloric content is also reduced.)

Cooking with wine is not as expensive as most people think. The amount of wine added to a dish for two rarely exceeds a cup. So there is no need to open a second bottle. You'll have enough left to serve with the meal. If you want to buy wine specifically for cooking, you need only look for an inexpensive, sound, natural wine. And you can always recork what you don't use and keep it in the refrigerator.

There are three ways of combining food and wine: in the glass, as a marinade or in the cooking pot. If your recipe calls for the use of wine or spirits in preparing a dish, here are some helpful tips.

MARINADES

- Wine is used as a marinade to tenderize, flavor and preserve meat and game. For best results use a cool marinade overnight in the refrigerator. If you're in a hurry, warm the marinade and let the meat marinate at room temperature.
- Most red-wine marinades require oil to help lock in the flavor and aroma of the wine.
- White-wine marinades are used for flavoring rather than tenderizing. Usually the marinade will be required for the sauce, so don't over-season it.
- Most wine marinades can be reused if kept in a sealed container in the fridge.

COOKING

- When a recipe calls for wine, don't waste your best bottle. Most of the flavor of wine is in its bouquet. When the wine is heated, the bouquet evaporates. On the other hand, don't use wine that you would not drink by itself. An oxidized bottle will give the dish a bitter taste.
- Store wines you intend to use for cooking in containers that allow the minimum of air. A good idea is to pour remnants into a half bottle. Cork it firmly and refrigerate. Or pour a light film of olive oil on the top of the wine to keep out the air.
- Spicy sauces will mask any deterioration in a wine, but in delicate sauces the taste of a poor wine will come through.
- The character of the wine should match the dish you are preparing. Don't use heavy wines with delicate fish or meat. Above all, the wine should be flavory.
- If a sauce takes two or three hours to cook, it's pointless to put in the wine at the start. Add it halfway through the cooking time.
- If the dish calls for Champagne and you would rather drink the wine than cook with it, substitute Gewürztraminer and a little lemon juice (this tip comes from the chef at the Champagne house Charles Heidsieck).

FLAMBÉING

- Flambéing is mostly show; it does little for the food except warm it up if the waiter has allowed it to go cold. Flambéing does, however, get rid of alcohol in a hurry, and leaves a dominant flavor of the spirit.

If you want to flambé, there's no need to reach for your exquisite XO Cognac or Paradis, but don't use the cheapest brandy you can find. (What you are left with once you burn off the alcohol is the taste of a cheap product.)

THE WORLD OF FOOD AND WINE

"Wine is perhaps the supreme convenience food because it can transform the most straightforward fare into a fine meal, yet the most elaborate and extravagant cuisine can do nothing to improve upon an indifferent bottle."

—Pamela Van Dyke Price

France

Nowhere on this globe are the pleasures of the table taken more seriously than in France. While other nations might discuss and dispute politics and religion over the dinner table, the French talk food. Interminable conversations and heated debates arise from such solemn matters as the right oil to use in a salad, or the ripeness of a cheese.

The history of France has been changed because of this national preoccupation: in the early seventeenth century the Duc de Guise lost a battle because he dallied over the dinner table to finish his melon. The great diplomat Talleyrand regained almost as much territory over the dinner table as his country lost during the Napoleonic Wars—by plying his peers with sumptuous dishes and wines at the Congress of Vienna in 1815.

For the man in the street, tips about good restaurants are more appreciated than tips on the stock market, and a "little recipe" from an old aunt is a treasured family heirloom. French chefs are accorded a status that other nations bestow upon opera singers, television stars and football players. Their restaurants are places of awe.

To the chef himself (and in French the word is solidly masculine), the success of a meal is a question of honor. Louis XIV's chef, Vatel, committed suicide because the fish he ordered did not arrive in time for the king's dinner.

In France, gastronomic recognition is more important than mineral wealth—and much more bankable. Yet French cuisine is not merely the legacy of the great chefs like Escoffier or Bocuse. There is another tradition that goes hand in hand with the classical style—provincial cooking. The dishes created and served in the homes of farmers and peasants and in roadside inns and cafés have contributed to the mainstream of French culinary arts. A dish of field mushrooms gathered after the rain, or a trout caught from the village bridge may rival in taste the most elaborate haute cuisine dishes gilded with their twenty garnishes.

France is perfectly situated to benefit from a whole range of climates and regional specialties. The southern Mediterranean brings olive oil, basil and garlic. The coasts of Brittany and Normandy supply lobster, Dover sole and oysters. From the fertile plains of the mid-west come flour for French bread, eggs and dairy products; the middle east provides the poultry of Bresse and the prized Charolais beef.

France is a splendid patchwork of provincialism. Each province is rich in tradition and local specialties. Just as the Bordelais think their wine is superior to Burgundy, so each province believes itself to be the center of the universe. Such competition keeps everyone busy creating new dishes to prove the point.

Although the classical haute cuisine created by the great chefs has set the standard for the rest of the world since the French Revolution, it is provincial cooking that provides the basis for French cuisine as we know it today. Traditional dishes with elaborate sauces, garnishes and minute attention to detail are still served in top restaurants and are studied in all cooking schools. But many of France's unique food specialties have evolved from bourgeois or provincial cuisine so rich in flavors and colors that a mere reading of the recipe unlocks a symphony of gustatory sensations: fragrant bouillabaisse from the south with garlic, saffron, olive oil, fresh fish and crusty bread; the mysterious black truffle mingling its earthy aromas with the unctuous flavor of pink foie gras, accompanied by a glass of cool Sauternes or Gewürztraminer; crisply glazed leg of Prés-salé lamb cooked on a spit, oozing succulent juices over flageolets au beurre sprinkled with chervil and served with a bottle of Château Palmer; escargot, lobsters in cream and tarragon sauce; flamed veal kidneys in Armagnac and mushrooms—the mouth-watering list is endless.

And let's not forget the over 360 cheeses, the thousands of wines and ciders, aperitifs, liqueurs, not to mention fruits, fresh or preserved, basted in syrup or frozen in sorbets. And when it comes to the breads, brioches, croissants and pastry, the mind goes numb.

There are fashions in food as there are in everything else. The names may change, but the basic concepts and craft remain the same, waiting to be reinvented by a new generation of chefs, professional or amateur. So varied are the techniques and recipes of the two arms of French cuisine that they embrace virtually every style that a gourmet might pursue.

BURGUNDY

Burgundy, whose golden slopes are uniquely favored by Nature, has enjoyed prosperity for centuries. The Abbey of Cluny was called "the light of the world" by Pope Urban II, and, together with the monastery at Vezelay it kept knowledge and culture alive during the Dark Ages.

In the late Middle Ages the powerful Duchy of Burgundy attracted artists and craftsmen from all over Europe. Castles and elaborate manor houses, hospices and abbeys multiplied. Wealthy landowners, ecclesiastical and temporal, held banquets to entertain visiting kings, and that meant cooks, vineyards, farms and cellars.

By the fifteenth century the capital, Dijon, was the most brilliant city of Europe. Its university rivaled that of Oxford, but unlike Oxford, the city fed the stomach as well as the mind. Today Dijon remains the gastronomic capital of France, with its own special contributions to world cuisine—Dijon mustard, Crème de Cassis and pain d'épices (spiced honey gingerbread).

With Chablis to its north and the Côte d'Or, Chalonnais, Mâconnais and Beaujolais to the south, Dijon is admirably situated to enjoy the best of Burgundy's wines. Driving south, the names of the villages flash by like a celestial wine list—Gevrey-Chambertin, Nuits-St-Georges, Vosne-Romanée, Meursault, Puligny-Montrachet.

If Burgundy produces arguably the best red and white wines in the world, the region is also blessed with the finest beef (Charolais) and chicken (from Bresse) raised in France, to say nothing of fine game, pork, snails, geese, frogs' legs, pike and cheeses such as Epoisse, Soumaintrain, Saint Florentins and Chaource.

The reputation of Burgundian gastronomy does not rest solely on high-quality ingredients, but on the skills of the region's chefs and farmers. Tending vineyards, raising beef and making cheese are not pastimes for weekend squires. The numerous starred restaurants throughout the region are testimony to a long-recognized fact: such is the creativity of Burgundian chefs (they taught the world how to deal with snails and the bony pike) that they have even found a way to cook eggs in red wine—and delicious it is, too!

Escargots à la Chablisienne

Snails Chablis Style
(Serves 4)

The use of Chablis makes this recipe a milder version of the traditional Escargots à la Bourguignonne. The snails should be served piping hot, with French bread as a dinner first course, or on toast with a green salad as a main course for lunch.

BUTTER COMPOUND:

3/4	cup unsalted butter, at room temperature	175 mL
2	tsp finely chopped shallots	10 mL
1	clove garlic, pasted	1
1	tsp chopped fresh parsley	5 mL
1	tsp salt	5 mL
1/4	tsp freshly ground black pepper	1 mL

SNAILS:

24	snails (canned)	24
2	tsp meat glaze or concentrated beef juice	10 mL
2	tbsp finely chopped shallots	30 mL
1	tsp chopped fresh parsley	5 mL
1	cup Chablis	250 mL
	Salt and freshly ground black pepper	

- Combine all the ingredients for the butter and reserve.
- Preheat the oven to 325°F/160°C.
- Drain the snails and rinse under warm water.
- In a skillet, melt the meat glaze or warm up the concentrated beef juice. Add the shallots, parsley and Chablis. Season with salt and pepper to taste. Bring to a boil, then remove from the heat.
- Add the snails to the wine mixture and let cool completely.
- Pour a few drops of the liquid into each snail shell. Place one snail in each shell and seal with the butter compound.
- Place the snails in a snail dish, butter side up, and bake until the snails begin to boil in the shells.

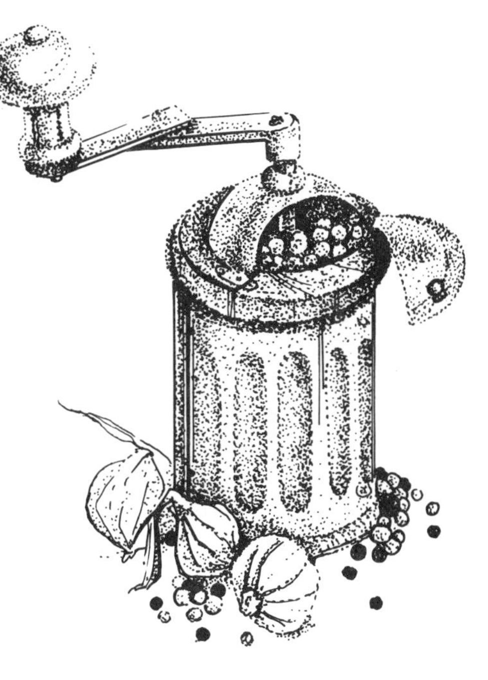

Wine serving suggestions:
Regional: Chablis
National: Sancerre, white Châteauneuf-du-Pape, Alsatian Tokay, Arbois white
International: Californian or Australian Chardonnay, Rioja whites (wood fermented)

Tony Aspler's choice: Corton-Charlemagne
Jacques Marie's choice: Chablis Premier Cru
Chef's choice:____

Mousseline de Brochet Dijonnaise

Pike Mousseline with Crayfish
(Serves 4)

Pike is a remarkable freshwater fish underestimated by many fishermen and cooks because it contains so many bones. But the firm, white, flaky flesh is delicious, and essential to the texture of quenelles.

This mousseline can be served as a main course, accompanied by a rice pilaf. The mixture can also be poached as individual quenelles and served as a lunch dish or appetizer with the same sauce before a roast meat or poultry main course.

1 lb	raw, fresh, boneless pike meat	500 g
3/4 cup	unsalted butter, melted	175 mL
8	eggs (2 whole eggs and 6 egg yolks)	8
	Salt and freshly ground black pepper	
1 tbsp	fresh chervil leaves	15 mL
2 tbsp	fresh parsley leaves	30 mL
1	small head Boston lettuce, parboiled	1
Pinch	freshly grated nutmeg	Pinch
2 cups	heavy cream	500 mL
1 lb	pike bones	500 g
1 cup	dry white Burgundy	250 mL
1 cup	water	250 mL
1 tbsp	tomato paste	15 mL
1/4 cup	unsalted butter	50 mL
24	mushroom caps	24

24	crayfish tails, shelled	24
2 tbsp	unsalted butter	30 mL

- Make sure that all the ingredients are very cold.
- Chop the pike meat in a food processor. Gradually blend in 3/4 cup/175 mL melted butter, 2 eggs and 2 egg yolks. Season with salt and pepper.
- Blend in the chervil, parsley, lettuce and nutmeg. Place the mixture in a bowl and refrigerate.
- Whip 1 cup/250 mL cream and stir into the cold pike mixture.
- Place the mousse in a buttered ring mold, ensuring that the mixture does not fill more than two-thirds of the mold. Place the ring in a pan of hot water and poach on the stove for 30 minutes, or until cooked and expanded.
- Prepare the sauce by cooking the fish bones in the white Burgundy and water seasoned with salt and pepper.
- After boiling lightly for 5 minutes, add the remaining cream, tomato paste, 1/4 cup/50 mL butter and simmer for a few minutes. Strain.
- Unmold the mousseline onto a round serving dish.
- Sauté the mushroom caps and crayfish tails in 2 tbsp/30 mL butter until hot and place in the center of the mousseline. Keep warm.
- Stir 4 egg yolks into the sauce and cook over low heat for 3 minutes without boiling, just until thickened. Adjust seasonings and pour over the mousseline. Serve hot.

Wine serving suggestions:
Regional: Montrachet or Meursault
National: white Hermitage, Condrieu, Pouilly-Fumé, white Burgundy
International: white Zinfandel, Australian Chardonnay, Greco di Tufo, Viña Sol

Tony Aspler's choice: López de Heredia Viña Tondonia 6 ano
Jacques Marie's choice: Le Montrachet
Chef's choice:________________________

Boeuf à la Bourguignonne

Beef Bourguignon
(Serves 4)

This rich, flavorful stew is a classic French dish that tastes even better when reheated the following day. The secret is to cook it slowly and let the sauce become rich by reduction rather than by adding too much flour. The marc de Bourgogne will give the dish a special flavor—it's made from the distilled skins, seeds and pulp that remain after the grapes have been pressed. It has a more pungent and earthy flavor than brandy (in Italy this distilled spirit is called grappa).

3 lb	top round or rump of beef	1.5 kg
4 tbsp	olive oil	60 mL
6 tbsp	butter	90 mL
8 oz	salt pork, diced	250 g
2	large onions, diced	2
	Salt and freshly ground black pepper	
4 tbsp	marc de Bourgogne	60 mL
3 tbsp	flour	45 mL
2 tbsp	tomato puree	30 mL
2	cloves garlic, pasted	2
1	bottle good red Burgundy	1
1	bouquet garni (1 sprig thyme, 2 bay leaves, 1 celery stalk, 5 sprigs parsley)	1
2	large carrots, quartered lengthwise	2
20	small white (pearl) onions	20
1 tsp	sugar	5 mL

12	mushroom caps	12
1	lemon	1
1/4 cup	finely chopped fresh parsley	50 mL

- Preheat the oven to 300°F/150°C.
- Cut the beef into 1-in/2.5-cm cubes. In a large skillet heat 2 tbsp/30 mL olive oil and 4 tbsp/60 mL butter and sauté the diced salt pork until golden. Remove the salt pork and place in a casserole.
- Add to the fat the diced onions and sauté until golden. Remove the onions and reserve with the pork.
- Add the beef to the fat and brown. Season with pepper. Moisten with the marc de Bourgogne and ignite.
- When the flames burn away, sprinkle with flour, mix well and cook for 3 minutes. Stir in the tomato puree and garlic and transfer to the casserole.
- Pour three-quarters of the bottle of Burgundy into the casserole and enough cold water to cover the meat. Add the bouquet garni and the carrots. Cover, bring to a boil and cook in a slow oven for 1 1/2 hours. Remove the bouquet garni and continue to cook for about 30 minutes, or until the meat is tender.
- Meanwhile, brown the pearl onions in 1 tbsp/15 mL butter and the sugar. Add the rest of the red Burgundy to the onions and cook until tender.
- In a separate pan, sauté the mushroom caps in the remaining butter and olive oil. Sprinkle them with the juice of the lemon, salt and pepper.
- Add the pearl onions with the wine and mushroom caps to the beef. Sprinkle with chopped parsley and serve hot with boiled potatoes.

Wine serving suggestions:
Regional: red Burgundy used in cooking
National: Côtes-du-Rhône, Châteauneuf-du-Pape, Cru Beaujolais
International: Zinfandel, Chianti Classico Riserva, Oregon Pinot Noir, Rioja reds, Hermitage or Syrah from the New World

Tony Aspler's choice: Pommard
Jacques Marie's choice: Morey-Saint-Denis
Chef's choice:____________________

GUYENNE AND GASCONY (BORDEAUX)

There has always been a great rivalry between Bordeaux and Burgundy, and if the Burgundians win hands down in terms of cuisine, the Bordelais more than hold their own with the products of their extensive vineyards.

The city of Bordeaux has justifiably been called the wine capital of France. Since Roman times, the wines of this and other regions have been shipped from its quays to the tables of the world. The ships that carried "claret" to the New World returned with its produce—pumpkins, tomatoes, bell peppers and corn—introducing these strange new vegetables to the chefs of France.

Not that the region lacked for its own local delicacies: Périgueux provides the rare black truffle and the unctuous cèpe; from the area of Mont-de-Marsan comes another species of wild field mushroom, as well as the confit de canard and confit d'oie (duck and goose preserved in their own spicy fat). The foie gras of Dax is justly famous as is the ham of Bayonne farther south. The Armagnac region (where the local eau-de-vie rivals Cognac at its best) offers a range of game birds, such as woodcock, guinea fowl, partridge, wood pigeons and the tiny thrush. The Atlantic coast, from Arcachon to Biarritz, complements the menu with grey mullet, tuna, sardines, squid, eel, trout and crayfish as well as oysters and lampreys.

Yet all of this gastronomic wealth seems to be there for one purpose—to set off the glorious complexities of Bordeaux wines. The red Médoc and Graves based on the Cabernet Sauvignon grape are the epitome of finesse and structure while the fleshy opulence of St-Emilion and Pomerol offer a richer, softer taste. For dessert wines there are few to rival the honeyed sweetness of Sauternes and Barsac.

Beyond these world-renowned regions are many less glamorous areas—Bourg, Blaye, Fronsac, Monbazillac, Jurançon, Madiran, Cahors and Gaillac. But the virtue of their wines is now being recognized, as prices for fine claret and dessert whites continue to rise.

Until the late seventeenth century, Bordeaux wines were not sold by name. Haut Brion in the Graves was the first chateau to receive recognition as a wine in its own right, thanks to the enterprise of the president of the Guyenne parliament, Arnaud de Pontac. De Pontac was a winegrower who opened a fashionable restaurant to increase his wine sales. The fame of Haut Brion spread. In 1668 Samuel Pepys recorded in his diary dining at the Royall Oake tavern in London where he drank "a sort of French wine called Ho Bryen, that hath a good and most particular taste that I have never met with."

Today the wines of Bordeaux are generally more consistent in quality than those of Burgundy. The Englishman's claret, the name the British gave to red Bordeaux, is now the yardstick for every wine-growing country that seeks to produce a wine from the ubiquitous Cabernet vine. But as close as California, Australia, Chile and Argentina come to matching claret quality, ultimately the great chateaux of Bordeaux steal the laurels for producing wines that best complement lamb, beef and game.

Steak Bordelaise

(Serves 4)

This is a simple way to turn an ordinary steak into a special dish that goes very well with red wine. Buy the steaks a few days ahead of time and let them age in the refrigerator to render them more tender. If you object to the meat turning a dark color while aging, brush the steaks lightly with oil first.

4	8-oz/250-g tender strip loin, porterhouse or rib eye steaks	4
	Salt and freshly ground black pepper	
2 tbsp	olive oil	30 mL
1/4 cup	finely chopped onions	50 mL
3	shallots, finely chopped	3
1 tbsp	flour	15 mL
1 cup	red Bordeaux wine	250 mL
2 tbsp	finely chopped fresh parsley	30 mL
2 oz	beef marrow, diced	60 g

- Remove the steaks from the refrigerator at least 30 minutes before cooking. Sprinkle both sides with salt and pepper.
- Pan fry the steaks in the olive oil to desired degree of rareness. Remove the steaks and keep warm on a serving platter.
- Sauté the onions and shallots in the oil until they are soft but not brown. Stir in the flour, cook for 30 seconds, then add the red wine. Turn up the heat to high and cook until the sauce bubbles, stirring constantly.
- Lower the heat and simmer, still stirring. Add the parsley and beef marrow. Cook for 1 minute, then taste and adjust the seasonings. Pour the sauce over the steaks and serve immediately with French-fried or pan-fried potatoes.

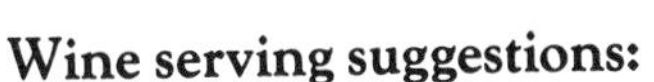

Wine serving suggestions:
Regional: red Bordeaux used in cooking
National: St-Joseph, Cornas, Nuits-St-Georges, red Sancerre
International: Tignanello, Rubesco, Californian or Australian Cabernet, Rioja reds, Chilean or South African Cabernet

Tony Aspler's choice: château-bottled St-Emilion
Jacques Marie's choice: St-Estèphe (Château Montrose or Cos d'Estournel)
Chef's choice: ______________________________

Rognons de Veau Flambés

Veal Kidneys Flamed with Armagnac
(Serves 4 to 6)

Armagnac is a brandy produced in the region southeast of Bordeaux. Distilled from the Ugni blanc, the same grape used to make Cognac, its flavor is earthier and more robust. The secret to this dish is not to overcook the kidneys. Use high heat and sauté them in small batches. They can be served with toast as an hors d'oeuvre, or as a main dish with a rice pilaf.

6	veal kidneys	6
1 tbsp	vegetable oil	15 mL
1/2 cup	Armagnac or brandy	125 mL
8 oz	button mushrooms, sliced	250 g
2/3 cup	butter	150 mL
2	large shallots, finely chopped	2
1/2 cup	dry white wine	125 mL
1 tbsp	dry mustard	15 mL
	Salt and freshly ground black pepper	
1	sprig thyme	1
1/2 cup	cream	125 mL

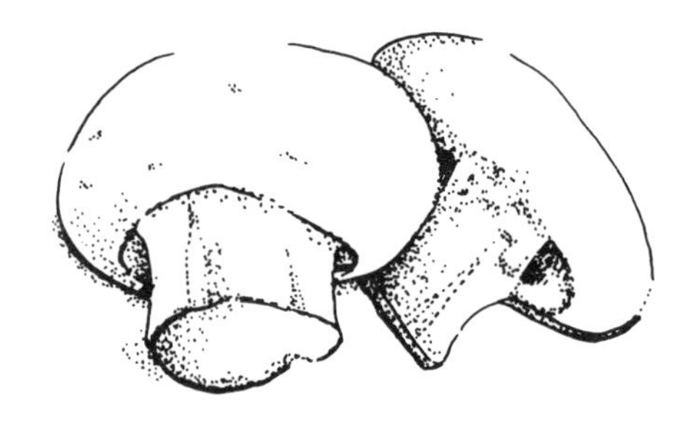

- Remove the membrane, fat and centers from the kidneys before slicing into thin strips. Sauté the kidney pieces in the oil on high heat, just until they curl slightly and change color. Keep them rare at the center.
- Add the Armagnac and flame. Remove the kidney pieces, drain the juices and reserve separately.
- Add the mushrooms to the frying pan with 1/3 cup/75 mL butter. Sauté over brisk heat until they start to render some liquid. Drain the mushroom liquid and add to the kidney juice. Reserve the mushrooms with the kidneys.
- In the same pan melt the remaining butter, add the shallots and brown lightly.
- Add the white wine, the combined kidney and mushroom juices, mustard, salt, pepper and thyme. Reduce the liquid to half its volume. Lower the heat and add the cream, mushrooms and kidneys. Stir well and simmer for a few minutes. Serve immediately.

Wine serving suggestions:
Regional: red Bordeaux
National: Côtes-du-Rhône, Côte-de-Nuits, dry Champagne
International: red Rioja, Bairrada, Californian and Australian Cabernet Sauvignon

Tony Aspler's choice: Gevrey-Chambertin
Jacques Marie's choice: first growth St-Emilion (Château Figeac or Pavie)
Chef's choice:______________________________

RHÔNE

The Rhône Valley, stretching south from Lyons to Orange, twists through dramatically rugged scenery. It was through this valley that the Greeks and Romans marched to spread their culture and teach the local inhabitants about grapes and wine making.

But if the Rhône is an autonomous wine region, the same cannot be said of its cuisine. The mighty river passes through several distinct areas, each with its own claims to culinary fame. Lyons is recognized as one of the great gastronomic centers of France, famous for its quenelles de brochet (pike dumplings), deep-fried whitebait, matelote au vin rouge (fish stew in red wine) and pan-fried potatoes.

On the left bank of the Rhône from Vienne to Montelimar the traveling gourmet will find such tempting dishes as gratin Dauphinois (sliced potatoes in cream baked with cheese), pâtés and salmis, tournedos with chanterelles.

Near Orange in the south of the region the specialties are braised duck with olives, trout with almonds, and frogs' legs in herbs and garlic. In the Ardèche on the right bank is the town of Lamastre, home of poularde en vessie (chicken cooked in the bladder or caul of a pig), stuffed trout, partridge cooked in pastry and the famous cayette—an unusual pork sausage prepared with spinach and cabbage. The region is also rich in cheeses—Bleu de Montbrisson, Dauphiné, Fourme, Rigotte, Pelardon, Chevreton and Picodon.

Wherever you travel in the Rhône Valley, the outdoor markets are a riot of color. The vegetables grown here are enormous and plentiful. The Mediterranean climate supports the olive tree, which means that olive oil rather than butter is the basis of the local cuisine.

The out-going people of the Rhône Valley have a sweet tooth which they satisfy with marrons glacés of Aubenas, berlingots from Carpentras, nougat from Montelimar, fruit jellies and chocolates filled with bilberries or raspberries and Williams pear tarts—all often enjoyed with the locally made dessert wine, Muscat de Beaumes-de-Venise.

As the hottest zone of France, the wines of the Rhône are the deepest in color, fullest in body and most powerful in alcohol. The northern Rhône produces such illustrious wines as Hermitage, Côte-Rotie and Condrieu; and the southern Rhône is the home of Châteauneuf-du-Pape, Côtes-du-Rhône Villages and the best rosés in the world—Tavel and Lirac.

Gratin de Queues d'Ecrevisse au Condrieu

Crayfish au Gratin
(Serves 2)

You can use large shrimps instead of crayfish in this recipe, but the combination of the crayfish with the Condrieu (made with Viognier grapes) will give the dish a very distinctive flavor. If a Condrieu is not available, use a not-too-sweet Riesling, Sauvignon or Chardonnay.

1 cup	dry white wine (Condrieu)	250 mL
2 cups	water	500 mL
1	small carrot, sliced	1
1	small onion, sliced	1
2	bay leaves	2
1	sprig thyme	1
10	whole black peppercorns	10
2	sprigs Italian parsley	2
1 tsp	salt	5 mL
3	cloves	3
24	raw crayfish or large shrimps	24
1/4 cup	butter	50 mL
1/4 cup	flour	50 mL
1 cup	cream	250 mL
	Cayenne pepper	
1	egg yolk	1
1/2 cup	grated Swiss cheese	125 mL

- In a saucepan, prepare a court bouillon by combining the wine, water, carrot, onion, bay leaves, thyme, peppercorns, parsley, salt and cloves. Bring to a boil and simmer for 10 minutes.
- Add the crayfish. Bring to a boil and simmer for 4 minutes. Remove the crayfish. Peel, devein and keep warm. Strain the cooking liquid and reserve 1 cup/250 mL.
- Melt the butter in a saucepan. Add the flour and cook the mixture until it is sandy in texture and light golden in color. Let the mixture cool until warm.
- Gradually add the cream and cooking liquid, mixing continuously with a whisk. Bring to a boil and simmer for 10 minutes, stirring from time to time to prevent scorching. Remove from the heat, add a touch of cayenne to taste and correct the salt if necessary.
- Blend in the egg yolk. Add the crayfish tails to the sauce.
- Pour into a buttered ovenproof dish and sprinkle with grated cheese. Place under the broiler for a few minutes, or until the cheese melts and turns golden.

Wine serving suggestions:
Regional: Condrieu, white Châteauneuf-du-Pape
National: dry Vouvray, Pouilly-Fuissé, white Macon, Chablis Premier Cru, Alsatian Riesling
International: Orvieto, Viña Sol, Californian Chardonnay, fruity Sauvignon, Australian Chardonnay

Tony Aspler's choice: Pomino (Frescobaldi)
Jacques Marie's choice: young Viognier
Chef's choice: ____________________

Terrine de Grives

Thrush Terrine

A terrine is a coarse pâté covered with lard (never aspic!) and usually served in the earthenware container in which it is cooked. If you want to be able to slice the terrine, pack it into a loaf pan or pâté mold and place a weight on top of the terrine while it is cooling. But traditionally a terrine is simply spooned out, while pâté and galantine are sliced.

If thrush are unavailable, substitute quail, partridge, pigeon or deer. This terrine will keep for about one week in the refrigerator.

1 tbsp	salt	15 mL
1 tsp	freshly ground black pepper	5 mL
1/4 cup	Cognac or Armagnac	50 mL
2 lb	chicken livers	1 kg
3 lb	thrush or game bird meat	1.5 kg
1 cup	unsalted butter	250 mL
8	juniper berries	8
2 cups	dry white Rhône wine	500 mL
1 lb	lard	500 g
2	large cloves garlic, crushed	2
1	large bay leaf	1
1	sprig thyme	1

- Preheat the oven to 300°F/150°C.
- Stir the salt and pepper into the brandy.
- Trim the chicken livers and soak them in the brandy.
- Bone the birds and remove the tendons. Pass the bird meat, butter, chicken livers and brandy through a medium meat grinder. Combine well.
- Place the mixture in a terrine or mold. Place the mold in a pan filled with hot water coming halfway up the sides of the terrine. Bake for 40 minutes.
- Meanwhile, soak the juniper berries in the white wine.
- Remove the terrine from the oven and pour the white wine and juniper berries over the top. Cook for another 20 minutes.
- Pass the terrine through a medium grinder, or blend for a very short time in a food processor. Let cool. Adjust seasonings.
- Melt the lard, garlic, bay leaf and thyme in a saucepan until the lard is clear.
- Strain out the garlic and the herbs and beat the melted lard well.
- Pack the meat mixture back into the terrine and cover with a layer of lard. Cool before serving.

Wine serving suggestions:
Regional: red or white Côtes-du-Rhône, white Hermitage
National: Rosé de Béarn, Jurançon, older Vouvray, Pinot Gris, Cru Beaujolais, Chinon
International: Pinotage, Shiraz, Zinfandel, Petite Sirah, Chianti

Tony Aspler's choice: Château Bordieu (Côtes-de-Blaye)
Jacques Marie's choice: Tavel rosé
Chef's choice:____________________

ALSACE

The late Jean Hugel, whose family has been growing wine in Riquewihr since 1639, once claimed that where one finds high-quality wines, one will also find good food. The gastronomy of Alsace bears out this assertion. Yet while Alsatian white wines—Riesling, Tokay, Pinot Blanc, Gewürztraminer and Muscat—are fascinatingly dry, complex and full of character and wines of great aristocracy, the robust, hearty cuisine of this region is largely rooted in peasant traditions.

The Alsatian likes his food, whether it be an everyday pot roast, onion tart, baeckenoffa (beef, lamb and pork slowly casseroled with potatoes, onions and white wine in a baker's oven) or saddle of hare baked in cream and served on a bed of noodles. And the portions served in homes and restaurants will reflect this trencherman approach.

The hilly, forested area of Alsace sheltered behind the Vosges mountains, is rich in game and fish, but historically the pig has ruled the kitchen. Pork dishes, especially as spiced sausage served with sauerkraut, reflect the German influence on Alsace, as do many of the other specialties of the region such as Kugelhopf (the sponge cake base for rum baba), the odorous Münster cheese and a fine cherry eau-de-vie called Kirschwasser.

But the glory of Alsace is its wines, particularly Gewürztraminer and Riesling, which marry so well with the national dishes of many other countries. These French varieties have greater intensity and dryness than their German counterparts; so much so that the Alsatian version of coq au vin, which produces a white sauce rather than a brown sauce from a red wine, is as rich and satisfying as the Burgundian version which calls for Chambertin! Alsatian wines are extremely versatile; they deserve a permanent place in the discriminating gourmet's cellar.

Pâté d'Alsace en Croute

Alsatian Pâté

The Alsatians used to relish enormous, heavy meals with generous portions of hot meat pies, charcuterie and plenty of local white wine. This recipe is based on one used by Madame Jean Hugel of one of the foremost wine-producing families in Alsace. It can be served hot as a starter with a good glass of Tokay d'Alsace, or cold as a snack.

PASTRY:		
1/2 cup	unsalted butter	125 mL
1 1/4 cups	pastry flour	300 mL
1 tsp	salt	5 mL
1/2 cup	water	125 mL
FILLING:		
1 1/2 lb	boned lean pork shoulder	750 g
1 cup	white wine	250 mL
2 tsp	salt	10 mL
1/2 tsp	freshly ground black pepper	2 mL
1 1/2 tsp	allspice	7 mL
2 tbsp	chopped fresh parsley	30 mL
2 tbsp	chopped onion	30 mL
1 cup	coarse breadcrumbs	250 mL
1	egg yolk	1

- To make the pastry, cut the butter into the flour.
- Dissolve the salt in the water and add to the flour and butter. Combine well. Roll the dough into a ball, cover and let rest for a few hours.
- To make the filling, cut the pork lengthwise into long strips.
- Combine the wine, salt, pepper and allspice. Marinate the meat in the wine for 4 hours at room temperature. Drain the meat well and combine with the parsley and onions.
- Preheat the oven to 375°F/190°C.
- Roll out one-third of the dough into a rectangle that is 2 inches/5 cm longer than the meat strips. Place on a floured baking sheet and sprinkle with the breadcrumbs (leave 2 in/5 cm around the edge of the rectangle free of breadcrumbs).
- Layer the meat strips on top of the breadcrumbs.
- Combine the egg yolk with 2 spoonfuls of cold water and brush on the edges of the dough.
- Roll the remaining dough out on a floured surface. Place on top of the meat, wrapping it lightly. Pinch the edges of dough together to seal well. Puncture the top with two or three holes 1/2 inch/1 cm in diameter. Decorate the surface of the pastry with dough remnants molded into leaves or flower shapes and secure with a little egg yolk. Insert a small chimney of paper into each hole to allow steam to escape.
- Bake for 45 minutes, then brush the top of the pâté with the remaining egg yolk and water mixture. Lower oven temperature to 325°F/160°C and bake until a small knife inserted into the center of the meat for 5 seconds comes out very hot.

Wine serving suggestions:
Regional: Tokay d'Alsace, Sylvaner, Riesling
National: dry Vouvray, Sancerre, white Bordeaux
International: Riesling Kabinett, Soave, Grüner Veltliner

Tony Aspler's choice: Rheingau Riesling Spätlese
Jacques Marie's choice: Gewürztraminer Sporen (Hugel's vineyard)
Chef's choice:________________________________

Tarte à l'Oignon

Onion Tart
(Serves 4)

When cooked, onions can be very sweet and tasty, as their strong and acrid flavor dissipates with the application of heat. This recipe is simple and very good. It will serve four as a main course, or eight as an appetizer.

PASTRY:

6 tbsp	butter	90 mL
1 cup	pastry flour	250 mL
1 tsp	salt	5 mL
6 tbsp	water	90 mL

FILLING:

4 oz	bacon	125 g
2 tbsp	butter	30 mL
6	medium onions, thinly sliced	6
1/2 tsp	salt	2 mL
pinch	freshly ground black pepper	pinch
pinch	freshly grated nutmeg	pinch
1 tbsp	flour	15 mL
1 1/4 cups	heavy cream	300 mL
4	large eggs	4

- To make the pastry, cut the butter into the flour.
- Dissolve the salt in the water and add to the flour mixture. Combine well. Roll the dough into a ball, cover and reserve.
- Preheat the oven to 400°F/200°C.
- Cut the bacon into thin strips and sauté lightly. Drain on paper towels and reserve.
- Roll out the pastry and line a 10-in/25-cm pie dish. Bake blind for 15 minutes.
- Melt the butter in a heavy skillet, add the onions and cook until soft. Remove from the heat and add the salt, pepper, nutmeg and flour.
- Add the cream and combine well.
- Beat the eggs well in a bowl. Add to the onions and cream mixture, combining well.
- Pour the mixture into the pie shell, sprinkle with bacon and bake for 35 minutes, or until the custard is set. Serve warm.

Wine serving suggestions:
Regional/National: Pinot Blanc, Sylvaner, Tokay d'Alsace, light Gewürztraminer, Riesling
International: Tavel, Chinon, Anjou white or rosé, fruity white Rioja, German Riesling Kabinett, Austrian Neuberger, Clare Watervale Riesling

Tony Aspler's choice: Kremser Müller-Thurgau
Jacques Marie's choice: Sylvaner
Chef's choice: ____________________

Choucroute à l'Alsacienne

Alsatian Sauerkraut
(Serves 8)

This royal dish is unique to the Alsace region of France. The local variations are usually found in the trimmings rather than the basic ingredients, although the juniper berries are very Alsatian. If you can't find the regional sausages or smoked meats, you can substitute corned beef, smoked goose or turkey, but be careful not to overcook the meat.

In Alsace the two most famous sauerkrauts come from Strasbourg and Colmar. La Maison des Têtes in Colmar makes a distinctive choucroute with chicken liver dumplings.

6½ lb	sauerkraut	3 kg
¾ cup	lard	175 mL
1	medium onion, chopped	1
2 cups	Riesling	500 mL
1 cup	bouillon	250 mL
2 lb	salted pork loin or shoulder of pork	1 kg
1 lb	smoked bacon, cut into 8 pieces	500 g
1 lb	salted bacon, cut into 8 pieces	500 g
	Salt and freshly ground black pepper	
3	cloves	3
1	bay leaf	1
1	clove garlic	1
18	juniper berries	18
8	small Strasbourg, Frankfurt or Vienna sausages	8

8	smoked pork (Montbeliard) sausages	8
8 oz	white (veal) sausages	250 g
8 oz	blood pudding sausages	250 g
8	medium peeled potatoes, boiled	8

- Rinse the sauerkraut several times in hot water and squeeze dry thoroughly.
- Melt the lard in a large, deep saucepan and lightly fry the chopped onion. Pour in the Riesling and the bouillon.
- Add the pork and the two types of bacon. Place the sauerkraut on top and add salt and pepper.
- Tie the cloves, bay leaf, garlic and juniper berries in a piece of cheesecloth and place in the sauerkraut. Cook, covered, on low heat for 1½ hours.
- Poach the Strasbourg and Montbeliard sausages, ensuring they do not boil. Fry the white sausages and blood sausages. Slice each sausage into 8 pieces.
- Place the sauerkraut in the center of a warm serving platter and pile sausages around it. Surround it all with boiled potatoes and serve very hot.

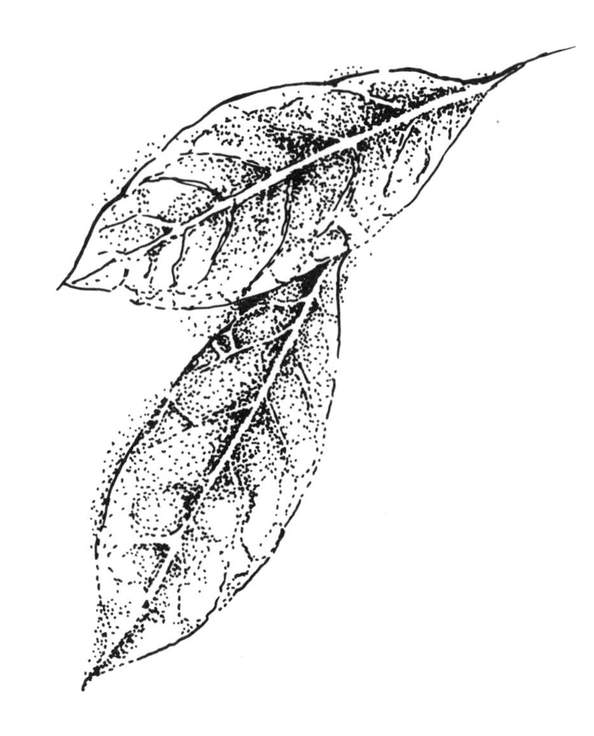

Wine serving suggestions:
Regional/National: Alsace Riesling, Gewürztraminer, Sylvaner
International: Aligoté, Mosel Riesling, Auxerrois, Fendant

Tony Aspler's choice: Traminer from Alto Adige
Jacques Marie's choice: Alsatian Riesling
Chef's choice:______________________________

LOIRE

The Loire Valley is the garden of France, the place where north meets south, where the French language is spoken without accent and where everything appears peaceful and serene. As early as the fourteenth century members of the French court were quick to appreciate the calm beauty and mild climate of the region. Their extravagant chateaux line the banks of the Loire River today like a twin set of pearls.

The river—the longest in France—has provided the region with a variety of fish and shellfish so fresh that they need no embellishment. Fresh grilled salmon or pike stuffed with sorrel served with a chilled glass of Sancerre and followed by Pithiviers (almond cakes) or a slice of Tarte Tatin (caramelized apple) accompanied by a sweet Vouvray is the quintessential dining experience of the Loire.

Or you could choose other local specialties such as thrush pâté (in the Loire a stronger dish than the Rhône version), hare stuffed with calf's liver, jugged goose or sheeps' tongues with turnips and quince paste.

Historically, the nobility hunted game on their estates while the peasantry raised pigs. Pork as a staple food requires some imagination to ensure a varied diet, and the kitchens of Touraine and Anjou provided some tantalizing answers—porc aux pruneaux (pork with prunes in a rich cream sauce), pork braised in white wine, rillons (pork ribs), rillettes (pork belly paste) and pigs' trotters.

As the garden of France the vegetables of the Loire are unparalleled for quality. Asparagus, leeks, lettuce, cabbage, broad beans and plump garlic are prepared without pretension and served simply. And no other region of France offers such a variety of wines in taste and style: the crisp Muscadet, the tart Gros Plant, the pink Anjou, the sparkling wines of Saumur, the sweet wines of Vouvray and Coteaux du Layon and the delightful reds of Chinon and Bourgueil. The full-bodied, dry, fruity Sancerre and Pouilly-Fumé are a wonderful complement to the goat's cheese of the area, especially the traditional hard version, Crottin de Chavignol, and the creamy Sainte Maure and Valencay.

Moules Marinières

Mussels in White Wine
(Serves 4)

Muscadet is one of the driest wines of France. Its high acidity makes it ideal for seafood and especially for the locally gathered mussels at the mouth of the Loire.

Make sure that the mussels are tightly closed when you buy them; discard any that are open. The fresh thyme in this recipe is important. Pull the sprig between your fingers to loosen the leaves and bruise them in the palm of your hands to release the oil before using.

2 tbsp	butter	30 mL
1 tbsp	chopped Italian parsley	15 mL
4 tbsp	chopped shallots or onions	60 mL
1	sprig fresh thyme	1
1	fresh bay leaf	1
2 cups	dry white wine (Muscadet)	500 mL
4 lb	small black mussels, trimmed, scraped and rinsed	2 kg
	Salt and freshly ground black pepper	

- In a thick pot combine the butter, parsley, shallots, thyme, bay leaf and wine.
- Bring almost to a boil over high heat. Then immediately add the mussels. Grind some black pepper over them and cover tightly. Steam until the mussels open, tossing from time to time.
- When the mussels open, remove them from the liquid. Remove the top shell from each and place them in a hot serving bowl. Keep hot.
- Remove the bay leaf from the liquid. Taste and adjust the salt. Pour the liquid over the mussels. Serve hot.

Wine serving suggestions:
Regional: Muscadet
National: dry Sauvignon Blanc, Aligoté, Alsatian Riesling
International: Verdicchio, Mosel Riesling, Chasselas

Tony Aspler's choice: Quincy
Jacques Marie's choice: Muscadet de Serve-et-Maine sur lie
Chef's choice:____________________

Rillettes

This terrine can be used as a spread on crusty French or Italian bread, or it can be shaped into small sausages and served as an appetizer or hors d'oeuvre.

4 oz	coarse salt	125 g
2 cups	water	500 mL
1 lb	pork fat, diced	500 g
2	onions, finely diced	2
4 lb	lean pork, cut into 1-in/3-cm cubes	2 kg
1 tsp	whole black peppercorns	5 mL
5	bay leaves	5
3	sprigs thyme	3
10	cloves	10

- Preheat the oven to 300°F/150°C.
- Combine the salt and water.
- Fry the diced pork fat in a large, ovenproof skillet until golden.
- Add the diced onions and pork. Cook for 10 minutes on medium heat.
- Add the salt water. Tie the peppercorns, bay leaves, thyme and cloves in cheesecloth to make a spice bag. Add to the skillet. Cook, covered, in the oven for 4 to 6 hours, until the meat falls apart to the touch. Stir from time to time to avoid sticking.
- When the meat is very tender, remove from oven. Discard the spice bag. Strain out 1/4 cup/50 mL fat and reserve. Let the pork cool in the remaining fat until it turns milky in color but has not set firmly.
- Crush the pork with a fork or a beater. Adjust seasonings and preserve in a clay or an earthenware pot covered with the reserved, melted fat, or shape the pork into sausages.

Wine serving suggestions→

CHAMPAGNE

For almost three hundred years, the sparkling wine of this region northeast of Paris has been the world's companion for celebration and victory. No other wine has been more flattered by imitation than Champagne; yet wine makers elsewhere have yet to equal the elegance and breed of this most labor intensive of all wines. From the picking of the grapes to the popping of the cork, thousands of pairs of hands manipulate it during its life in the cellars.

One would have thought that such a beverage would have inspired local chefs to create dishes that belong on the pinnacles of haut cuisine—either with Champagne as part of the recipe or dishes to complement its ethereal nature. But in truth, the fare of the Champagne region is very down to earth, simple and homely. Pike braised in Champagne and poularde (roast chicken) au Champagne are about as adventuresome as the local dishes go.

Local delicacies like the fragrant andouillettes of Troyes (sausages containing anonymous spare parts of the pig) and pig's trotters à la Sainte-Menehoulde have been praised by gourmets from novelist Alexander Dumas to Louis XVI, who was reportedly arrested at Varennes when he stopped there to indulge his passion for pieds de porc.

Other local specialties include smoked lamb's tongue, thrush cooked in Champagne, black pudding made from rabbit, carp and eel stewed in wine, braised mutton neck, and white sausage.

The cuisine of the Champagne district may lack the delicacy and subtle flavors of Burgundy, but it stands second to none in the fame of its cheeses. This is the home of nutty-tasting Brie and its cousin the Coulommiers. Less known but equally delicious are the fruity-lactic Chaource and the Cendré of Riceys and Langres, a soft cheese matured in the ashes of beechwood, poplar or vine stalks, which give it a grayish-black rind and a strong, pungent taste.

In short, Champagne is a region where the wine is made of stars and the cheeses of silk. What comes between is an ample and amiable diet that is both delicious and filling.

Wine serving suggestions:
Regional: Bourgueil, Chinon, dry Vouvray
National: Côtes-du-Rhône, Fitou, Corbières, Minervois, Pinot Blanc
International: Chianti, Petite Sirah, Shiraz, Chilean Cabernet Sauvignon

Tony Aspler's choice: Sancerre
Jacques Marie's choice: Alsatian Pinot Noir
Chef's choice:____________________

Pieds de Porc à la Sainte-Menehould

Pigs' Trotters
(Serves 4)

During my apprenticeship in Paris, my fellow young cooks and I sometimes used to eat at Les Halles after work, at one or two in the morning. I always chose one of three dishes—onion soup au gratin, oysters or pieds de porc, a simple but memorable dish, especially when accompanied by plenty of fresh Muscadet or Beaujolais from the keg (a true feast for young men trying to survive on meagre salaries!).

This dish should be served very hot with Dijon mustard and French-fried potatoes. Try adding a half bottle of inexpensive, fruity white wine to the court bouillon—it makes all the difference.

4	pigs' feet, cut in half lengthwise	4
	Medium coarse salt (enough to cover pigs' feet)	
2	carrots, washed, trimmed and cut into 2-in/5-cm lengths	2
2	onions, peeled and quartered	2
1	stalk celery, trimmed and diced	1
3	cloves garlic	3
30	whole black peppercorns	30
6	cloves	6
1	whole chili pepper	1
1	sprig thyme	1
1	large bay leaf	1
4 qt	water	4 L
1 cup	melted butter	250 mL
4 cups	breadcrumbs	1 L

- Sprinkle the halved pigs' feet generously with salt and refrigerate for 24 to 36 hours.
- Wash off the salt well and wrap the pigs' feet in cheesecloth secured with kitchen twine.
- Prepare a court bouillon by simmering the carrots, onions, celery, garlic, peppercorns, cloves, chili pepper, thyme and bay leaf in the water for 15 minutes.
- Add the pigs' feet to the court bouillon, cover and cook very slowly for 4 to 5 hours, or until very tender. Remove from the heat and allow the pigs' feet to cool in the liquid.
- Remove the pigs' feet from the cold court bouillon and discard the cheesecloth.
- Roll each halved foot in melted butter and cover with breadcrumbs.
- Barbecue or grill on a slow fire until golden on all sides.

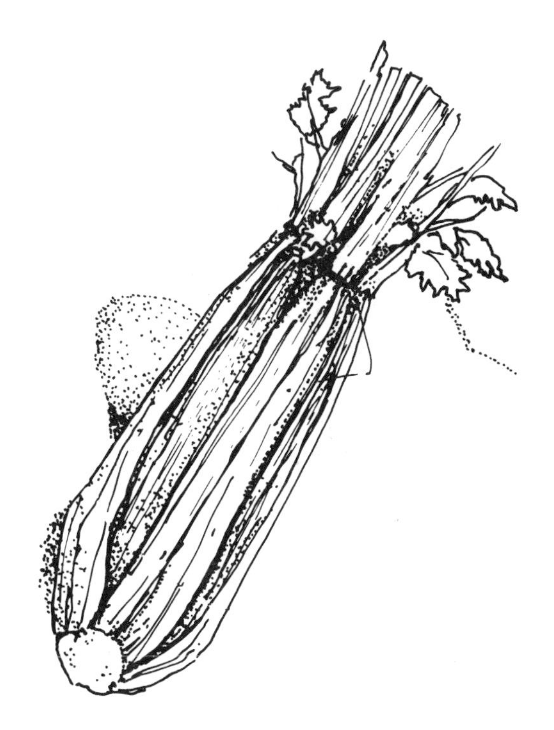

Wine serving suggestions:
Regional: Coteaux Champenois
National: Pouilly-Fumé, Beaujolais
International: Californian Fumé Blanc, Valpolicella, Rhine Riesling QbA

Tony Aspler's choice: Rosé de Marsannay
Jacques Marie's choice: Tavel
Chef's choice:________________________

Poularde au Champagne

Chicken with Sweetbreads in Champagne
(Serves 4)

This recipe was a specialty of the Rotisserie Perigourdine in Paris, where I served as an apprentice in the 1950s. It's an expensive dish, but delicious. The quality of the chicken is important—it may not be possible to buy poulet de Bresse, the famous chicken from Burgundy, but try to buy the freshest bird you can find. And if you can buy crème fraîche or Devon cream, the dish will be even more spectacular (if not, substitute heavy cream). This dish uses Coteaux Champenois, the still wine of the Champagne region. When this wine undergoes a secondary fermentation in the bottle, it becomes sparkling wine.

8 oz	sweetbreads	250 g
1	chicken, approx. 3-4 lb/1.5-2 kg, cut into 8 serving pieces	1
1/4 cup	unsalted butter	50 mL
1/4 cup	Cognac	50 mL
4	large shallots, finely chopped	4
8 oz	white mushrooms, sliced	250 g
1	black truffle, fresh or canned, thinly sliced	1
	Salt and freshly ground white pepper	
1 1/2 cups	still Champagne (Coteaux Champenois)	375 mL
1 tbsp	unsalted butter	15 mL
1 tbsp	flour	15 mL
2	egg yolks	2

1 cup	crème fraîche or Devon cream	250 mL
4	slices white bread	4

- Soak the sweetbreads in cold water overnight. Blanch them by simmering in salted water for 10 minutes. Dice them.
- Sauté the chicken pieces in butter in a heavy skillet, until golden brown. Remove the chicken from the pan and keep warm.
- In the same pan, sauté the sweetbreads until golden. Return the chicken to the pan. Douse the chicken and sweetbreads with Cognac, then toss together and ignite.
- Add the shallots, sliced mushrooms and truffle. Season with salt and pepper.
- Stir in the wine and bring to a boil.
- Prepare a beurre manier by making a paste with 1 tbsp/15 mL butter and 1 tbsp/15 mL flour. Stir into the wine. Simmer over low heat until the chicken is tender.
- Mix the egg yolks and cream together and add to the sauce a few minutes before the end of the cooking time. Cook over very low heat for a few minutes, mixing well with a wooden spoon just until the sauce coats the back of the spoon. (Do not allow the sauce to boil or the egg yolks will curdle.)
- Cut out 8 heart-shaped croutons from the bread slices and fry them in some butter.
- Adjust the seasonings and serve the chicken garnished with croutons.

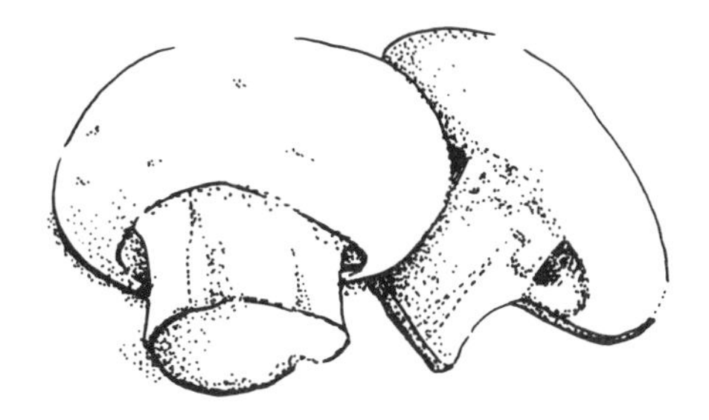

Wine serving suggestions:
Regional: extra dry Champagne
National: white Burgundy, Alsatian Sylvaner, Cabernet d'Anjou
International: Sekt, Californian Chenin Blanc Dry, dry Orvieto

Tony Aspler's choice: Marco Felluga's Pinot Bianco
Jacques Marie's choice: Pol Rouge brut
Chef's choice:________________________________

NORMANDY

The fertile soil, an Atlantic climate tempered by the Gulf Stream and a lengthy coastline make Normandy, in northwestern France, a region rich in produce of all kinds. Lush pastures nourish some of the best beef and lamb in France. The milk from the cows makes the famous nutty Normandy butter, thick cream and a range of world-renowned cheeses. The fruit of the apple orchards is pressed into cider and distilled to make Calvados, an eau-de-vie that, at its finest, can rival Cognac.

From the rivers come trout, shad and salmon; the rocky coastal waters produce lobster, scallops, shrimps, mussels and oysters as well as sole and turbot. And from its fields and forests hunters bag pheasant, woodcock and snipe.

But above all, the pride of Normandy is its cheeses; more than twenty are produced in the region, including Camembert (which was developed by a local woman named Marie Harel in 1790 and now accounts for twenty percent of all French cheese production), the square Pont-l'Evêque (the oldest of Normandy cheeses) and the highly flavored Livarot wrapped in the traditional five strips of reed.

Since no wine is produced in Normandy, the local cuisine has developed around cider and Calvados. The Romans brought back one particular dish when they captured Gaul—salted and smoked ham boiled in cider, then panfried in fresh butter and herbs. Consumed at the end of a meal, it was known as the "Spur of Bacchus." Other specialties of the region include Andouille fumée (smoked pork sausage), pressed duck from Rouen, shad basted with cider, tripes à la mode de Caen, poulet vallée d'Auge (a rich concoction of chicken with cream sauce and Calvados), sole à la Normande.

The Normans have heroic appetites, and it's not surprising that they invented the practice of taking a digestive between courses. Invariably, it's a glass of Calvados—known as "le trou Normand."

Sole à la Normande

Dover Sole Normandy
(Serves 4)

Sole is the best of the flat fish—its flesh is lean, white, firm and delicate. Dover sole has a different texture and taste from lemon sole, gray sole or flounder. It can be prepared in an infinite number of ways, but this recipe is one of the best—it was often served by my grandmother in her restaurants in Deauville and Houlgate. When properly prepared, it's an outstanding dish. Make sure you reserve your finest dry white wine for the occasion!

4	whole Dover sole, approx. 12 oz/350 g each	4
1/3 cup	dry white wine (Muscadet or Sylvaner)	100 mL
1	large bay leaf	1
1	sprig thyme	1
4	sprigs Italian parsley (flat leaves)	4
1	stalk celery, trimmed	1
15	whole white peppercorns	15
8	medium white mushrooms	8
	salt	
7 tbsp	unsalted butter	105 mL
4	large shallots, finely chopped	4
8	oysters	8
24	baby shrimps, shelled	24
16	large raw mussels	16
1/4 cup	all-purpose flour	50 mL
1/3 cup	heavy cream	100 mL

pinch	cayenne pepper	pinch
4	croutons (crescent- or "N"-shaped)	4
8	smelts or gudgeons, deep-fried	8

- Fillet the sole. Put all the trimmings (heads, bones, white skins) in a heavy saucepan with the wine, bay leaf, thyme, parsley, celery, white peppercorns, mushroom stalks, salt, 1 tbsp/15 mL butter and enough water to cover. Simmer for 30 minutes, partly covered.
- Fold the sole fillets (skin side in) and place them, seam side down, in a skillet that has been buttered and sprinkled with the shallots. Strain the stock over the fish, cover and bring to a boil. Turn down the heat and simmer gently for 5 minutes, or until cooked but still firm.
- Meanwhile, in a skillet toss the oysters, shrimps and mussels in 1 tbsp/15 mL butter over low heat until firm. Remove. Poach the mushroom caps in the oyster and mussel juices.
- Remove the sole fillets and place on a warm platter. Add the oysters, mussels, shrimps and mushroom caps and keep warm.
- In a heavy saucepan melt 5 tbsp/75 mL butter and add the flour. Cook on low heat until the mixture swells and foams without coloring. Remove from the heat and mix in 2 cups/500 mL fish stock and the oyster liquid, a little at a time. Simmer for 10 minutes, then add the cream.
- Adjust the seasonings and add the cayenne pepper. Pour the sauce over the sole fillets and garnish with croutons and deep-fried smelts.

Wine serving suggestions:
National: dry Riesling or Pinot Blanc d'Alsace, Macon Lugny, Pouilly-Vinzelles, dry Sauvignon
International: Soave, light Californian Chardonnay

Tony Aspler's choice: Rosemount Chardonnay
Jacques Marie's choice: Montrachet
Chef's choice:________________________

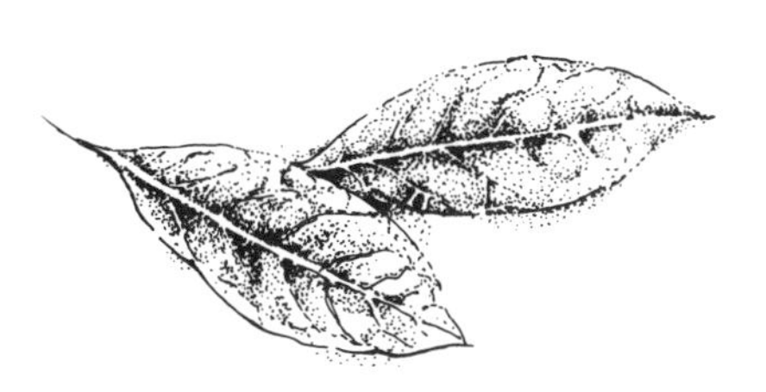

Gigot de Prés-Salés

Roasted Leg of Lamb
(Serves 4)

The Prés-salés ("salted meadows") near Mont St-Michel in Normandy produces famous lamb. The animals are fed on the rich, thick grass flavored with sea salt and iodine, giving the meat a distinctive taste that is prized by gastronomes. The word "gigot" means little leg. The legs of lamb from this region are small but very tender. They are traditionally accompanied with flageolets—small, pale-green kidney beans served swimming in butter with chopped parsley.

1	leg of lamb	1
5	cloves garlic, peeled and cut into slivers	5
3	carrots, washed and trimmed but not peeled	3
3	onions, peeled	3
3	stalks celery, trimmed	3
	Salt, freshly ground black pepper and oil	
1 tsp	whole black peppercorns	5 mL
6	cloves	6
3	large bay leaves, crushed	3
1½ tsp	fresh thyme	7 mL
1½ tsp	fresh rosemary	7 mL
4 cups	hard cider (unpasteurized)	1 L
⅓ cup	unsalted butter	75 mL
1 tbsp	finely chopped fresh parsley	15 mL

- Preheat the oven to 450°F/230°C.
- Trim the skin and fat from the leg of lamb. Reserve the fat. Remove the hip bone and chop it roughly with a cleaver.
- Cut tiny slits in the meat and insert slivers of garlic.
- Coarsely chop the carrots, onions and celery.
- Rub the lamb with salt, freshly ground black pepper and oil. Place in a roasting pan in the oven and cook, turning from time to time until slightly colored.
- Meanwhile, chop the lamb fat and melt in a skillet. When the lamb fat is half melted, add the carrots, onions and celery and sauté over a brisk heat until the onions turn golden.
- Add the peppercorns, cloves, bay leaves, thyme and rosemary and toss rapidly for 30 seconds. Place this garnish around the leg of lamb with the chopped hipbone.
- Lower the oven temperature to 325°F/160°C and cook the lamb until medium rare. Remove the lamb from the roasting pan and keep warm. Degrease the roasting pan and deglaze with the cider. Cook over medium heat until reduced by half. Strain and degrease the sauce. Whisk in the butter and parsley, and adjust seasoning.
- Carve the lamb and serve hot with the sauce on the side.

Wine serving suggestions:
Regional: Normandy cider
National: red Bordeaux (St-Emilion or Pomerol)
International: South African Cabernet, Rioja red, Devon cider

Tony Aspler's choice: Cru Classé Pauillac
Jacques Marie's choice: Margaux (Château Palmer)
Chef's choice:____________________________

Lapin au Cidre

Rabbit with Cider and White Turnips
(Serves 4)

Almost every farm in Normandy has a hutch full of rabbits busily munching their way to the pot, and city dwellers can always find fresh rabbit at the market. When I visit my Normand cousin Michel Anée in Vimoutiers, his wife, Ginette, always prepares this recipe. With its creamy, Calvados-flavored sauce, the dish makes a great meal accompanied by a bottle of *cidre bouché* and Calvados from their own distillery.

1	rabbit, cut in pieces	1
	Salt and freshly ground white pepper	
6 tbsp	unsalted butter	90 mL
2 tbsp	olive oil	30 mL
3	onions, sliced	3
3	shallots, sliced	3
3	cloves garlic, crushed	3
1/4 cup	Calvados	50 mL
1 tbsp	flour	15 mL
3 cups	dry cider (brut)	750 mL
1	bouquet garni (4 sprigs Italian parsley, 2 fresh bay leaves and 2 sprigs fresh thyme)	1
2 lb	small white turnips	1 kg
1 tsp	sugar	5 mL
2/3 cup	crème fraîche or Devon cream	150 mL
	Freshly chopped parsley	

- Season the rabbit with salt and pepper.
- In a large skillet, heat 3 tbsp/45 mL butter and the oil. When the butter becomes golden brown, add the pieces of rabbit and sauté until golden on all sides. Remove and keep warm.
- To the same pan add the onions, shallots and garlic. Sauté until golden.
- Return the rabbit pieces to the pan and mix well. Douse the rabbit with Calvados and ignite. Stir until the flames die out.
- Sprinkle the rabbit with flour and toss well. Add the cider and blend in with a wooden spoon.
- Add the bouquet garni, adjust the seasonings and simmer for 45 minutes.
- Meanwhile, peel the turnips, cut in quarters lengthwise and parboil in water for 5 minutes. Drain and sauté in the remaining butter. When they begin to color, sprinkle with sugar and brown (caramelize), tossing them from time to time.
- Deglaze the turnips with a ladle of sauce from the rabbit, then add the turnips to the rabbit.
- Add the cream, combine well and adjust seasoning. Simmer for another 15 minutes.
- Remove the bouquet garni, sprinkle with freshly chopped parsley and serve very hot.

Wine serving suggestions:
Regional: dry cider
National: Tokay d'Alsace, white Graves, dry Champagne
International: Australian Sauvignon Blanc, Orvieto (secco)

Tony Aspler's choice: Cahors
Jacques Marie's choice: cidre bouché or Sauvignon de St. Bris
Chef's choice:______________________________

Charlotte Normande aux Pommes

Apple Charlotte
(Serves 6)

There are two kinds of Charlotte—one is served cold and made with Bavarian cream lined with lady fingers. The other kind is made with fruit (usually apples) and buttered bread and is served hot. The following recipe is a rich variation of the second type, made with brioche. Traditionally it is served garnished with pan-fried apples, glazed cherries and plenty of crème fraîche, crème anglaise or fresh raspberry jelly.

1 lb	cooking apples	500 g
12 oz	brioche or egg bread	300 g
1 cup	milk	250 mL
3 cups	sweet cider	750 mL
1 cup	brown sugar	250 mL
2/3 cup	raisins	150 mL
1	cinnamon stick	1
1	vanilla bean, cut lengthwise	1
1/3 cup	chopped almonds or hazelnuts	100 mL
2 tbsp	slivered orange peel	30 mL
5	eggs, well beaten	5
1/4 cup	unsalted butter	50 mL
	crème fraîche or raspberry jelly for garnishing	

- Preheat the oven to 200°F/90°C.
- Peel, core and dice the apples.
- Cut the brioche into cubes and let soak in the milk.
- In a saucepan, combine the apples with the cider, brown sugar, raisins, cinnamon and vanilla. Cook until the apples are tender but still firm. Remove the cinnamon stick and vanilla bean.
- Remove the saucepan from the heat and add the chopped nuts, orange peel and brioche. Add the eggs and combine well.
- Grease a Charlotte mold (7 to 8 in/18 to 20 cm in diameter) with the butter. Coat the mold with brown sugar. Pour in the pudding mixture. Place the mold in a larger pan filled with hot water coming halfway up the sides of the mold. Bake for 1 hour.
- Remove the pudding from the mold while still warm and place on a round platter. Serve with crème fraîche or fresh raspberry jelly.

Wine serving suggestions:
Regional: sweet new cider
National: Barsac, Muscat, Sainte Croix-du-Mont
International: Tokaji (3 puttonyas), dry Marsala, Piccolit, Riesling Auslese to Beerenauslese.

Tony Aspler's choice: Coteaux-du-Layon
Jacques Marie's choice: Crémant d'Alsace
Chef's choice:________________________________

FRANCHE-COMTÉ (JURA)

Situated on the Swiss border between the better-known wine regions of Burgundy and Alsace, Franche-Comté is a forgotten corner of France where few tourists venture. Below its forests, lush pastures and craggy mountains lie huge veins of salt. Innumerable streams cut through rocks, fall from rocky cliffs and disappear underground only to emerge several kilometers away. These cold mountain rivers support a wealth of crayfish, pike, salmon and trout to supplement the game in the fields and forests. When simply prepared in the local manner they are delicious with the piquant wines of Arbois—white and red.

Unique to this region is vin jaune, reminiscent of fino sherry in its taste and production. The grapes are late picked and kept for a long time to dry before pressing. When barrel-fermented, the wine develops a film of yeast, called *flor*, as in the dry sherries of Jerez. The local vin de paille (where the grapes are left to dry on straw before pressing) can live for fifty years or more. Like the region itself, wines from Château-Chalon, Pupillin, L'Etoile and Poligny are too often overlooked by connoisseurs for more expensive and classic labels.

Franche-Comté has its own style of charcuterie: sausages spicy with cumin, a red sausage irreverently called "Jesus de Morteau" and the long gendarmes, the sausage of Besançon. A little higher on the gastronomic ladder are such specialties as hot pigeon pâté, blood omelet, frogs' leg soup and the famous Jura cheeses—blue, the Gruyère-like Comté and a type of cheese spread called Cancoillote. Chicken with morilles (the fragrant mushrooms of the region) and stuffed tongue are about as haut as the cuisine gets.

But if the cuisine of the region is little known, the wines have long been famous in Europe. Arbois was a favorite of Emperor Frederic Barbarossa and the French kings, Henry IV and Louis XIV. And it was at Arbois that Louis Pasteur conducted his experiments on fermentation, which were to usher in the new science of oenology.

Wine serving suggestions:
Regional: Arbois, Pupillin, Côtes-du-Jura
National: Beaujolais, Chinon, Côtes-de-Bourg or Blaye, red Macon, Sylvaner, Chardonnay
International: Valpolicella, Oregon Pinot Noir, light Zinfandel, Maréchal Foch

Tony Aspler's choice: l'Etoile from Lons-le-Saunier
Jacques Marie's choice: Arbois red or rosé
Chef's choice: ________________

Tranches de Porc Comtoise

Loin of Pork with Ham and Cheese
(Serves 6)

The Comté cheese is a type of Gruyère—rich and flavorful without being too fat. This high-calorie dish is sustaining fare made for the severe winters of the Jura region.

This dish is easy to prepare, but it should not be overcooked. (The fear of trichinosis has led some people to cook pork until it is as dry and tough as an old boot!) Serve it with a dry white wine with enough acidity to balance the richness of the food, or with a fruity red or rosé.

3	eggs	3
4 tbsp	oil	60 mL
	Salt, freshly ground black pepper and freshly grated nutmeg	
6	4-oz/125-g slices pork loin (or veal or turkey)	6
1/4 cup	flour	50 mL
1 cup	fresh white breadcrumbs	250 mL
6	slices Comté cheese (or Gruyère or Jarlsberg)	6
6	slices smoked ham	6
3/4 cup	butter	175 mL

- Preheat the oven to 375°F/190°C.
- Beat the eggs in a bowl with the oil, salt, pepper and nutmeg.
- Trim the fat from the pork slices and place them between two sheets of foil. Pound the meat until very thin but not perforated.
- Dust each pork slice with flour and dip into the egg mixture.
- Coat each side with breadcrumbs, pressing the crumbs lightly into the meat. Place a slice of cheese on top of each breaded pork slice.
- Dip each slice of ham in the flour, egg mixture and breadcrumbs and place on top of the pork and cheese.
- Heat half the butter in an ovenproof skillet until it foams. Place the breaded "sandwiches" pork side down and cook until golden, then baste the tops with hot butter. (Do this in batches if necessary.) Transfer to the oven and cook until tender. Serve on a hot serving tray with the remaining butter melted on top.

PROVENCE, CÔTE D'AZUR AND NICE

This southern triangle of France, bounded by Aix-en-Provence, Toulon and Cannes, is a region of contrast, passion, light and color—a land forged in the fires of invasion by Greeks, Romans, Carthaginians and Moors and shaped by the ferocious mistral wind that blows down the Rhône Valley.

Above the beaches of the Riviera rise the pine-covered mountains fragrant with lavender, rosemary and thyme and loud with the incessant chirping of the cicada. This is not the gentle rolling Loire or pastoral Brittany. The land here is rugged and wild, symbolized by the tortuous limbs of the olive trees that stand black and forbidding against an azure sky.

It is the olive tree that has shaped the cuisine of the region. In Provence they say, "a fish lives in water and dies in oil." The bouillabaisse, the bourride (cream fish soup) and brandade (pounded salt cod cooked with oil and garlic) are the proof of this proverb. The culinary term "à la provençale" means to cook in tomatoes and garlic, two staples that are as ancient a part of the local culture as the language of the region—langue d'Oc.

The garlic, known as the truffle of Provence, is sweeter and less pungent here than the varieties grown farther north. The Provençales use it with abandon in sauces like rouille and aioli and in local specialties such as the pieds et paquets of Marseille, the loup grillé au fenouil of St. Tropez and the saucisson d'Arles.

The quality of light that attracted artists like van Gogh, Cézanne, Matisse and Picasso is a gift of endless days of sunshine which nourish a cornucopia of vegetables, fruits and herbs. The abundance of artichokes, aubergines, asparagus, zucchini, fennel, cabbage, lettuce and the ubiquitous tomato finds expression in such popular dishes as ratatouille, pistou, pissaladière and salade Niçoise.

The vineyards of Provence are the oldest in France—as old as Massalia, the name the invading Greeks gave to the port we now know as Marseille. The wines they produce are like the people themselves—lively, cheerful, outgoing and delightful companions for the flavorful seafood dishes of the coast. They may lack the finesse and elegance of a great Bordeaux or Burgundy, but their fresh, fruity charm never fails to please. And the appellation controlée wines of the Côte de Provence such as Château de Selle, Domaine Ott, Château Romassan, Château Simone and such local appellations as Bandol, Bellet, Cassis and Palette are worthy of the most discerning palate.

Bouillabaisse

Provençal Fish Soup
(Serves 6)

Bouillabaisse is a hearty Mediterranean fish soup and, like pot au feu, is substantial enough to constitute a whole meal. There is no definitive recipe for this dish, since it originated as a kind of pot-luck fish stew—a fisherman's "catch of the day" made with garlic, olive oil, saffron, tomatoes, pastis and day-old bread.

In the Provençal dialect, *boui-abaisso* means "boiling down," which describes the way this soup is cooked. Today there are more recipes for bouillabaisse than there are cooks; every chef adapts ingredients according to their availability and his or her own culinary style. In this recipe I have indicated traditional Mediterranean fish ingredients, as well as substitutes if these species are not available (the more variety of fish, the better).

Sauce rouille is a traditional accompaniment to a bouillabaisse. The hot red pimentos should not be confused with allspice or Jamaican peppers (also called pimentos in English). The peppers used in this recipe (*Capsicum annuum*) are known for their thick, sweet-fleshed red fruit; they come from the same family as paprika. (You can also buy these pimentos, already seeded and peeled, in jars.) To increase the hotness of the sauce, add tabasco or cayenne pepper. But remember—the hotter the sauce, the number the palate!

Aioli, the popular mayonnaise made with garlic and olive oil, is also typical of Provence, where it is used without discretion with all types of hot or cold dishes—especially bouillabaisse and boiled fish. The local people sometimes add a little stewed pulp of cold boiled potato to give more body to the sauce and minimize curdling during hot summer days.

FISH:

1 lb	conger eel (Substitute: eel)	500 g
2 lb	coarse fish such as sard, grondin, rouquier, galiente rascasse, gurnet, fielan, chapon, angler (Substitutes: porgy, mackerel, cod, sea bass, haddock, red grunard)	1 kg
2 lb	delicate fish such as whiting, John dory, dorade, red mullet (Substitutes: sole, flounder, mullet, red snapper, halibut)	1 kg

MARINADE:

2 tsp	whole saffron, crushed	10 mL
2 tbsp	Pastis, Pernod or anise liqueur	30 mL
1/4 cup	extra-virgin olive oil	50 mL
1/2 tsp	chopped fresh thyme	2 mL
1/2 tsp	chopped fresh savory	2 mL
1/2 tsp	chopped fresh rosemary	2 mL
1/2 tsp	chopped fresh fennel leaves	2 mL
1 tbsp	finely grated orange rind	15 mL

FISH STOCK:

2 tbsp	butter	30 mL
7 tbsp	extra-virgin olive oil	105 mL
2	onions, chopped	2
2	stalks celery, chopped	2
2	carrots, chopped	2
1 tbsp	chopped fresh savory	15 mL
1 tbsp	chopped fresh basil	15 mL
2 tsp	chopped fresh thyme	10 mL
2 tsp	chopped fresh rosemary	10 mL
2	bay leaves	2
1	large sprig fresh fennel	1
5	sprigs Italian parsley	5

8 cups	water	2 L
2 cups	dry white wine	500 mL
3 lb	raw lean sea fish bones such as halibut, sole, flounder, turbot	1.5 kg

3	leeks, white part only, cleaned and cut into fine julienned pieces	3
1	bulb fennel, cleaned and finely chopped	1
4	cloves garlic	4
4	ripe steak tomatoes, peeled, seeded and chopped	4
3	1½-lb/750-g lobsters, cut in half lengthwise, optional	3
	Salt and freshly ground black pepper	
1	stale French bread stick	1

- Cut all the fish into slices 2 in/5 cm thick (unless the fish are very small—8 oz/250 g or less).
- Place the fish in a stainless steel or glass bowl. Add all the ingredients for the marinade and toss well. Marinate for 1 to 2 hours in a cool place, turning the fish occasionally.
- To make the stock, heat the butter and 2 tbsp/30 mL olive oil in a large pot (not aluminum or cast iron, unless enameled). Sauté the onions, celery and carrots over low heat until they are soft. Do not color.
- Sprinkle the herbs over the vegetables. Add the water, white wine and fish bones cut into pieces 2 to 3 in/5 to 8 cm long. Bring to a boil and simmer for 20 to 25 minutes, or until the fish bones separate easily.
- Strain through a fine sieve or cheesecloth. Reserve the liquid and keep very hot.
- Heat 5 tbsp/75 mL olive oil in a large enamel cooking pot. Cook the leeks and fennel until slightly colored.
- Crush 2 cloves garlic with some salt to make a paste. Add the garlic, tomatoes, fish, lobsters and marinade to the boiling fish stock, adding water if necessary to cover the fish. Season with pepper and bring to a boil over brisk heat for 15 minutes.
- Cover, turn down the heat very low and let soak for 10 to 15 minutes, or until the delicate fish has broken down and the coarse fish is cooked but remains in pieces.
- Rub the remaining garlic cloves on the crust of the French stick. Slice the bread on a 45 degree angle about ½ in/1 cm thick. Toast the slices in the oven, sprinkled with a little olive oil.
- To serve, line the bottom of a very hot soup tureen or soup plate with the slices of bread. Ladle the piping-hot bouillabaisse over the bread and serve immediately. Serve the sauce rouille and aioli separately as accompaniments.

SAUCE ROUILLE
Cold Pepper Sauce

2	large cloves garlic, peeled	2
2	hot red pimentos	2
2	egg yolks	2
1/2 cup	extra-virgin olive oil	125 mL
	Salt and freshly ground black pepper	
1 tbsp	fish stock or water	15 mL

- In a mortar pound together the garlic and pimentos until smooth, or grind through a food mill or blender.
- Add the egg yolks and beat in the oil, a little at a time, as for mayonnaise. Season to taste with salt and pepper.
- Add the fish stock and mix vigorously. Serve in a sauce boat.

AIOLI
Garlic Mayonnaise

8	cloves garlic, peeled	8
1/2 tsp	salt	2 mL
2	egg yolks	2
1/4 tsp	freshly ground white pepper	1 mL
2 cups	extra-virgin olive oil	500 mL
1/2	small lemon	1/2

- In a mortar pound the garlic with the salt to form a paste.
- Add the egg yolks and pepper and blend well. Transfer mixture to a mixing bowl.
- As for mayonnaise, add the olive oil very slowly, whisking continuously to form a thick paste. Blend in the juice of half a lemon. (If desired, the sauce can be thinned by mixing with a little tepid water at the end.)

Wine serving suggestions:
Regional: Bandol, Cassis whites, Provence rosé
National: Entre-Deux-Mers, Muscadet-sur-lie, Pouilly-Fumé
International: Soave, white Rioja, Chilean Sauvignon Blanc

Tony Aspler's choice: Schlumberger's Pinot Blanc from Alsace
Jacques Marie's choice: Château Romassan "Coeur de grain," Cuvée Marcel Ott
Chef's choice: ____________________

Italy

Italy produces more wine—and more individual wines—than any other country in the world, and the products of its kitchens, from the Alps to Sicily, are equally diverse and varied. Those who have not ventured past the stereotypical Italian restaurant menu of minestrone, spaghetti Bolognese, veal Marsala and cassata have missed a whole range of gustatory experiences.

Italian food is artfully simple. It depends on the ingredients that can be grown in a small plot of land, augmented by what can be hunted, netted or snared. This local concentration means that each of the twenty provinces has its own unique style of cooking dictated by its geography, climate and traditions. In Piedmont, for instance, I have eaten donkey stew and cows udders. Mercifully, I was informed only after the fact.

Pasta, that most Italian of dishes, is said to have been introduced to Venice by Marco Polo, who brought the recipe back from the court of the Great Khan in China. And it was the Venetians who, in the sixteenth century, gave the world the fork as a dining utensil. Catherine de Medici took her Florentine chefs with her to Paris when she married the future Henri II, thereby introducing the French to Europe's most sophisticated cuisine of the time—a cuisine influenced by the Greeks and Romans.

Although pasta is now available the length and breadth of the peninsula, it was originally a southern specialty. Northerners, especially those living in the Venetian plains, prefer rice dishes. Their creamy, textured risottos are flavored with everything from frogs' legs to apples and are even stained black with cuttlefish ink.

In the distinctive Trentino-Alto Adige area in the northeast, the influence of Austrian neighbors can be seen both in the local dishes and in the wines which still bear German names: local menus include such rib-sticking dishes as speck (bacon), Wiener Schnitzel, Apfelstrudel and a

delicious Tyrolean specialty called Schulzkrapfen (ravioli stuffed with cheese and sauerkraut).

The basis of northern Italian cooking is butter, while south of Umbria olive oil is the staple. In the north the emphasis is on rice and corn dishes served with meat and game; in the south the emphasis is on fresh vegetables, especially tomatoes, peppers, aubergines and broccoli. Throughout Italy the basic spices used are basil, marjoram, oregano and thyme, added more liberally as you travel south. And in a country surrounded almost entirely by coastline, seafood is always a specialty.

Just as there are dozens of pastas in all shapes and sizes so, too, does Italy boast an enormous range of cheeses—from the bland Mozzarella, nutty Fontina, and creamy Caciotta to the silky, piquant Gorgonzola, sharp Pecorino, smoked Provolone and delicious Parmigiano Reggiano.

Each region has its locally made wines which marry well with the specialties of the area: the meat and game and white truffles of Piedmont and Tuscany go well with the full-bodied Barolos, Barbarescos and Chiantis. The crisp whites of Friuli and Veneto complement the fish and seafood of the Adriatic. Frascati could have been made for Roman artichokes, and the robust reds and full-bodied whites of the south complement the highly flavored olive oil and tomato-based dishes of Calabria and Apulia. Even the desserts, especially beloved by southern Italians (the best gelati come from Sicily), have their accompanying wines in Vin Santo, Piccolit, Verduzzo and the sweet sparkling Muscatos of Asti.

Gnocchi alla Romana

Semolina Patties with Parmesan
(Serves 6)

Gnocchi are fresh pasta dumplings made from corn or wheat flour, semolina, or potato flour. They make good garnishes for stews or could be served as a main course in a cream, tomato or meat sauce. They are easily reheated but are best served fresh.

4 cups	milk	1 L
2 tsp	salt	10 mL
	Freshly ground black pepper	
1/2 tsp	freshly grated nutmeg	2 mL
1 cup	semolina	250 mL
3	eggs	3
1 1/4 cups	grated Parmesan cheese	300 mL
1 cup	butter	250 mL

- In a heavy saucepan, bring the milk to a boil. Add the salt, pepper and nutmeg, mixing well.
- Add the semolina, stirring constantly, and cook until the mixture forms a thick paste. Remove from heat.
- Beat the eggs and 1 cup/250 mL Parmesan together with a fork. Add the mixture to the semolina.
- Pour the hot semolina paste onto a buttered baking sheet. Spread the paste evenly over the baking sheet. Cool.
- Preheat the oven to 400°F/200°C.
- When cool, cut the semolina in squares or triangles, 1 1/2 to 2 in/4 to 5 cm in diameter.
- Melt the butter over low heat. Dunk each gnocchi in the butter and place in a baking dish.
- Sprinkle 1/4 cup/50 mL Parmesan over the gnocchi. Bake on the top shelf of the oven until golden. Serve hot with a fresh tomato sauce.

Wine serving suggestions:
Regional: Sangiovese, Montecompatri, Zagarolo
National: Chianti, Rubesco, Rosato del Salento, Chiaretto, dry Verduzzo, Tocai di Lison
International: Chablis, white Graves, Pinot Blanc, Rosé d'Anjou, Chenin Blanc, light Sauvignon, Chassagne-Montrachet, Chiroubles, red Sancerre, red Rioja, German Riesling Kabinett, Grüner Veltliner, white Garrafeira

Tony Aspler's choice: Barbera d'Asti
Jacques Marie's choice: Santa Maddalena
Chef's choice:____________________

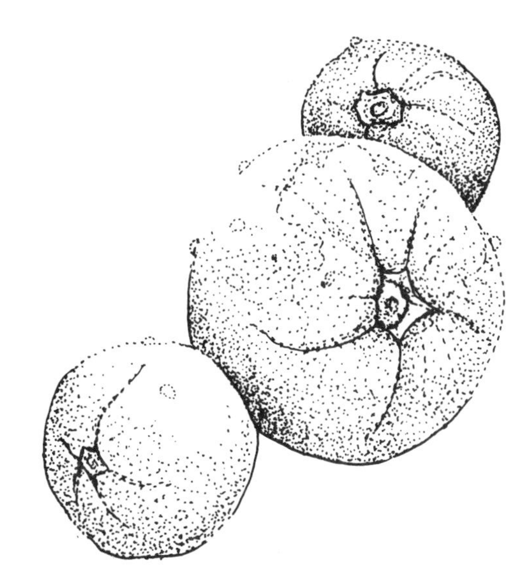

Spada alla Siciliana

Swordfish Sicilian Style
(Serves 4)

The swordfish, one of the best of the Mediterranean sea fishes, can reach weights of 350 lb/160 kg. The flesh is firm and resembles a cross between veal and tuna in taste and texture. This Sicilian specialty makes a convenient and delicious summer picnic meal and can be prepared a day ahead. Serve it cold with fresh bread.

1	onion, finely chopped	1
1 cup	olive oil	250 mL
1/2 cup	tomato puree	125 mL
1/4 cup	white wine or water	50 mL
1	stalk celery, chopped	1
	Salt and freshly ground black pepper	
4	slices swordfish, approx. 8 to 12 oz/250 to 350 g each	4
4 tbsp	flour	60 mL
24	green olives, pitted	24
4 tsp	capers	20 mL
1 tbsp	sugar	15 mL
3 tbsp	wine vinegar	45 mL

- Fry the onions in 1/2 cup/125 mL olive oil until golden.
- Add the tomato puree, wine and celery. Season with a little salt and pepper and cook over low heat for 10 minutes.
- Season the fish with salt and pepper and sprinkle each side with flour.
- Fry the fish in the remaining olive oil (less 2 tbsp/30 mL) on both sides over medium heat until golden. Remove and reserve.
- Add to the sauce the olives, capers, sugar, vinegar and remaining 2 tbsp/30 mL oil and cook for 5 minutes. Place the fish in the sauce and cook for a further 5 minutes. Remove and let cool completely before serving.

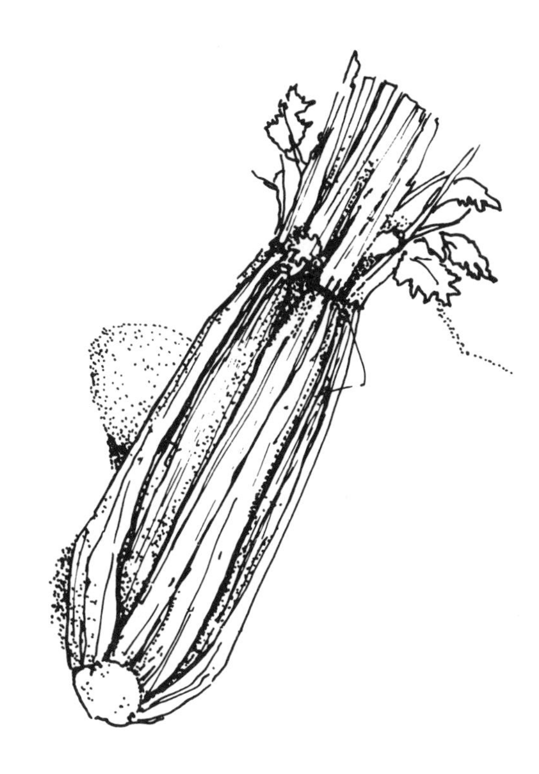

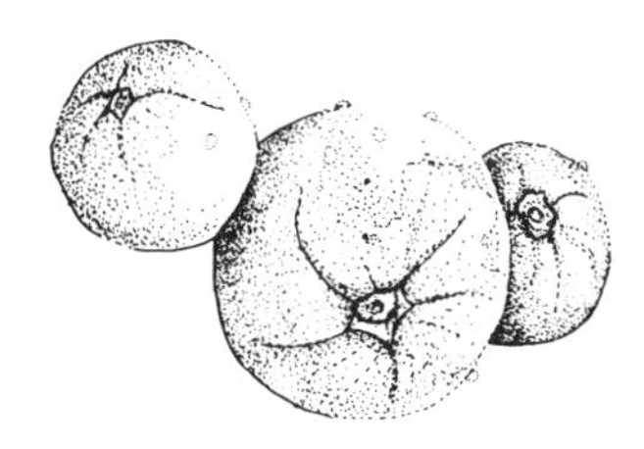

Wine serving suggestions:
Regional: Bianco di Alcamo, white Valledolmo or Vallelunga, white Corvo, Damaschino
National: Soave, Bianchello del Metauro, Est! Est! Est!, Lacrima Christi, Orvieto, Portofino, Verdicchio, Vernaccia di San Gimignano
International: Muscadet sur lie, Sancerre, Entre-Deux-Mers, Sylvaner, Rhine Riesling, Viña Sol, Grüner Veltliner, Vinho Verde, Traminer, Californian Semillon

Tony Aspler's choice: white Regaleali (Count Tasca)
Jacques Marie's choice: Verdicchio dei Castelli di Jesi
Chef's choice:______________________________

Stracotto

Braised Steak
(Serves 4)

The province of Arezzo produces some of the best beef in Italy. Chianina steers have been raised here for over three thousand years. They are the largest cattle in the world—4,000 lb/1,800 kg—and the beef is highlighted in the many meat dishes that Tuscany is famous for.

This recipe is a favorite of the house of Antinori—one of the classic wine estates in Tuscany. Marchese Piero Antinori serves it to his guests to set off his Villa Antinori Chianti Classico.

1	carrot	1
1	onion	1
1	stalk celery	1
4	leaves basil	4
1	sprig rosemary	1
5	sprigs Italian parsley	5
1/4 cup	olive oil	50 mL
2	cloves garlic	2
2	slices bacon	2
1 1/2 lb	flank steak	750 g
	Salt and freshly ground black pepper	
1 cup	Chianti	250 mL
2 tbsp	tomato paste	30 mL
1 cup	water	250 mL

- Chop the carrot, onion, celery, basil, rosemary and parsley. Fry in the olive oil until lightly colored.
- Cut the garlic cloves into quarters and cut the bacon into 2-in/5-cm pieces. Cut slits in the steak at a 45 degree angle and insert the pieces of garlic and bacon. Season with salt and pepper.
- Brown the steak on both sides with the vegetables. Add the Chianti and cook slowly until reduced by half. Add the tomato paste blended with the water. Cook slowly, covered, for 1½ hours, or until the steak is very tender.

Wine serving suggestions:
Regional: Chianti, Tignanello, Vino Nobile di Montepulciano, Tegolato
National: Barbera, Cabernet, Carema, Cellatica, Cinqeterre, Corvo, Falerno, Fracia, Gattinara, Grumello, Rubesco, Sassella, Spanna, Taurasi, Venegazzu
International: Rioja red, Gran Coronas, Dão, Cahors, Pomerol, St-Emilion, Shiraz, Californian Pinot Noir, Chilean Cabernet

Tony Aspler's choice: Villa Antinori Chianti Classico Riserva (what else?)
Jacques Marie's choice: Carmignano
Chef's choice:____________________

Ragu Bolognese

Bolognese Sauce
(Serves 6)

In Bologna, tagliatelle (a ribbon-shaped egg pasta) is often served with a meat sauce called ragu. (The word *ragu* is a corruption of the French *ragoût*, which means stew—the old French verb *ragoûter* means to arouse the taste buds or appetite.)

This unctuous sauce is a masterpiece of Bolognese cooking. Make sure you cook it slowly, allowing time for the flavors to develop. The freshness and quality of the herbs is important. This sauce is delicious served with all kinds of pasta. It should keep well if refrigerated.

4 tbsp	butter	60 mL
4 oz	smoked ham or bacon, coarsely chopped	125 g
	Freshly ground black pepper	
1 cup	chopped onions	250 mL
1/2 cup	chopped celery	125 mL
1/4 cup	chopped carrots	50 mL
4	cloves	4
1/4 tsp	nutmeg	1 mL
2	bay leaves	2
1/4 tsp	thyme	1 mL
3 tbsp	olive oil	45 mL
1 lb	lean beef, finely ground	500 g
8 oz	lean pork, finely ground	250 g
1/2 cup	dry white wine	125 mL
2 cups	beef stock	500 mL

3 tbsp	tomato paste	45 mL
1/4 tsp	basil	1 mL
1/4 tsp	oregano	1 mL
1/2 cup	sliced mushrooms	125 mL
8 oz	chicken livers, roughly chopped	250 g
1 tsp	salt	5 mL
1/2 cup	heavy cream	125 mL

- In a large, heavy skillet, melt the butter over moderate heat. Add the ham or bacon and cook until golden. Add freshly ground black pepper to taste.
- Add the onions, celery and carrots. Cook until soft and slightly golden.
- Add the cloves, nutmeg, bay leaves and thyme. Mix well.
- In another frying pan, heat the olive oil. Add the beef and pork. Stir constantly over medium-high heat until lightly browned, breaking up any lumps.
- Turn up the heat to very high and immediately add the white wine. Boil for 1 minute.
- Add the meat to the vegetables in the first skillet. Add the stock and tomato paste. Cook for 45 minutes over low heat, just simmering, stirring occasionally.
- Add the basil and oregano. Remove the bay leaves and cloves.
- Add the mushrooms and chicken livers. Mix well and cook for 5 minutes.
- Add the salt and stir in the cream (the sauce should be very thick).

Wine serving suggestions:
Regional: Lambrusco di Sorbara
National: Chianti, Sangiovese, Barbera, Gattinara
International: Côte-de-Bourg, Côte-de-Nuits, red Sancerre, light Zinfandel, Bairrada

Tony Aspler's choice: Rubesco
Jacques Marie's choice: Barbaresco
Chef's choice:________________________

Osso Bucco

Braised Veal Shanks
(Serves 6)

When osso buchi are very fresh, the marrow from the round bone of the shin is the prize of the dish. But if the bones are not fresh, the marrow could be sour or rancid.

Some chefs prefer to cut the osso buchi only two fingers thick. In this recipe from northern Italy, the veal shanks are thicker and as a result take longer to cook (they must be cooked slowly or they will dry out).

Osso bucco is traditionally served with gremolata. In Italy minced anchovy fillets are sometimes added to this garnish.

6	veal shanks or shins, approx. 1 lb/500 g each and 4 in/10 cm thick	6
1 tsp	salt	5 mL
1/2 tsp	freshly ground black pepper	2 mL
	Flour	
4 tbsp	butter	60 mL
1/2 cup	olive oil	125 mL
1 cup	finely chopped onions	250 mL
1/2 cup	grated carrots	125 mL
1/2 cup	finely chopped celery	125 mL
1 cup	dry white wine	250 mL
1 cup	beef, veal or chicken stock	250 mL
1/2 tsp	basil	2 mL
1/2 tsp	thyme	2 mL
1/2 tsp	marjoram	2 mL
1/2 tsp	rosemary	2 mL

4	small bay leaves	4
1 tsp	garlic, pasted	5 mL
3 cups	drained whole tomatoes, coarsely chopped	750 mL
6	sprigs Italian parsley	6

GREMOLATA:

1 tbsp	grated lemon peel	15 mL
1 tbsp	finely chopped garlic	15 mL
3 tbsp	finely chopped Italian parsley (flat leaves)	45 mL

- Preheat the oven to 300°F/150°C.
- Tie the veal shanks around the outside circumference with butcher's string. Season the shanks with salt and pepper and dredge lightly in flour.
- Using a thick-bottomed casserole large enough to accommodate the veal in one layer, melt the butter and olive oil at medium heat. Brown the veal shanks on all sides. Remove them and reserve in a warm place.
- Add the onions to the casserole and cook for 2 minutes, stirring continuously. Add the carrots and celery and cook for a further 2 minutes, stirring continuously.
- Stir in the wine, stock, basil, thyme, marjoram, rosemary, bay leaves, garlic, tomatoes and parsley. Season with salt and pepper.
- Raise the heat and bring to a simmer. Cook for 5 minutes.
- Add the veal shanks standing upright, with the larger cross-sections of marrow facing upwards. Baste the shanks with sauce. Cover and cook in the oven for 2 hours, or until the meat is tender.
- Prepare the gremolata by combining the lemon peel, garlic and parsley.
- Transfer the veal shanks to a hot serving platter. Carefully remove the string. Spoon the sauce around and over the meat.
- Sprinkle the gremolata over the veal shanks and serve with risotto or rice pilaf.

Wine serving suggestions:
Regional: Valtellina Superiore
National: Brunello di Montalcino, Barbaresco, Merlot, Valpolicella
International: St-Emilion, Mercurey, red Penedes, Garrafeira

Tony Aspler's choice: Taurasi
Jacques Marie's choice: Barolo Brunate (Vigneto Zonchetta)
Chef's choice:______________________________

Pollo alla Cacciatore

Braised Chicken Hunter Style
(Serves 4)

The French version of this dish, poulet à la chasseur, is mainly garnished with white wine, mushrooms, shallots and tarragon; the Italians use red wine, olive oil and green peppers. This recipe has a distinctive Mediterranean touch, adding anchovies, black olives and red wine vinegar.

You can use the discarded chicken fat to sauté some new or small potatoes and serve them as an accompaniment.

3 lb	roasting chicken	1.5 kg
	Salt and freshly ground black pepper	
1/4 cup	olive oil	50 mL
1	small onion, chopped	1
2	cloves garlic, finely chopped	2
1	green pepper, seeded and sliced	1
1/2 tsp	chopped fresh oregano	2 mL
1/2 tsp	chopped fresh rosemary	2 mL
3	medium tomatoes, peeled, seeded and coarsely chopped	3
2 tbsp	red wine vinegar	30 mL
3/4 cup	red wine	175 mL
1/2 cup	chicken stock or water	125 mL
12	black olives, Mediterranean style	12
3	anchovy fillets, chopped	3
1 tbsp	chopped Italian parsley	15 mL

- Cut the chicken into serving pieces. Season with salt and pepper.
- Heat the olive oil to a haze in a heavy-bottomed skillet. Brown the chicken in the oil, four pieces at a time and skin side first. Remove the chicken and keep warm.
- Discard most of the fat from the skillet, leaving sufficient to coat the bottom of the pan. Add the onion and garlic to the skillet and cook until slightly colored.
- Add the green pepper, oregano, rosemary, tomatoes, vinegar, red wine and stock. Mix well and season with salt and pepper. Bring to a boil and cook for 5 minutes.
- Add the chicken pieces and simmer, covered, for 30 minutes, or until the chicken is tender.
- To serve, arrange the chicken pieces on a hot serving platter. Add the olives, anchovies and parsley to the sauce. Bring to a boil (degrease if necessary) and adjust seasoning. Ladle the sauce over the chicken pieces and serve hot.

Wine serving suggestions:
Regional: Ravello, Aglianico
National: Sangiovese, Chianti, Nebbiolo
International: Côtes-du-Rhône, Tavel, Zinfandel, Petite Sirah, Dão, Faustino, Chilean Cabernet, Shiraz

Tony Aspler's choice: Ruffino Chianti Riserva Ducale
Jacques Marie's choice: Montepulciano d'Abruzzo
Chef's choice:______________________________

Cassata alla Siciliana

Sicilian Cheesecake with Chocolate
(Serves 8)

There are two types of cassata. Gelato is made with two flavors of ice cream, almonds and candied fruits soaked in liqueur. The recipe given here is for dolce, a rich, sweet cheesecake made with cream cheese and chocolate. Chocolate is a very difficult food to appreciate wine with, because of its blandness. Ideally, the wines suggested here should be served after the dessert.

1	fresh pound cake, 9 by 3 in/22 by 8 cm	1
1 1/4 lb	ricotta cheese	625 g
1/4 cup	heavy cream	50 mL
1/4 cup	confectioner's sugar	50 mL
1/4 tsp	salt	1 mL
1/2 tsp	vanilla	2 mL
1/4 cup	Strega or Curacao or orange-based liqueur	50 mL
4 oz	mixed candied fruit, chopped	125 g
2 oz	semi-sweet chocolate, grated	60 g

FROSTING:

1/2 cup	espresso coffee	125 mL
14 oz	semi-sweet chocolate, grated	450 g
1 cup	unsalted butter, very cold	250 mL

- Trim off the end and top crust of the pound cake with a bread knife. Cut the cake horizontally into 1/2-in/1-cm slices.
- Mash the ricotta cheese in a bowl with a fork. Beat it with an electric beater, adding the cream (a little at a time), sugar, salt, vanilla and liqueur until smooth.
- Lightly mix in the candied fruit and chocolate with a rubber spatula or wooden spoon.
- Starting with the bottom slice of cake, spread generously with the cheese mixture. Add the next slice of cake and repeat the process until all the slices are used. (Do not cover the top slice with the mixture.)
- Press the cake lightly with the palm of your hand to make sure the slices stick together. Refrigerate for 4 hours. (The cake should feel firm.)
- To prepare the frosting, place a stainless-steel bowl over a double boiler and pour in the espresso coffee.
- Add the chocolate, stirring constantly until it is completely melted.
- Add the butter a few small pieces at a time, stirring continuously until a smooth texture is achieved. Refrigerate until cold but still soft enough to spread.
- With a spatula, cover the cake with the chocolate mixture, reserving a small amount. Using a piping bag, decorate the cake with the rest of the frosting. Decorate the top and sides with candied fruit.

Wine serving suggestions:
Regional: Marsala Vergine
National: Malvasia, Asti Spumante
International: Muscat Beaumes-de-Venise, Frontignan, Lunel, German Auslese, Moscatel de Setúbal, sweet Champagne

Tony Aspler's choice: Malvasia delle Lipari
Jacques Marie's choice: Moscato Passito di Pantelleria
Chef's choice:______________________________

Charles de Gaulle once said about France: "How can you govern a country that has 320 cheeses?" The same might hold true of Germany in terms of sausages. There are some 1,500 varieties which are celebrated annually at the Wurstmarkt (sausage market) in Bad Durkheim, one of many such festivals dedicated to the pleasures of the table. The French, Italians, Spanish and Portuguese may drink more wine than the Germans, but no other nationality celebrates the vintage with more fervor. Every village and hamlet within staggering distance of a vineyard has its own wine festival. Any excuse to dress up in national costume, parade through the streets and knock back wine is welcomed.

Bismark may have unified Germany in 1871 under the King of Prussia, but a national cuisine does not emerge at the stroke of a pen. The patchwork of principalities and duchies still retain their own local culinary traditions to this day.

The unifying feature, apart from the ubiquitous sausage, is the zest with which the Germans approach their meals. Hearty appetites demand hearty fare. By contrast, their wines are light and delicate, so they tend to drink them on their own and order beer with their meals instead.

Regional cooking styles are based on climate and agricultural potential. In the northern coastal area the diet is rich in fish, particularly halibut, herring, flounder and eel. The sandy soil here is ideal for the cultivation of potatoes, grains, cabbage and beets.

The North Sea climate calls for lusty soups of cabbage and smoked bacon reinforced with dumplings (sweet and sour eel soup is a local specialty), roast goose and potatoes, smoked fish and meat in sweet and sour sauces. This particular taste predilection extends to mixing fruit and meat as well.

Between the northern plain and the mountains of southern Germany lie the rich, fertile central plateau and the Rhine and Mosel valleys—a landscape of vineyards, orchards, wheat fields and pastureland. Westphalia ham and broad beans, Sauerbraten (marinated pot-roast of beef), Thuringian Bratwurst grilled over an open fire and Blindhuhn, a casserole of vegetables, apples, beans and bacon, are the dishes to look for when travelling in the region.

The forested, mountainous area to the south supports a prosperous dairy industry. The wheat and barley of its fields produce those two staples of the German pantry—bread and beer. This is the home of Black Forest cake, a dish that is now de rigueur for any North American coffee shop with pretensions. Other local favorites include veal shanks in pickle sauce, calves' liver fritters and a wealth of game birds, wild boar and venison. The forests provide a harvest of mushrooms—chanterelle, morel, boletus and field varieties. This region is also the center for Schnapps and German eaux-de-vie, especially Kirsch.

What German cuisine may lack in delicacy and finesse is made up for in the elegance of its wines. No other country offers such an appealing range of light, flowery wines that balance sweetness with fruity acidity. A Riesling from the Rhine or Mosel can range from tartly dry to unctuously sweet depending on the level of sugar in the grapes at the time they were picked. In fact, a single vineyard can produce the same wine in styles ranging from Kabinett to Trockenbeerenauslese, depending on the sugar values.

Those adventurous diners who have tried Riesling of Kabinett quality with fish and light meat are delighted to discover how well the wine goes with the food. And German wines are invariably lower in alcohol than their French, Italian or Californian counterparts.

Hasenpfeffer

Braised Hare in Wine Sauce and Pepper
(Serves 6)

Hare has been praised by civilizations from the Egyptians to the Gauls, who found it far superior to rabbit. Hare has dark meat and a stronger flavor than rabbit, which is tender but not as tasty.

In Germany, Hasenpfeffer is a traditional dish which was popular in medieval times, when pepper was a precious spice and Hasenpfeffer was a dish enjoyed only by the rich and mighty.

8 oz	lean bacon	250 g
8 to 10 lb	hare	3.5 to 5 kg
1 tsp	salt	5 mL
3/4 tsp	freshly ground black pepper	4 mL
1/2 cup	flour	125 mL
1/2 cup	finely chopped onions or shallots	125 mL
3	cloves garlic, pasted	3
2 cups	red wine	500 mL
1 cup	stock	250 mL
2 tbsp	brandy	30 mL
1 tbsp	red currant jelly	15 mL
1	bay leaf	1
1/4 tsp	thyme	1 mL
1/4 tsp	rosemary	1 mL
3	cloves	3
1/2	lemon	1/2

- Finely dice the bacon and cook over moderate heat until crisp. Remove and place on paper towels to dry. Reserve the bacon fat.
- Cut the hare into serving pieces. Season with salt and pepper and sprinkle with the flour.
- Heat the bacon fat in a large 6-qt/6-L ovenproof skillet. Fry the hare pieces on all sides until golden. Remove and keep warm.
- Reserve 3 tbsp/45 mL fat in the skillet. Fry the onions until golden.
- Add the garlic and fry for 1 minute. Then add the wine and stock.
- Add all the remaining ingredients except the lemon juice. Return the hare to the skillet. (The hare should be almost covered by the liquid.) Simmer over low heat, covered, for 1 to 1½ hours, or until the hare is very tender.
- When tender, remove bay leaf and add the lemon juice. Adjust the seasonings (the sauce should be peppery) and serve with parsley potatoes or dumplings.

Wine serving suggestions:
National: Spätburgunder Spätlese, Franconian white, Scheurebe Kabinett, Riesling Spätlese
International: Pinot Noir, Barbaresco, Barolo, Amarone, Pomerol, St-Emilion, Crozes-Hermitage, St-Joseph, Vega Sicilia, Barca Vehla, Garrafeira, Shiraz

Tony Aspler's choice: Assmannshauser Höllenberg Spätburgunder
Jacques Marie's choice: Chambertin
Chef's choice:____________________________________

Sauerbraten

Beef Pot Roast
(Serves 8)

Sauerbraten is probably one of the best-known German dishes. But it is not "sour," as the name implies. The meat is marinated in vinegar, wine or buttermilk to tenderize and flavor it. This was necessary in ancient times when the meat used came from animals that were too old to work and consequently tough. Today the marinating time can be kept to a minimum. The tender, rich flavor of the dish goes well with a semi-sweet white German wine or a rich warm red. Serve it hot with dumplings, boiled potatoes or buttered noodles.

4 lb	boneless beef roast (front end or top round)	2 kg
1½ cups	red wine vinegar	375 mL
1 cup	dry red wine	250 mL
2 cups	water	500 mL
2 tbsp	salt	30 mL
2 tsp	whole black peppercorns, crushed	10 mL
4	cloves, crushed	4
1 tsp	caraway seeds	5 mL
2	bay leaves, crushed	2
2	large onions, sliced	2
2	large carrots, chopped	2
2	celery stalks, chopped	2
½	lemon, sliced	½
10	juniper berries	10
5	allspice berries	5

6	sprigs Italian parsley, chopped	6
9 tbsp	lard	135 mL
6 tbsp	flour	90 mL
2 tbsp	brown sugar, or 1/4 cup/50 mL raisins	30 mL

- Trim the fat from the meat if necessary.
- To prepare the marinade, in a saucepan combine the vinegar, red wine, water, salt, peppercorns, cloves, caraway seeds, bay leaves, onions, carrots, celery, lemon, juniper and allspice. Bring to the boil and simmer for 3 minutes.
- Cool the marinade and add the parsley. Pour the marinade into a stainless steel, glass or earthenware bowl.
- Place the meat in the marinade and turn it several times. Cover the bowl with kitchen wrap and refrigerate for 4 to 7 days, depending on the toughness of the meat, turning the meat twice a day.
- Preheat the oven to 350°F/180°C.
- Remove the meat from the marinade and pat dry with paper towels. Reserve the marinade.
- Melt 6 tbsp/90 mL lard in a large Dutch oven. Sprinkle the meat with 3 tbsp/45 mL flour and brown in the hot lard on all sides.
- Pour the marinade over the meat and cover tightly. Cook in the oven for 2 1/2 to 3 hours, or until the meat is tender.
- Pour the liquid off the meat and cover the meat. Strain the liquid and skim off the fat if necessary.
- Melt the remaining lard in a saucepan and blend in the remaining flour with the brown sugar or raisins. Cook until slightly browned.
- Gradually add the strained liquid. Stirring constantly, cook for 20 minutes on very low heat. Adjust seasonings.
- To serve, slice the meat thickly and place slices on a warm serving tray. Ladle the sauce over the meat and pour the rest into a sauce boat.

Wine serving suggestions:
Regional/National: Rheingau Riesling Spätlese Trocken, Rheinhessen and Franken Sylvaner Kabinett, Riesling Kabinett
International: Côtes-du-Rhône, Amarone, Australian Hermitage, Zinfandel

Tony Aspler's choice: Venegazzu
Jacques Marie's choice: Châteauneuf-du-Pape (Château des Fines Roches)
Chef's choice:________________________________

Austria's lasting legacy to world cuisine has been the gift of the Wiener Schnitzel, the Wiener sausage and the famous Sachertorte (chocolate cake with apricot jam filling). Their communal birthplace was Vienna (Wien), the former capital of the Austro-Hungarian Empire. As the glittering heart of Europe in the nineteenth century, Vienna attracted the finest chefs from Hungary, Czechoslovakia, Romania, Yugoslavia and the Alto Adige—all of whom brought their local traditions with them.

The Empire is no more, but its ghost still haunts the kitchens of the great Viennese restaurants and hotels where the culinary traditions of Central Europe are fused in the elaborate pastries, cakes, cookies and confections beloved by Austrians today. Semolina puddings, cream cheese pancakes, cream-filled meringues, apple strudel, coffee with whipped cream—Austrian cuisine is for the sweet-toothed. For those who cannot while away the afternoons in Vienna's coffee houses or would rather skip dessert, Austria also offers a whole range of dishes that remind one of its former sphere of influence: carp simmered in beer stock (Poland), goulash (Hungary), pork and sauerkraut (Germany), roast goose and dumplings (Czechoslovakia) and risotto (Venice), as well as fried trout (Adriatic coast).

Today Austria has no coastline, but lakes near the Hungarian border provide salmon, trout, pike, perch, sturgeon and crayfish. Game is also readily available, especially during Wildbretwochen (game festival week)—partridge, pheasant, wild boar, hare, woodcock and three species of deer.

Austrian wines are classified in the same manner as German wines, but they are drier and higher in alcohol. The workhorse grape of the Austrian industry is the Grüner Veltliner, which produces a crisp dry white. The best come from the towns of Krems and Gumpoldskirchen.

Lusciously sweet dessert wines, far cheaper than their German counterparts, are made in Burgenland around the shores of Neusiedlersee.

The Austrian equivalent of Beaujolais nouveau is called Heurige—a cloudy, spritzig wine served in inns and taverns a few weeks after the harvest. The proprietors advertise its arrival by hanging a switch of fir twigs or a straw wreath outside their establishments. They serve it in jugs with roast chicken, and the unwary tourist could easily be carried away by the contagious party atmosphere, as the locals enjoy the first fruits of the new vintage.

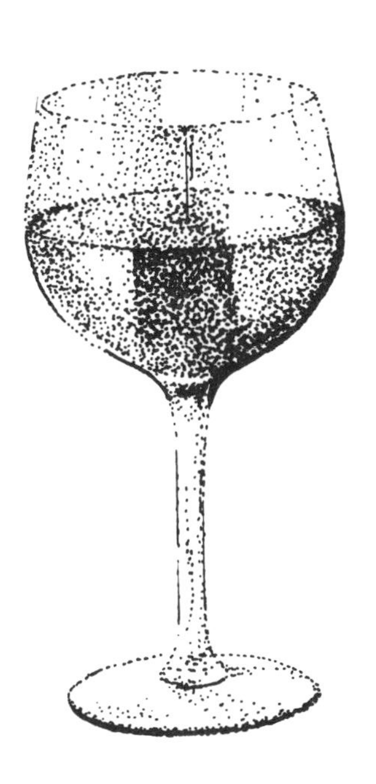

Rahmschnitzel

Veal Cutlets with Mushrooms
(Serves 4)

The famous Austrian dish, Wienerschnitzel, is actually a variation of Scaloppine alla Milanese. Rahmschnitzel, a less well-known specialty, are veal cutlets in a rich mushroom and cream sauce. The key is to cook the cutlets very quickly, or they will become tough.

4	veal cutlets, approx. 6 oz/175 g each	4
1 cup	dry white wine	250 mL
	Salt and freshly ground black pepper	
1/3 cup	flour	75 mL
8 tbsp	unsalted butter	120 mL
1 cup	sliced white mushrooms	250 mL
1/2 cup	heavy cream	125 mL
1 tsp	paprika	5 mL
2	slices white bread	2
1 tbsp	finely chopped fresh parsley	15 mL

- Soak the veal cutlets in white wine for 30 minutes, turning them from time to time.
- Remove the cutlets from the wine and dry them on paper towels. Reserve the marinade. Season the cutlets with salt and pepper and dust them with a light coating of flour.
- In a thick skillet, melt 4 tbsp/60 mL butter. When foaming, add the cutlets and cook them on both sides over medium heat without browning the butter. (Do not overcook. The cutlets should be moist in the center.)

- Place the cutlets on a serving platter and keep them in a warm oven.
- Discard half the butter from the skillet and sauté the mushrooms over brisk heat. When the mushrooms turn golden, add the wine from the marinade and cook until reduced by half.
- Add the cream and paprika. Cook until the sauce begins to thicken.
- Remove the crusts from the slices of bread. Cut each slice diagonally in half and trim to make 4 heart shapes. Fry the croutons in the remaining butter to a light golden color on both sides.
- To serve, pour the mushroom sauce over the veal cutlets arranged on a serving platter. Stick the points of the croutons into the sauce around the cutlets and sprinkle with chopped parsley. Serve immediately.

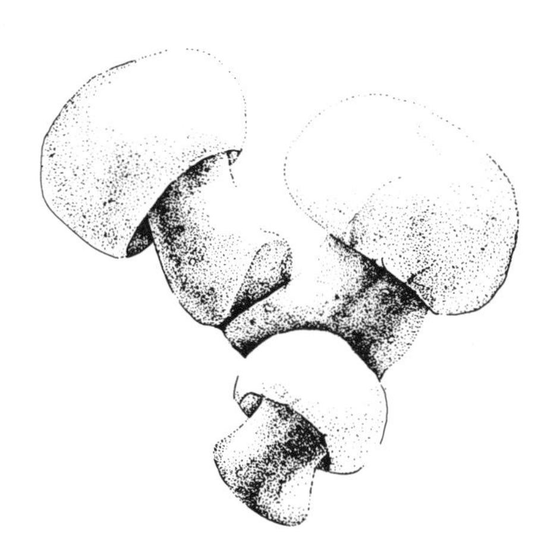

Wine serving suggestions:
National: Austrian Rhine Riesling, Müller-Thurgau Kabinett, Weissburgunder
International: Mercurey, Pinot Grigio, Cape Riesling, Australian Semillon, red Rioja, Tavel rosé, Jurançon, German Kabinett

Tony Aspler's choice: Torre di Giano
Jacques Marie's choice: Gumpoldskirchener
Chef's choice: ______________________

Spanish cuisine is deceptively simple, based as it is on the ingredients readily available in each of the country's self-contained regions. The weight and style of the dishes reflect the climate and temperament of these ancient kingdoms—from the heavy soups and substantial pork and lamb dishes of the Basque country and Galicia in the north to the light fish dishes and pastries of Andalusia in the south and the classic paella of Valencia.

Paella, a treasure trove of chicken and shellfish mixed with saffron rice, is the quintessential Spanish dish—a meal that can be prepared in a single pot, indoors or out. Its quality depends on the freshness of the ingredients and the skill of the cook.

Spanish cuisine has been influenced by foodstuffs rather than techniques. (The only indigenous creation that has been wholeheartedly embraced by other nations is mayonnaise. Cardinal Richelieu tasted the velvety cold sauce at Port Mahon on the island of Minorca and brought the recipe back to France in the early part of the seventeenth century.) The Romans were responsible not only for planting the vine in Spain, but the orange and lemon groves of the south and the fields of sugar cane. During their seventeenth-century occupation the Moors introduced a variety of spices such as saffron, aniseed and cumin, as well as planting almond orchards.

In the seventeenth century the Conquistadores brought back from the New World the potato, the tomato and the pimento—novel foodstuffs which were eventually cultivated throughout Europe.

The major wine-growing areas are perhaps the easiest keys to the style of food in Spain. Rioja and Navarre, which produce the best red wines of the country, boast fine lamb while the crisp, elegant whites (sparkling and still) of Catalonia marry well with the fish, lobster and prawns of the Penedes coast. The influence of Provence across the Pyrenees is evident here, too. The sherries of Jerez, from the light Manzanillas and Finos to the rich, nutty Olorosos set up the palate for the fish stews and cod of the southwest or accompany the tapas—snacks of shrimp, deep-fried whitebait, toasted almonds, pieces of ham or the ubiquitous spicy red sausage known as chorizo, made from the pork of black, long-legged Spanish pigs. This fiery sausage can be found in a variety of regional dishes from traditional stews and paellas to the pride of Rioja—patas a la riojana, layers of potato, tomato, onions, red pepper and chorizo baked in stock.

Spanish wines, particularly from Rioja and Catalonia, both red and white, still and sparkling, have improved so dramatically in quality in the last decade, that they now rival the great wines of France and Italy. And in terms of price, they are currently often the best value to be had in the wine store.

Bunuelos de Caracoles

Snail Fritters
(Serves 6)

Snails are very popular in Spain, France and Italy—particularly those that feed on vine leaves. These fritters make good appetizers and in Spain are sometimes served as hot tapas. Tapas (from *tapa*, meaning "top") are snacks or appetizers served on top of the counter in bars or *tascas* (taverns) with pre-dinner drinks, such as a cold glass of Fino.

72	snails, canned	72
4 tbsp	oil	60 mL
8	shallots, chopped	8
2	cloves garlic, chopped	2
	Salt and freshly ground black pepper	
1/2 cup	dry sherry	125 mL
1/2	lemon	1/2
1 tsp	chili powder	5 mL
1 cup	flour	250 mL
2	egg yolks	2
4	egg whites	4
	Oil for deep frying	

- Rinse the snails under cold water and drain well.
- In a skillet heat 4 tbsp/60 mL oil and fry the shallots and garlic until golden.
- Add the snails, salt, pepper, sherry, lemon juice and chili powder. Toss and cook for 1 minute.
- Remove from heat and let cool. Drain off the juices and reserve.

- Place the flour in a bowl. Form a well in the center and add the egg yolks and the cooking juices from the snails. Combine to form a fairly thick batter, adding a little water if necessary.
- Whip the egg whites with a pinch of salt until they hold peaks. Fold them into the batter with your hand, without working the batter too much.
- Preheat a deep-fat fryer to 375°F/190°C.
- Dip the snails in the batter and deep fry until the batter is crisp and golden. Serve immediately.

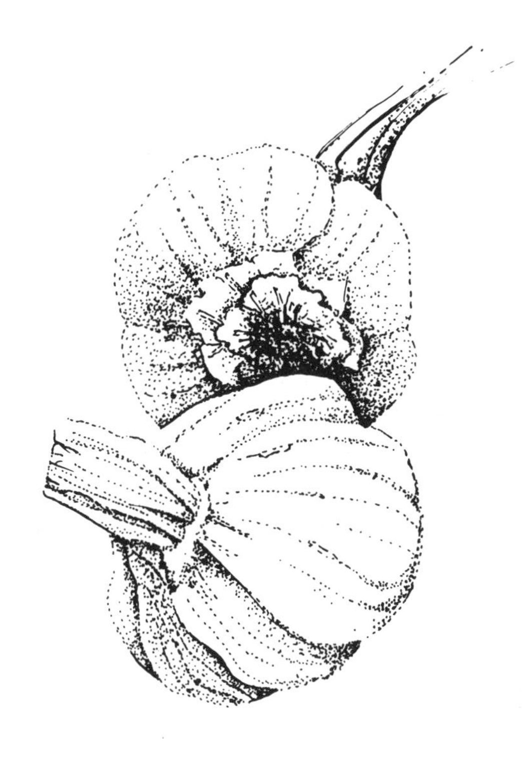

Wine serving suggestions:
National: Dry sherry, Montilla, Alella, Canamero
International: Portuguese whites, White Côtes-du-Rhône, Pinot Blanc, Verdicchio, Washington Riesling, Chilean Sauvignon, Seyval Blanc

Tony Aspler's choice: chilled Manzanilla
Jacques Marie's choice: chilled fino sherry
Chef's choice: ______________________

Pastel de Champinones

Mushroom Pie
(Serves 6)

In Spain, this dish is often prepared at Christmas time with *revellon*, a field mushroom with a pungent and distinctive flavor. The pastry is a bit tricky because it is high in fat and very low in moisture. The dough should be rolled when it is still warm, fairly soon after mixing. If it is too flaky, add a few drops of water.

Although the traditional pastel de champinones is a covered pie, this version resembles a lighter quiche, which makes a wonderful lunch or brunch dish served with a dry sherry or a fruity white wine.

PASTRY:

1/2 cup	unsalted butter	125 mL
1 tbsp	dry sherry	15 mL
1/2 tsp	salt	2 mL
1/2 tsp	sugar	2 mL
1	egg yolk	1
1 cup	pastry flour	250 mL

FILLING:

3 tbsp	olive oil	45 mL
2 tbsp	butter	30 mL
2	shallots, finely chopped	2
1/4 cup	finely chopped onions	50 mL
1 lb	mushrooms, sliced	500 g
5 oz	lean, boned chicken, minced	150 g
5 oz	lean ham, minced	150 g

	Salt and freshly ground black pepper	
1 tsp	savory	5 mL
1/3 cup	dry sherry	75 mL
4	eggs	4
1/3 cup	cream	75 mL

- To make the pastry, melt the butter in a saucepan without browning. Remove from heat.
- Add the sherry, salt, sugar and egg yolk. Combine well.
- Add the flour, a little at a time, combining well until smooth. Roll the dough into a ball. Do not refrigerate.
- Preheat the oven to 325°F/160°C.
- To make the filling, place the olive oil and butter in a saucepan over medium heat. Sauté the shallots and onions until soft.
- Add the mushrooms and cook until their juice has reduced.
- Add the minced chicken and ham. Season with salt, pepper and savory. Cook for 10 minutes over medium heat, stirring occasionally.
- Add the sherry and cook over low heat for 15 minutes.
- Roll out the pastry on a floured table top and line a 10-in/25-cm pie dish with the dough.
- Place the mushroom mixture in the pastry-lined dish.
- Beat the eggs and mix with the cream. Pour over the mushroom filling. Bake for 1 hour.

Wine serving suggestions:
Regional/National: Fino, Manzanilla sherry, Montilla, wood-aged Rioja whites, Gran Viña Sol, Jean Léon Chardonnay
International: Portuguese white Garrafeira, Vin jaune, Condrieu, Vouvray, Pouilly-Fumé, Alsatian Pinot Gris, Sylvaner, Sercial, Riesling Kabinett, Chenin Blanc

Tony Aspler's choice: Manzanilla
Jacques Marie's choice: Müller-Thurgau
Chef's choice:____________________

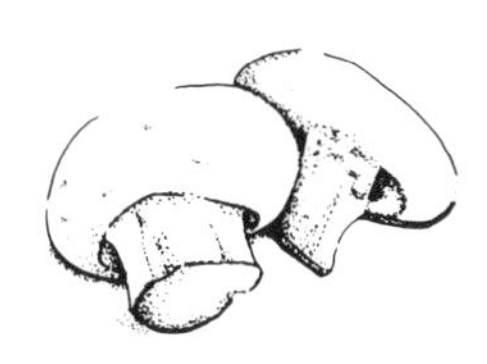

Langosta Catalana

Lobster Catalan
(Serves 4)

Most Spaniards believe that lobster is best simply broiled or grilled with a little olive oil and fresh herbs. Though I generally agree with that approach, this Catalan recipe is one of the best lobster dishes I have ever tasted. There are many versions of this dish, but the use of unsweetened cocoa in this recipe is authentically Catalan. Serve it with a rice pilaf and slices of bread fried in olive oil.

2	2-lb/1-kg live lobsters	2
1/2 cup	olive oil	125 mL
4 tbsp	finely chopped onion	60 mL
1 tbsp	salt	15 mL
3/4 tsp	cayenne pepper	4 mL
6	medium tomatoes, peeled and chopped	6
4	green peppers, seeded and cut into strips	4
2 tbsp	tomato puree	30 mL
2 cups	dry white wine	500 mL
2	bay leaves	2
1/2 tsp	oregano	2 mL
1/2 tsp	thyme	2 mL
1/4 cup	finely chopped fresh parsley	50 mL
1 tsp	saffron	5 mL
4	cloves garlic, pasted	4

1 oz	unsweetened cocoa	30 g
1/2 cup	brandy	125 mL

- Preheat the oven to 375°F/190°C.
- Cut the lobsters in half lengthwise. Discard the stomach and intestine. Remove the coral and liver and reserve. Separate the claws and split them in two. Separate the head and cut the tail in two.
- Heat the olive oil in a large, shallow ovenproof casserole and fry the lobster pieces over medium-high heat for a few minutes, or until they start to turn red. (If necessary, add more oil.) Remove the lobster pieces.
- In the same oil, sauté the onion until golden brown.
- Add the lobster pieces with the juices, salt, cayenne pepper, tomatoes, green peppers, tomato puree, white wine, bay leaves, oregano, thyme and half the parsley. Mix well, cover tightly with foil and bake for 20 minutes.
- Pound the saffron, garlic, cocoa, coral and liver to a smooth paste.
- Remove the lobster from the oven and place on the stove over high heat. Add the brandy and ignite. When all the flames have disappeared, remove a cup full of sauce and add to the cocoa and saffron paste. Mix well.
- Return the diluted paste to the lobster, stir and cook for 5 minutes. Correct seasoning if necessary. Discard the bay leaves and place the lobster pieces on a platter.
- Pour the sauce over the lobster and sprinkle with the remaining parsley.

Wine serving suggestions:
Regional: Viña Sol, Gran Viña Sol, Raimat Casal
National: Marques de Murrieta or Tondonia white, Marques de Riscal white, Viña Berceo, Marques de Caceres rosé
International: Gewürztraminer, Pinot Gris, Müller-Thurgau, Mosel Riesling Spätlese, Greco di Tufo, Pomino, Portuguese white, Chilean white

Tony Aspler's choice: Jean Léon Chardonnay
Jacques Marie's choice: Torres Viña Esmeralda
Chef's choice:____________________

Pato Valenciana

Duck Valencia Style
(Serves 4)

Whether wild or domesticated, duck is always a special treat. The flavor and texture of the dark meat is a considerable cut above the humble chicken. Choose a young duck that is not too fat (a young duck will have a soft and flexible beak), though even a lean duck will be a little fatty.

This dish is rich, spicy and exotic—a little like a paella. Choose a spicy, sturdy wine and good peasant bread to accompany it and complete the meal with a light fruit salad or fruit mousse, followed by a siesta!

1	lean duck, approx. 5 lb/2.5 kg	1
1 cup	olive oil	250 mL
2 tsp	salt	10 mL
1/2 tsp	freshly ground black pepper	2 mL
2	medium onions, sliced	2
1	large green pepper, diced	1
1	large red pepper, diced	1
3	cloves garlic, minced	3
8 oz	ham, cubed	250 g
2	smoked sausages (Spanish), sliced	2
3	tomatoes, peeled, seeded and quartered	3
6 cups	stock	1.5 L
1 tsp	saffron	5 mL
2 tsp	paprika	10 mL
1/4 tsp	cayenne pepper	1 mL

1½ cups	long-grain rice	375 mL
4 oz	cauliflower florets	125 g
4 oz	green beans, halved	125 g
4 oz	green peas	125 g
2 oz	mushrooms, sliced	60 g
12	large shrimps, peeled and deveined	12
8 oz	lobster or crab meat	250 g
12	large mussels or ½ cup/125 mL canned clams	12

- Preheat the oven to 350°F/180°C.
- Cut the duck into serving pieces.
- Heat half the olive oil in a frying pan. Degrease the duck pieces if necessary. Season with salt and pepper. Fry the duck in the oil, coloring the pieces on all sides.
- Remove the duck. In the same oil, fry the onions, green and red peppers, garlic, ham and sausages for 5 minutes over medium heat.
- Add the tomatoes and toss well.
- Transfer the vegetables to an ovenproof casserole. Add the stock, saffron, paprika, cayenne, salt, pepper and the duck pieces. Cover and cook in the oven for 20 minutes.
- Fry the rice in the remaining oil and add to the casserole. Mix well and bake for 30 minutes.
- Add the cauliflower, green beans, peas, mushrooms, shrimps, lobster and mussels. Cover and cook for a further 30 minutes, or until the rice is tender. (Add more liquid if the casserole becomes dry.) Adjust seasonings and serve very hot.

Wine serving suggestions:
Regional: Jumilla or Alicante reds
National: Sangre de Torro, Utiel-Requena rosé, Priorato, Campo Viejo, Faustino, Rioja Baja, Montilla-Moriles
International: Jura Vin jaune, Crozes-Hermitage, Cahors, Shiraz, Zinfandel, Petite Sirah, Aglianico del Vulture, Cabernet di Pramaggiore, Rosso Conero, Castel del Monte

Tony Aspler's choice: Doble Capa (Bodegas Salvador Poveda Luz, Alicante)
Jacques Marie's choice: Vega Sicilia
Chef's choice:______________________________

Pollo a la Aragonesa

Chicken Aragon
(Serves 4)

Aragon was one of the medieval kingdoms of Spain situated between Catalonia and Castile. Today the cuisine of this northwestern province of Spain is known for its excellent sauces. One of the most famous dishes is Pollo a la Chilindron, a combination of tomato, garlic, peppers and ham, but Pollo a la Aragonesa is more subtle in taste and less common. The dish is delightful served with rice and either a good fruity white wine, or a smooth red wine.

1	chicken, with neck and wings, approx. 3 lb/1.5 kg, cut into serving pieces	1
3 cups	water	750 mL
2	bay leaves	2
1 tsp	salt	5 mL
4	medium onions, diced	4
2	cloves garlic, crushed	2
6 tbsp	olive oil	90 mL
	Salt and freshly ground black pepper	
1 cup	dry white wine	250 mL
1/4 tsp	cumin	1 mL
1/4 tsp	coriander	1 mL
1/3 cup	heavy cream	75 mL
3	slices white bread, cubed	3
2 tsp	chopped fresh parsley	10 mL

- Make a chicken broth by simmering the chicken neck and wings in the water with the bay leaves and salt.
- Sauté the onions and garlic in 4 tbsp/60 mL olive oil until golden. Remove from the oil.
- Season the chicken pieces with salt and pepper. Sauté the chicken in the oil until golden on all sides. Remove the chicken pieces.
- When the stock is reduced to 1 cup/250 mL, remove the neck, wings and bay leaves. Add the chicken, onions, garlic, wine, cumin and coriander. Cover and simmer for 30 minutes.
- Remove the chicken, degrease the juices and pass through a blender until smooth. Return to the saucepan and bring to a boil.
- Add the cream. Taste and adjust the seasoning.
- Fry the bread cubes in 2 tbsp/30 mL olive oil until golden. Pat dry on paper towels.
- Place the chicken pieces on a serving tray. Cover with the sauce and sprinkle with the parsley and fried bread cubes.

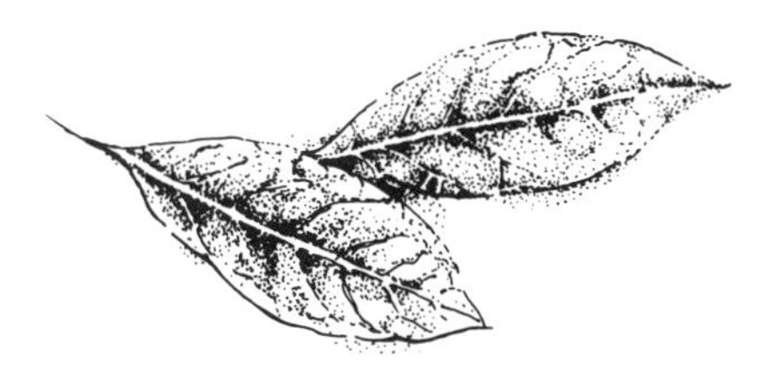

Wine serving suggestions:
Regional: Cariñena reds
National: Rioja reds, Navarra reds, Gran Coronas Reserva, Santa Digna, Jean Léon Cabernet
International: Bairrada, Alentejo, Conde de Santar, St. Joseph, cru Beaujolais, Côte-de-Bourg or Côte-de-Blaye, Chianti Classico Riserva, Taurasi, Californian Pinot Noir, Maréchal Foch, Chilean Cabernet

Tony Aspler's choice: Gran Coronas Black Label
Jacques Marie's choice: Marques de Murrietta Castillo Ygay
Chef's choice: ______________________________

Pisto Manchego

Vegetable Stew
(Serves 4)

Pisto and menestra are the two most popular vegetable stews in Spain. Like the Italian caponata and the French ratatouille, this dish, made with green peppers, tomatoes and olive oil, has a distinctive Mediterranean character. Serve it as a main course, or as an accompaniment to roasted or grilled meats.

4 oz	lean pork or chicken	125 g
5 tbsp	olive oil	75 mL
4	onions, diced	4
2	large green peppers, diced	2
1/2 cup	diced pimento	125 mL
1 lb	zucchini, sliced	500 g
4	tomatoes, peeled, seeded and diced	4
	Salt and freshly ground black pepper	
6	eggs	6

- Cut the meat into very small pieces (the size of chickpeas). In a heavy skillet, lightly sauté the meat in 3 tbsp/45 mL olive oil.
- Add the onions and green peppers. Cook over low heat until the onions become soft but not brown.
- Add the pimento and cook for 20 minutes over low heat.
- Meanwhile, sauté the sliced zucchini separately in 1 tbsp/15 mL olive oil over medium heat for 2 minutes. Add the diced tomatoes and continue to sauté until the tomatoes become soft.
- Add the zucchini and tomatoes to the meat, peppers and onions. Season with salt and pepper and cook for a further 15 minutes.

- Meanwhile, beat the eggs with salt and pepper. In the remaining olive oil, cook two flat omelets, cooking them on both sides. Cut into thin strips and set aside.
- To serve, place the pisto on a large hot plate and garnish the top with the strips of omelet.

Wine serving suggestions:
National: Mancha whites, Valdepeñas reds, Valdeorras, Viña Sol, Solar de Samaniego
International: Aveleda, Cartaxo, Dolcetto, Barbera del Monferrato, Chiaretto, Carema, still Vouvray, White Côtes-du-Rhône, Sancerre, Pinot Gris

Tony Aspler's choice: Albariño de Fefinanes
Jacques Marie's choice: Montecillo Cumbrero
Chef's choice:________________________________

Portuguese cuisine naturally resembles that of its Spanish neighbor, although it does have its own special identity, particularly in the use of spices.

The influence of the seven-hundred-year Moorish occupation is more evident in the nation's kitchens. The Moors planted extensive almond orchards in the south as well as introducing rice, figs, citrus fruits and oriental spices such as cardamom, coriander, cumin and aniseed.

Portuguese cooking is based on such local staples as olive oil, garlic, bread, tomatoes, beans and chickpeas. A combination of these ingredients can make a soup or one-pot meal when chicken, sausage or pork is added.

Simple practicality is the essence of Portuguese cooking. Meat and fish are either grilled or stewed, with no accoutrements other than a brush of olive oil or a squeeze of lemon juice. The flavor is in the freshness of the ingredients.

In the northern provinces of Minho, Tras-os-Montes and Douro, where the land is rugged and uncompromising, you find some of the best cooking in Portugal. Lamprey stew, caldo verde (a kale and potato soup) with broa (cornbread) are examples of peasant dishes that have been raised to a gastronomic experience. Other local dishes not to be missed are presunto ham, the spicy chourico and linguica sausages and tripe casseroled with chickpeas.

But the pride of Portugal is its fish, netted along its lengthy Atlantic coastline. Sardines, hake, mullet, squid, shrimp, sea bass, oysters and—the nearest thing to a national treasure—the cod supplement a wealth of freshwater fish from the country's rivers and lakes.

The Portuguese, it is said, have a recipe for bacalhau (dried salt cod) for every day of the year. They also have a sweet tooth and enjoy such desserts as chocolate mousse prepared with port wine and ovos moles, a specialty of Aveiro made with a paste of egg yolk cooked with sugar in rice water.

Apart from its range of ports from white to vintage, Portugal also produces a host of fascinating table wines: Vinho Verde (the lively, tart "green" wine from Minho, both white and red—green refers to age not to color), the powerful reds and earthy whites of the Dao and Bairrada, the pre-phylloxera reds of Colares grown in sand dunes and the sweet Muscatels of Setubal. And, of course, the pink wines like Mateus, which introduced so many people around the world to wine.

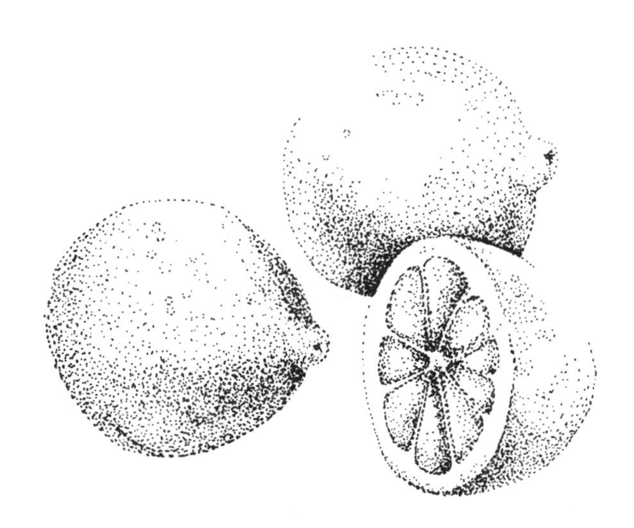

Caldo Verde

Cabbage and Potato Soup
(Serves 4)

I've always found it interesting that the most common soup in Portugal, a coastal country, does not contain any fish. Caldo verde is to Portugal what pea soup is to Quebec or minestrone to Italy. In Portugal kale is usually used, but cabbage or collard greens can be substituted.

Served with sweet cornbread, linguica (garlic pork sausage) and a glass of red Vinho Verde, this soup makes a fabulous meal.

1/2	small green cabbage, or 8 oz/250 g fresh kale or collard greens	1/2
6 cups	chicken broth or water	1.5 L
4 oz	chorizo, Linguica or garlic-seasoned smoked pork sausage	125 g
4	medium potatoes, peeled	4
2 tsp	salt	10 mL
1/2 cup	olive oil	125 mL
1/2 tsp	freshly ground black pepper	2 mL

- Wash the cabbage or greens. Trim away coarse veins, stems and blemished spots. Shred into very fine strips.
- Place the broth and sausage in a skillet and simmer for 20 minutes. Remove the sausage and set aside.
- Slice the potatoes and add to the broth with the salt. Cook until tender. Remove the potatoes and mash them roughly.
- Return the mashed potatoes to the water and stir them in with the olive oil and pepper. Bring to a boil over high heat. Add the greens to the soup and boil, uncovered, for 5 minutes.
- Add the sausages and simmer for 1 minute. Serve hot with cornbread.

Wine serving suggestions:
A soup of this nature really doesn't need a wine, but if you want to make a meal of it, try a Vouvray or red Vinho Verde.

Bacalhau Gomes de Sa

Dried Cod with Potatoes and Olives
(Serves 4)

The great French chef August Escoffier ranked fresh cod among the best of fish—the equal of salmon. Bacalhau is dried salted cod or green cod. This unspoilable provision was the staple food of the Vikings, who left it behind everywhere they went, and it was the pursuit of cod by Basque and Portuguese fishermen that led to the discovery of the New World.

Bacalhau is a very popular dish throughout Portugal, and each region (in fact, each family!) has its own variation. This version is simple to prepare and very tasty served hot, warm or cold. It goes well with any dry white wine, though the Portuguese themselves usually drink red wines with grilled sardines and cod.

2 lb	dried salt cod	1 kg
1	large bay leaf	1
2	sprigs fresh thyme	2
1	whole red chili pepper	1
2 lb	potatoes, peeled	1 kg
1 cup	good-quality olive oil	250 mL
4	medium onions, sliced	4
2	cloves garlic, crushed	2
16	oil-cured black olives	16
	Freshly ground black pepper	
1	lemon	1
1 tbsp	chopped fresh parsley	15 mL
4	eggs, hard-boiled	4
2	tomatoes, sliced	2

- Soak the cod in fresh cold water for 24 hours, changing the water twice.
- Place the cod in the pot and cover with water. Add the bay leaf, thyme and chili pepper. Bring to boil and simmer for 25 minutes.
- Slice the potatoes thickly, add to the fish and cook, covered, until tender.
- Remove the fish and potatoes and reserve the cooking liquid. Flake the fish on a warm serving plate. Keep warm and moist.
- Heat the oil in a skillet. Add the onions and garlic. Cook them until soft without coloring.
- Add the fish, sliced potatoes, olives and 2 cups/500 mL cooking liquid. Gently toss together. Season with pepper and lemon juice. Cook over gentle heat for 5 minutes.
- Sprinkle the fish with the parsley. Remove the bay leaf and chili pepper. Toss and serve with slices of hard-boiled egg on top and circled with sliced tomatoes.

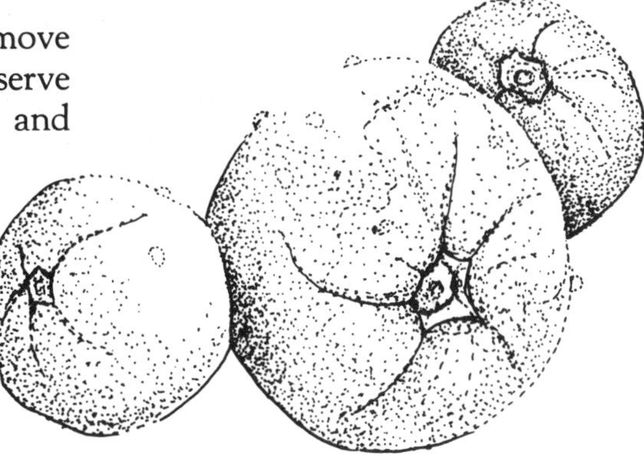

Wine serving suggestions:
Regional/National: Vinho Verde, any local dry white
International: Macon Blanc, white Bordeaux or Côtes-du-Rhône, Soave, Rioja white, Sylvaner

Tony Aspler's choice: Bucelas Garrafeira

Jacques Marie's choice: Quinta da Aveleda, Vinho Verde
Chef's choice:______________________________

Bifa a Portugese

Portuguese Steak
(Serves 4)

When I lived in Africa, I often used this recipe to cook camel steaks, although I had to marinate the meat for several hours instead of ten minutes to make it edible! (If you like a spicy steak you can increase the marinating time.) When cooking the steaks, be very careful not to burn the pepper and garlic coating.

6	large cloves garlic, peeled	6
1 tbsp	red wine vinegar	15 mL
1 tsp	salt	5 mL
1/4 tsp	freshly ground black pepper	1 mL
1/4 tsp	cayenne pepper	1 mL
3 tsp	olive oil	15 mL
4	sirloin steaks, 3/4 in/2 cm thick	4
2 tsp	butter	10 mL
1/2 tsp	thyme	2 mL
1	bay leaf	1
8	slices presunto ham or prosciutto	8
1	medium onion, sliced	1
1/2 cup	dry red wine (Dão)	125 mL
1/2	lemon	1/2
2 tsp	finely chopped fresh parsley	10 mL

- Crush 4 garlic cloves in a mortar and pestle with the vinegar, salt, pepper, cayenne and 1 tsp/5 mL olive oil, to make a paste.
- Rub the paste on the steaks and let them rest for 10 minutes.
- Preheat the oven to 300°F/150°C.
- In a heavy frying pan melt the butter and remaining olive oil over medium heat. When foaming, add 2 cloves garlic (sliced), thyme and bay leaf (crushed) and cook for 1 minute, stirring continuously.
- Strain the fat and pour it back into the frying pan.
- Add the steaks and cook them to the rare stage. Place the steaks in an ovenproof dish.
- In the same fat, sauté the ham on both sides. Place 2 slices on each steak.
- Fry the sliced onion until golden brown and tender. Place the onions on the ham.
- Add the red wine and the juice of half a lemon to the skillet and bring to a boil, scraping the food particles from the bottom of the pan. Adjust the seasonings and pour the sauce over the steaks. Sprinkle with parsley and serve hot.

Wine serving suggestions:
Regional/National: Douro or Dão red
International: Provence red, Australian/Chilean Cabernet, Zinfandel, southern Italian red, Pinotage

Tony Aspler's choice: Periquita from Azeitao
Jacques Marie's choice: Barca Velha, the rarest of all Portuguese wines made in the Douro
Chef's choice:____

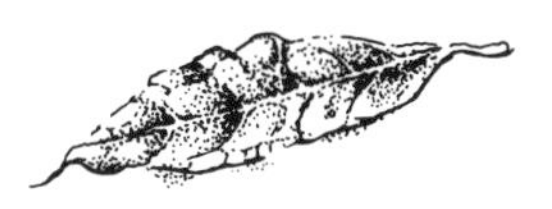

Central Europe

Centuries of political upheaval notwithstanding, the most persuasive culinary influence in Central Europe is still the Austro-Hungarian Empire, which dominated for more than six hundred years until the end of the First World War, and more particularly the cuisine of its capital, Vienna. The delicacy and finesse of Viennese cooking can still be found in the pastries and dumplings and thin schnitzels of the Balkan nations.

The other influences are Turkish and Muslim—the love of spices, honey and sweetmeats—and the exigencies of life for a peasant population perennially living in the path of warring kings and princes. The need to store food during long winters or sieges encouraged the art of pickling vegetables and the creation of sauces of yogourt and herbs for meats that were none too fresh.

Rich meat soups with feather-light dumplings and meat stews with peppers and onions were survival foods, which ingenious cooks turned into minor gastronomic triumphs. Landlocked countries such as Hungary and Czechoslovakia had to rely on lake fish—carp, pike and perch—while their neighbors had the benefit of the coastal waters of the Adriatic or the Black Sea.

Yet there are fascinating local differences that help to define a national cuisine: the Hungarian preference for cooking with lard instead of butter, the Czech love of dumplings, the Yugoslavian predilection for chestnuts and the unique sour soups prepared by the Romanians from fermented wheat bran. Charcoal grilling of minced meats with onions and peppers is practiced throughout the Balkans, washed down with the locally produced wines. (The whites tend to be better than the reds for cooling throats unused to paprika and chili peppers.)

The wines of Central Europe may lack the stylishness of their counterparts in France and Germany, but their personality fits the fiery cuisine of the region very well. Hungarian Tokay, however, need not take second place to any of the world's great dessert wines. The sweetness of Tokay is measured in puttonyos, the buckets of concentrated grape mash added to the fermentation of the Furmint grapes. The designation of 3, 4 or 5 puttonyos will appear on the label of the bottle. Best of all, and regarded as a wine of miraculous restorative powers, is Tokay Eszencia—the syrupy juice of the grapes in a state of noble rot, which drips from the berries without being pressed.

Ribji Guljaz

Pan-fried Fish Yugoslavian
(Serves 6)

Olive oil gives foods its own special flavor. There are basically two types of olive oil used in cooking. The cold-pressed oil has a greenish color, a distinctive nutty flavor and stays fresh for a long time. The heat-extracted oil is less expensive and paler in color, but turns rancid more quickly. Depending on the type of olives and their origin, olive oils have their own distinctive tastes. The best ones are used on salads or are simply poured on top of food for flavor—good olive oil is always present on all Mediterranean tables as a condiment.

1/4 cup	extra-virgin olive oil	50 mL
1	small onion, chopped	1
2 tsp	salt	10 mL
1 tsp	freshly ground black pepper	5 mL
2 tbsp	paprika	30 mL
6	sea bass fillets (or other sea fish)	6
1 tbsp	tomato paste	15 mL
1/2 tsp	thyme	2 mL
1	bay leaf	1
2 tbsp	lemon juice	30 mL
1	clove garlic, pasted	1
1 cup	dry white wine	250 mL
1 tbsp	finely chopped fresh parsley	15 mL
1	small sweet red pepper, finely diced	1

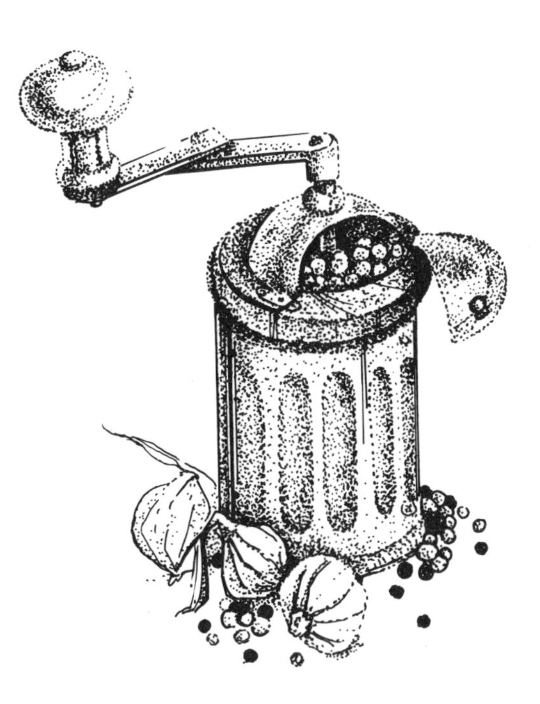

- Heat the olive oil in a large, thick-bottomed frying pan (enamel or cast iron if possible). Add the onions and fry to a light golden color.
- Mix the salt, pepper and paprika on a plate. Coat each fish fillet on both sides.
- Place the fillets in the pan with the onion and cook on both sides over medium heat.
- Combine the tomato paste, thyme, bay leaf, lemon juice, garlic and wine. Pour the mixture over the fish, cover and cook over low heat, basting from time to time, until the fish is tender. Serve hot, sprinkled with fresh parsley and red pepper.

Wine serving suggestions:
National: Jugoslavian Riesling, Sipon
International: dry Vouvray, Chablis, Sancerre, Pinot Blanc, Soave, Riesling, Pinot Grigio, Penedes whites

Tony Aspler's choice: sparkling Montlouis
Jacques Marie's choice: Traminer or light Gewürztraminer
Chef's choice:____

Brazant na Cesky Zpusob

Pheasant Czech Style
(Serves 4)

Since ancient Greece the pheasant has been regarded as a meal reserved for the tables of the nobility. This bird is particularly prized in Central Europe and in this recipe the Czechoslovakians have preserved its natural flavor enhanced with just a little spice. Braised red cabbage or Brussels sprouts and potato cakes are the classic accompaniments.

When buying pheasant, remember that the hens are usually tastier than the cocks and that young pheasants are more tender than older ones (the beak of a young bird will be pliable and the feathers at the tip of the wings pointed).

2	pheasants	2
1 tsp	salt	5 mL
1/2 tsp	freshly ground black pepper	2 mL
1/2 tsp	thyme	2 mL
4 oz	pork fat	125 g
1/2 cup	unsalted butter	125 mL
1/2 cup	diced onion	125 mL
20	juniper berries	20
20	allspice berries	20
20	whole black peppercorns	20
1	bay leaf	1
1 cup	chicken stock	250 mL
1 cup	dry white wine	250 mL
2 oz	smoked bacon	60 g
	flour	

- Preheat the oven to 425°F/220°C.
- Season the cavities of the pheasants with salt, pepper and thyme. Cover the breasts with thin strips of pork fat and secure with string.
- In a Dutch oven, place the butter, onion, juniper berries, allspice berries, peppercorns and bay leaf. Cook in the oven until the onions start to color. Then place the pheasant in the pan and roast, uncovered, for 20 minutes. Turn up the oven to 450°F/230°C.
- Remove the string and the pork fat. Add the stock, white wine and smoked bacon. Cook for 20 minutes, or until the pheasants are tender, basting 3 or 4 times during the roasting time.
- Remove the birds, strain the juices and thicken the gravy with flour. Carve the pheasant and serve hot with the gravy, braised red cabbage or Brussels sprouts and potato cakes (see below).

BRAMBORAK
Potato Cakes

1 lb	potatoes, peeled	500 g
2	eggs	2
4 tbsp	milk	60 mL
	Salt and freshly ground white pepper	
2	cloves garlic, pasted	2
1/4 tsp	marjoram	1 mL
1/2 cup	flour	125 mL
1 cup	vegetable oil	250 mL

- Grate the raw potatoes and dry.
- Add the eggs, milk, salt, pepper, garlic, marjoram and flour and combine well to form a paste.
- Pour the oil into a frying pan and heat to a haze.
- Spoon the potato mixture into the fat and fry on both sides until crisp and golden brown.

Wine serving suggestions:
National: Riesling, Bohemian Blauburgunder
International: Tokay d'Alsace, Gigondas, St-Emilion, Chianti Riserva, Napa Cabernet, Maréchal Foch

Tony Aspler's choice: Château Musar
Jacques Marie's choice: Hermitage
Chef's choice:____________________

Sarmale Umpluta

Stuffed Cabbage
(Serves 6)

Stuffing cabbage or vine leaves is probably one of the most ancient forms of cooking. The leaves are an edible wrapper that conveniently holds and seals in the flavor of the filling ingredients.

Stuffed cabbage is still popular among central European cooks, and the variations are endless. You can try using Savoy cabbage in this recipe—the leaves are more tender and easier to fold.

Drink a sturdy wine with this dish, since cabbage has a strong flavor; beer is also a good accompaniment. Serve the cabbage rolls with fried green peppers and cornmeal porridge.

1/4 cup	short-grain rice	50 mL
1	green cabbage, approx. 2 lb/1 kg	1
1 lb	sauerkraut	500 g
8 oz	ground pork	250 g
8 oz	ground beef	250 g
1	slice bread (soaked in water)	1
1/2 cup	finely chopped onion	125 mL
1 1/2 tsp	salt	7 mL
1/4 tsp	cayenne pepper	1 mL
1 tsp	dry thyme	5 mL
3	slices lean bacon, finely chopped	3
6	slices bacon, cut in half	6
2 cups	tomato juice	500 mL
1 cup	sour cream	250 mL

- Cook the rice in boiling water for 10 minutes.
- Trim the cabbage of outer leaves and immerse in boiling water for 10 minutes.
- Wash the sauerkraut under cold water and squeeze by hand until fairly dry.
- Peel the leaves from the cabbage (as many as you can without breaking any) until you obtain 12 large leaves (immerse the cabbage in boiling water again if necessary).
- Mix together the ground pork, beef, bread, onion, rice, salt, cayenne pepper and thyme until the mixture is smooth and fluffy.
- Preheat the oven to 350°F/180°C.
- Lay out the cabbage leaves flat and trim the thick rib end. Divide the pork mixture into 12 equal portions and place the filling in the center of each cabbage leaf. Roll each leaf, tucking the sides in carefully.
- Combine the sauerkraut and chopped lean bacon and place in the bottom of a thick ovenproof dish. Arrange the cabbage rolls on top and secure half a slice of bacon on the top of each with a toothpick. Pour in the tomato juice. Cover and cook for 1 hour. Uncover and cook for an additional 30 minutes, or until tender.
- Place the cabbage rolls on a serving dish.
- Add the sour cream to the tomato juice and sauerkraut. Mix well, adjust seasoning and warm briefly on the stove without boiling. Pour on top of the cabbage rolls.

Wine serving suggestions:
National: Romanian Cabernet, Merlot, Pinot Noir, Kadarka, Babeasca
International: Rhône reds, Provence reds, light Zinfandel, Barbaresco, Taurasi, Dão, Australian Shiraz

Tony Aspler's choice: Crozes-Hermitage (Jaboulet)
Jacques Marie's choice: Babeasca Focsani
Chef's choice:________________________________

Beef Pörkölt

Paprika Beef Stew
(Serves 6 to 8)

Although many people think that any stew containing paprika is called goulash, in Hungary there are important distinctions. *Gulayas* is a dish with plenty of gravy, resembling a soup more than a stew and containing onions, paprika, potatoes and dumplings. *Pörkölt* is also made with paprika, but contains more onions and the gravy is shorter and thicker. *Tokany* is a similar dish to pörkölt but contains fewer onions and the meat is cut in smaller pieces. *Paprikas* contains paprika and sour cream and is made with fish or fowl. *Szeklergulyas* is made with pork or mixed meats, paprika, sour cream and sauerkraut!

1 lb	onions, sliced	500 g
1 tbsp	lard	15 mL
2 tbsp	paprika	30 mL
2 lb	beef (rump or shin), cut into 1½-in/3-cm cubes	1 kg
	Salt and freshly ground black pepper	
4	cloves garlic, crushed	4
½ tsp	cumin seed, crushed	2 mL
1 cup	dry red wine	250 mL
½ cup	diced red pepper	125 mL
½ cup	diced green pepper	125 mL
4 oz	dried tomatoes or 4 fresh tomatoes, peeled and seeded	125 g
	Sliced green onions for garnish	

- In an ovenproof casserole, fry the sliced onions in the lard until golden brown. Add the paprika and mix well.
- Immediately add the meat. Combine thoroughly.
- Add the salt, pepper, garlic and cumin.
- Add the wine and cook, covered, over low heat until the meat is tender.
- Add the peppers and tomatoes and cook for 10 minutes. Serve sprinkled with sliced green onions.

Wine serving suggestions:
National: Bull's Blood, Szekzardi
International: Châteauneuf-du-Pape, Dão reds, Zinfandel, Australian Shiraz, Taurasi, Pinotage

Tony Aspler's choice: chilled Hungarian Kadarka
Jacques Marie's choice: Eger Medoc Noir
Chef's choice:______________________________

Mediterranean Basin

The Greeks taught the world how to think and also how to cook. They gave our language the term "epicure," and it was their chefs who worked the kitchens of imperial Rome and showed the Romans the art of fine cuisine. In the Middle Ages Greek chefs found employment in Orthodox monasteries where they wore tall white hats to distinguish them from the regular black-hatted monks. From that time the white stove-pipe hat became the international symbol of the profession.

Many Greek dishes have Turkish names, since the country was occupied by the Turks for nearly four hundred years after the fall of Constantinople in 1453. But at that time the Greeks had already an established cuisine that went back five hundred years before Christ. One of the first cookbooks ever written was assembled by the Greek poet Hesiod.

Greece exemplifies the common thread that runs through all the national cuisines of the Mediterranean rim. Meals are prepared and cooked in the open air, invariably over charcoal. Olive oil, lemons, garlic, rice and saffron are to be found in every kitchen, along with a range of herbs such as oregano, thyme, basil, rosemary and mint, usually gathered wild. As you move east to Turkey, Syria, Lebanon, Israel and Egypt, these are augmented by the perfumed and aromatic cardamom, rosewater and orange flower and a variety of spices such as cinnamon, ginger and coriander.

Add to this the abundant fish and seafood of the Mediterranean, lamb from the coastal plains, goat and ewe cheese, chickpeas, sesame seeds, beans, pine nuts, pistachios, walnuts, almonds and a colorful range of subtropical vegetables that blaze on the market stalls from Athens to Cairo, and you have the basis of the world's oldest cuisine.

For those with a sweet tooth, the countries of the Mediterranean Basin offer a range of tempting desserts from baklava (phyllo pastry with pistachio nuts and honey) to Turkish delight, halva and konafa (shredded dough pastries).

Wines are produced in all these Mediterranean countries—even Egypt—and perhaps the kindest thing that can be said of them is that they go well with the local dishes. Greek Retsina, a resinated white wine, is an acquired taste but one that should be cultivated if only as a satisfying accompaniment to taramasalata (creamy fish roe pâté) or hummus (chick-pea dip). There is, however, one exception: Château Musar in the Bekka Valley of Lebanon which, against all odds, produces some of the finest red wine in the world.

Honey Roasted Chicken

(Serves 4)

Ever since the Egyptians kept bees in 2600 B.C., honey has been used as a principal sweetener in middle-eastern cooking. Honey carries the distinctive flavor and color of the flower from which it is made, ranging from dark, strong buckwheat honey to honeys made from clover, orange or apple blossoms, rosemary, thyme, sage, heather, acacia and the peculiar resiny pine honey.

This recipe will give the chicken a nice golden color; the honey is tempered by the lemon juice, so the dish is not too sweet.

1	large lemon	1
1	chicken, approx. 3-4 lb/1.5-2 kg	1
2 tsp	salt	10 mL
1 tsp	freshly ground black pepper	5 mL
1 tbsp	olive oil	15 mL
4 tbsp	butter	60 mL
4 tbsp	honey	60 mL
2 tbsp	slivered almonds	30 mL
1 cup	water	250 mL
1 tsp	freshly grated ginger	5 mL

- Preheat the oven to 450°F/230°C.
- Squeeze the lemon juice into a large bowl. Roll the chicken in the lemon juice and pour the remaining juice into the chicken cavity. Mix together the salt and pepper and season the chicken inside and out.
- Coat a roasting pan with the olive oil and preheat in the oven for 3 minutes.
- Melt the butter and honey together and brush the chicken inside and out with the mixture.

- Place the chicken in the hot roasting pan, breast side up. Cook for 15 minutes, then reduce the heat to 350°F/180°C. Continue to cook for 20 minutes per pound/500 g, basting during cooking.
- About 15 minutes before the chicken is cooked, place the slivered almonds on a dry baking tray and toast them in the oven to a golden color.
- When ready remove the chicken and deglaze the pan with the water. Reduce by half and stir in the ginger.
- Carve the chicken. Pour the juices over the meat and sprinkle with the warm almond slivers.

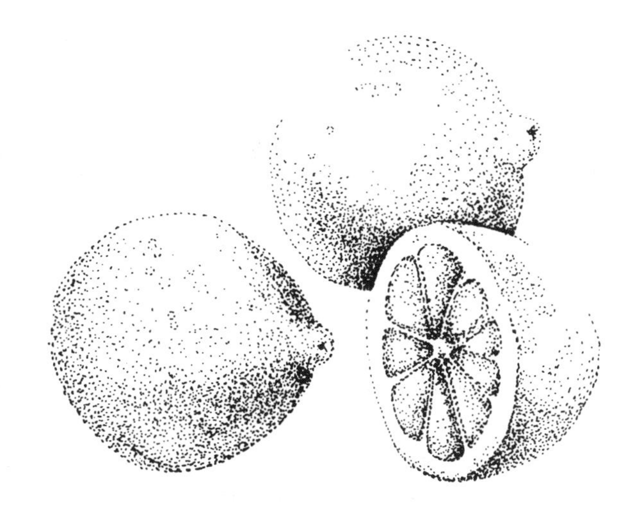

Wine serving suggestions:
National: Château Musar
International: St-Emilion, red Graves, St. Joseph, Cornas, Crozes-Hermitage, Spanna, Barbaresco, Chianti Classico, Australian Cabernet/Shiraz

Tony Aspler's choice: Tavel rosé
Jacques Marie's choice: Allesverloren Tinta Barocca
Chef's choice:____________________________________

Date Mousse

(Serves 4)

Dates, a staple food of desert regions, are extremely nutritious and can be used in a multitude of ways, including a fermented alcoholic beverage. The best dates have thin skins and are long and narrow. The worst are dry, hard, fibrous and are often sold in pressed blocks. Many varieties of dates exist; some are prized as great delicacies.

The Arabs prepare dry dates by cutting a hole in a watermelon and storing the dates inside for twenty-four to forty-eight hours. The dry dates swell from the melon moisture and are almost as good as fresh dates. Good dates are also grown in California in the Coachella Valley.

1 lb	Carmel dates, skinned, pitted and chopped	500 g
1/2 tsp	grated lemon rind	2 mL
1 cup	milk	250 mL
3	egg whites	3
pinch	salt	pinch
2 tbsp	fruit sugar	30 mL
3/4 cup	heavy cream	175 mL
2 tbsp	chopped pistachios	30 mL

- Reserve 4 dates for garnish.
- Place the remaining dates in a blender with the lemon rind and milk and puree.
- Whip the egg whites with the salt until they hold peaks. Add the sugar a little at a time and whip until the egg whites are stiff and glossy.
- Fold the egg white mixture into the date puree and refrigerate.
- Whip the cream until stiff. Fold the refrigerated mousse into the whipped cream.
- Chill for 3 hours and garnish with sliced dates and chopped pistachios before serving.

Wine serving suggestions:
National: Muscatel, Château Rishon, Golden Cream
International: Crémant d'Alsace, Blanquette de Limoux, German Auslese, sweet Champagne, sparkling Vouvray, Asti Spumante, Tokay Aszu, Muscat, Australian Semillon, Setubal, Vin Santo

Tony Aspler's choice: Beaumes-de-Venise
Jacques Marie's choice: Côteau-du-Layon
Chef's choice:______________________________

Dolmas

Stuffed Vine Leaves
(Serves 4)

Although dolmas are Turkish in origin, they are served throughout the Middle East. They are made with vine leaves that are first blanched and then stuffed with meat, rice and herbs before being braised in stock, oil and lemon juice. Fresh vine leaves have a finer taste, but those preserved in brine can be used as a substitute. (Fresh leaves should be blanched in salted boiling water for five minutes to soften them.) At a pinch, Swiss chard, cabbage, kale or the leaves of the fig or hazelnut tree can also be used, but they won't be as tender or tasty.

12	canned vine leaves	12
4 cups	water	1 L
2/3 cup	white rice	150 mL
1 lb	lean ground beef or lamb	500 g
1/2 cup	chopped onion	125 mL
2 tbsp	chopped fresh parsley	30 mL
2 tbsp	chopped fresh dill	30 mL
2	small lemons	2
	Salt and freshly ground black pepper	
1/4 cup	olive oil	50 mL
1/2 cup	pine nuts	125 mL
2 tsp	butter	10 mL
2 cups	plain yogurt	500 mL

- Blanch the vine leaves in boiling water for 30 seconds to rinse off brine.
- Bring 2 cups/500 mL water to a boil and add a little salt. Add the rice, cook for 6 minutes, then drain.
- When the rice is cool, combine with the meat, onion, parsley, dill, lemon juice, salt and pepper.
- Preheat the oven to 350°F/180°C.
- Spread out the leaves and pat dry if necessary. Divide the meat mixture and place some in the center of each leaf. Fold over the sides and gently but firmly roll into a cylinder.
- Place the filled leaves side by side in a baking dish with 2 cups/500 mL water, pinch of salt and the olive oil. Weight them down with a plate to keep them from unfurling and simmer in the oven for 45 minutes.
- Fry the pine nuts in butter over gentle heat until light golden. Drain on a paper towel and sprinkle with salt.
- When the nuts are cool, mix in the yogurt with a few twists of black pepper.
- When the stuffed vine leaves are cooked, place on a warm dish and serve with the yogurt on the side.

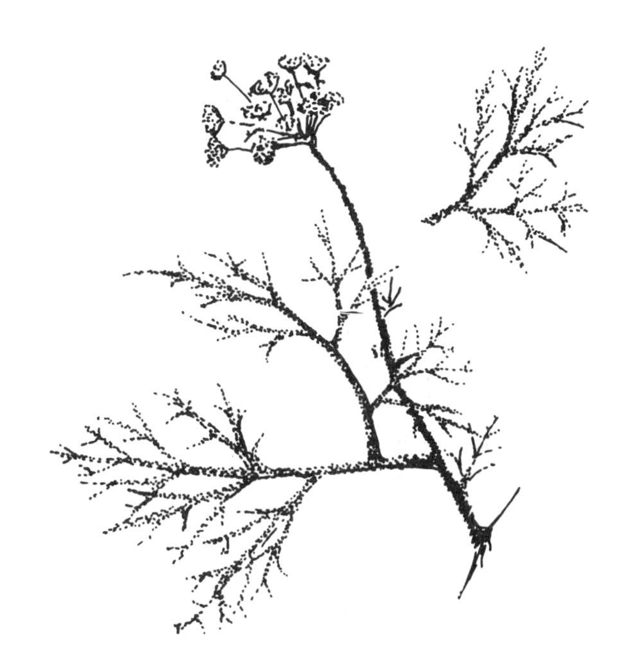

Wine serving suggestions:
National: Buzbag, Papazkarsi, Adakarasi (Turkish reds)
International: Zinfandel, southern Italian reds, Californian and Chilean Cabernet Sauvignon, Australian Shiraz, Pinotage, Rhine and Emerald Riesling, Steen, Jugoslavian Traminer, Cinsaut

Tony Aspler's choice: Retsina
Jacques Marie's choice: Villa Doluca red
Chef's choice:____________________________________

Ochtapodi Krassato

Octopus in Red Wine
(Serves 6)

Since ancient times, octopus has been an important source of food in the Mediterranean Basin. This unappetizing-looking creature has eight arms and should not be confused with the longer-bodied squid or calamar, which has ten.

If you want to prepare this dish the authentic Mediterranean way, you must buy a whole small octopus, remove the ink sac and reserve it. Add the ink with the wine when you make the sauce!

2 lb	octopus tentacles	1 kg
2 tbsp	coarse salt	30 mL
2	large cloves garlic, crushed	2
1/3 cup	extra-virgin olive oil	75 mL
1 lb	onions, finely chopped	500 g
3 tbsp	red wine vinegar	45 mL
2 cups	dry red wine	500 mL
1 lb	tomatoes, seeded, peeled and finely chopped	500 g
2 tsp	chopped fresh rosemary	10 mL
2	bay leaves	2
1/4 tsp	mace or nutmeg	1 mL
1/4 tsp	cinnamon	1 mL
2	cloves	2
1 tsp	salt	5 mL
3 tbsp	tomato puree	45 mL

1/2 tsp	fresh thyme	2 mL
1 tbsp	chopped Italian parsley	15 mL
2 tsp	chopped fresh coriander	10 mL

- Rinse the octopus tentacles in water salted with the coarse salt.
- Place the tentacles in a pot over medium heat and toss them with a wooden spoon until they turn red and render some liquid.
- Remove the tentacles and cut them into 1/2-in/1-cm lengths. Discard the liquid and dry the pot without washing.
- In the same pot, cook the crushed garlic in the olive oil until golden. Discard the garlic and add the octopus pieces. Cook the pieces until they brown slightly, tossing them with a wooden spoon.
- Add the onions and cook until golden.
- Add the remaining ingredients except for the parsley and coriander. Stir and cover. Simmer for 3 hours over very low heat, or until the octopus is tender.
- Remove the octopus and place on a hot serving dish. Strain the sauce over the octopus and sprinkle with the chopped parsley and coriander.

Wine serving suggestions:
National: Savatiano, Pallini, Santa Helena, Demestica
International: Orvieto, white Châteauneuf-du-Pape, Entre-Deux-Mers, Fumé Blanc, Australian Semillon

Tony Aspler's choice: Tokay d'Alsace
Jacques Marie's choice: Viognier (Guigal)
Chef's choice:____________________

Australia and New Zealand

The esoteric culinary arts are not really part of the Australian national character. Perhaps it has to do with the country's sunshine, which draws the Aussies out of doors to eat for most of the year. As a result, the barbecue plays a central role in households down under.

Australians are hearty eaters, preferring quantity to fussily displayed dishes. They are great meat lovers, with their excellent lamb and beef high on the list. The country also boasts a wealth of seafood (prawns, lobster, oysters, shark, flounder). Meat and fish are often prepared with the tropical and subtropical fruits that grow in the valleys along the southern and eastern coasts.

The early British settlers at the beginning of the nineteenth century established a meat and potatoes cuisine which was gradually influenced by the wealth of natural produce from the orchards and the fishermen's nets. From the Aborigines the pioneers borrowed the idea of baking meat in clay. The kangaroo, a staple of the Aborigines, was pressed into service by the new arrivals when they wanted soup; the oxen were too valuable to slaughter for meat.

With the waves of immigrants from a variety of ethnic backgrounds, other culinary ideas were absorbed into the Australian kitchen. But there are few dishes that can legitimately be claimed as authentic Australian creations, apart from the ubiquitous Carpetbag Steak and Pavlova.

Beer is a national pastime in Australia, though the wines of the Hunter and Barossa valleys rival Bordeaux and Burgundy, at their best, especially the Cabernets and Chardonnays.

New Zealand also has a thriving wine industry. The food on the islands is very similar to Australian fare, leaning heavily on lamb and first-rate dairy produce. Like Australia, the indigenous people of New Zealand, the Maoris, have a unique cuisine based on fruit, fish and seafood which they marinate or wrap in leaves and bake or steam over hot stones buried in the ground.

Carpetbagger Steak

(Serves 4)

The fondness that Australians have for both beef and seafood has resulted in this hearty combination of steak and oysters. The oysters should have a silky texture; the breadcrumbs will help retain their juices.

1	large clove garlic	1
1/2 cup	butter, melted	125 mL
4	thick strip loin or fillet steaks, approx. 1 1/2 in/4 cm thick	4
	Salt and freshly ground black pepper	
16	very large oysters, shucked	16
1 cup	soft white breadcrumbs	250 mL
1 cup	red wine	250 mL
1 tbsp	finely chopped fresh parsley	15 mL

- Crush the garlic clove to a paste and mix with the warm melted butter.
- With a sharp, pointed knife carefully cut a large pocket in the side of each steak. Season the steaks with salt and pepper, including inside the pocket.
- Roll 8 large oysters in the breadcrumbs, patting the crumbs lightly into the oysters.
- Place 2 breaded oysters in each steak pocket and close with small skewers.
- Brush each steak with garlic butter. Pan fry the steaks on each side to desired doneness. Remove the steaks and place on a heated serving platter.
- Remove the fat from the pan and add the red wine. Bring gently to a boil and reduce by half. Season with salt and pepper.
- Add the remaining oysters and toss in the wine for 1 minute.
- Place 2 oysters on each steak. Spoon the wine over them and sprinkle with parsley. Serve hot.

Wine serving suggestions:

National: Australian Shiraz and Cabernet Shiraz
International: Californian Zinfandel, Châteauneuf-du-Pape, Chilean Cabernet, Côtes-du-Rhône

Tony Aspler's choice: Primitivo di Manduria from the heel of Italy
Jacques Marie's choice: 1962 Brown Bros. Milawa Cabernet Shiraz Mondeuse
Chef's choice:______________________________

Rabbit Stew with Claret

(Serves 4)

Rabbit is not only delicious, but it's one of the healthiest meats. It is higher in protein and lower in saturated fat, cholesterol, sodium and calories than beef, lamb, pork, chicken or fish. The white meat is delicate and very tender, so turkey or chicken breast could also be used in this recipe. Avoid a heavy wine with this dish—a light Cabernet or Merlot wine would go well instead.

1	3 1/2- to 4-lb/1.5- to 2-kg rabbit (with liver) cut into serving pieces	1
4 tbsp	butter	60 mL
18	pearl onions, peeled	18
4 oz	bacon, diced	125 g
	Salt and freshly ground black pepper	
4 tbsp	flour	60 mL
2 cups	good-quality stock	500 mL
1	bouquet garni (3 sprigs parsley, 2 sprigs thyme, 2 bay leaves)	1
2	cloves	2
6	whole black peppercorns	6
3/4 cup	claret (red Bordeaux)	175 mL

- Chop the rabbit liver and reserve.
- Heat the butter in a skillet. When foaming, add the onions and bacon and fry until golden. Remove the onions and bacon and reserve.
- Season the rabbit pieces with salt and pepper and fry them on both sides in the bacon fat. Add the flour and brown well. Stir in the stock.

- Stir in the bouquet garni, cloves, peppercorns and salt to taste. Add the cooked onions and bacon and cover. Simmer gently for 1 hour, or until the rabbit is tender.
- Add the claret and the chopped rabbit liver. Let simmer for 10 minutes, then serve.

Wine serving suggestions:
National: Cabernet from Cooks, Corbans, McWilliams, Montana, Nobilos, Villa Maria, Pinotage
International: Merlot del Piave, Barbaresco, Chianti, Médoc, Mâcon, red Graves, Conde de Santar, light Rioja, Maréchal Foch

Tony Aspler's choice: Cabernet Sauvignon Rosé (made by Miguel Torres in Chile)
Jacques Marie's choice: Villa Maria Cabernet
Chef's choice:____________________

Pavlova

(Serves 6)

Anna Pavlova was a dancer and actress who took Australia and New Zealand by storm in 1926. The dessert named after her consists of a meringue that is crisp on the outside and soft in the center, covered with whipped cream and fresh fruits.

Meringues are delicate creatures—make sure there is no egg yolk in the whites and that the bowl and beaters are grease free before you whip the egg whites. And don't try to make this dish on a humid day, because the egg whites will never dry out properly.

4	egg whites, at room temperature	4
1 cup	fruit sugar	250 mL
1/2 tsp	salt	2 mL
1/2 tsp	cornstarch	2 mL
2 tsp	white vinegar	10 mL
1 tsp	vanilla	5 mL
3 cups	sliced fruits, such as bananas, peaches, kiwi, mango, strawberries, passionfruit or papaya	750 mL
1 1/2 cups	heavy cream, whipped	375 mL

- Preheat the oven to 300°F/150°C.
- Grease a 9-in/23-cm pie plate and cover the bottom with a circle of greased foil dusted lightly with cornstarch.
- Beat the egg whites in a large mixing bowl until they stand in peaks. Gradually add the sugar, a spoonful at a time, beating until all the sugar has been added. Add the salt and

beat well (the mixture should be very stiff at this stage).

- Combine the cornstarch, vinegar and vanilla. Lightly fold into the meringue.
- Heap the meringue in the pie dish. Smooth it around the edges and make a hollow in the center. Put the pie dish in the oven, turn the heat down to 225°F/110°C and bake for 1½ hours. Do not brown.
- Remove the meringue from the oven and let it cool in the dish in a dry place. When cool remove the meringue from the foil and place on a serving dish.
- Drain the sliced fruit well and place in the hollow of the meringue. Cover with whipped cream and serve immediately.

Wine serving suggestions:
National: Liqueur Muscat, Australian Sauterne
International: Barsac, Austrian Beerenauslese, Beaumes-de-Venise, sweet Champagne or sparkling

Tony Aspler's choice: Morris' Muscat from Rutherglen, Victoria
Jacques Marie's choice: Lindemans Hunter River Porphyry
Chef's choice: ________________

The Republic of South Africa, two-thirds the size of Europe, enjoys one of the world's most blessed and bountiful climates. The fertile coastal plain that beards the tip of the continent is as rich in agricultural and food products as it is in mineral wealth. The local populations of blacks, whites, Indians and Asians have turned an impressive national pantry of fish, tropical and subtropical fruits, vegetables, beef, lamb and game into a remarkable tartan of epicurean delights.

The agglomeration of races that make up South Africa has been integrated if only in terms of the kitchen: the national cuisine is an amalgam of bland English cooking, sturdy Dutch recipes, the flair of the French heightened by Malayan spices and the traditional produce and techniques of the indigenous black population.

But perhaps the greatest contribution South Africa has made to world gastronomy is its wines. The best Cabernets and Hermitages from both large and small estate wineries rival those of Bordeaux and the Rhône; the ports and sherries of the Cape take second place only to those of Portugal and Spain. Pinotage, a cross between Pinot Noir and Cinsaut, is a unique South African variety. The only problem is that these wines are often difficult to find.

Bobotie

Minced Meat Curry
(Serves 6)

This type of spicy minced meat pie is very typical of South African cooking. Bobotie is one of the great Cape Malay main dishes where traditionally game was the principal source of meat. This recipe provided a convenient way of rendering tough meat more palatable.

Today bobotie is made from fresh or leftover minced meat. It should always be moist. Serve it with hot boiled rice and chutney or other curry garnishes.

2	onions, peeled	2
3 tbsp	butter	45 mL
1	slice white bread	1
1 cup	milk	250 mL
1 lb	minced lean beef	500 g
1 lb	minced lean lamb	500 g
2	eggs	2
1 tbsp	curry powder	15 mL
4 tsp	sugar	20 mL
2 tsp	salt	10 mL
1/2 tsp	freshly ground black pepper	2 mL
1 1/2 tsp	turmeric	7 mL
2 tbsp	cider vinegar or lemon juice	30 mL
3 tbsp	chutney	45 mL

1/2 cup	seedless raisins	125 mL
4	lemon leaves or bay leaves	4
2 tbsp	slivered almonds	30 mL

- Preheat the oven to 350°F/180°C.
- Cut the onions into thin slices and sauté them in butter for about 10 minutes, until soft.
- Soak the bread in the milk and squeeze dry, reserving the milk.
- Crumble the soaked bread and mix in a bowl with the meat, cooked onions, 1 egg, curry powder, sugar, salt, pepper, turmeric, vinegar, chutney and raisins.
- Pat the mixture into a greased baking dish. Press the lemon or bay leaves and almonds half into the meat mixture. Bake for 1 hour.
- Beat the remaining egg and milk together and pour over the meat mixture. Continue baking for another 30 minutes. Serve with saffron rice and garnishes for curry.

Wine serving suggestions:
National: Tinta Barocca, Grenache rosé, Pinotage, Shiraz, Roodeberg
International: Châteauneuf-du-Pape, Zinfandel, Castel del Monte, Shiraz, Petite Sirah, Gewürztraminer

Tony Aspler's choice: Alsatian Gewürztraminer
Jacques Marie's choice: Sauvignon Blanc Fumé
Chef's choice:____________________

Van der Hum Flan

(Serves 8)

South Africa produces excellent brandy that tastes somewhat like Armagnac, particularly when it is aged in French Limousin oak barrels. Van der Hum is a liqueur made with Cape brandy, sugar, cinnamon, cardamom, cloves, nutmeg and the peels of "naartjies," the local tangerine.

PASTRY:		
1 cup	cake and pastry flour	250 mL
pinch	salt	pinch
2/3 cup	unsalted butter	150 mL
1/3 cup	fruit sugar	75 mL
2	egg yolks	2
1 tbsp	lemon juice	15 mL
FILLING:		
6	egg yolks	6
1 cup	fruit sugar	250 mL
4 tsp	gelatin	20 mL
1/2 cup	cold water	125 mL
1/2 cup	Van der Hum or other orange-based liqueur	125 mL
2 cups	heavy cream	500 mL

GARNISH:

24	seedless white grapes	24
2	egg whites	2
1/4 cup	fruit sugar	50 mL

- To make the pastry, sift the flour with the salt.
- Rub the butter lightly with the flour until it resembles coarse crumbs.
- Stir in the sugar, egg yolks and lemon juice and knead lightly. Roll the dough into a ball, cover and chill for 1 hour.
- Roll out the dough, line a 10-in/25-cm flan ring and bake blind at 350°F/180°C until cooked.
- To make the filling, whisk the egg yolks well. Add the sugar and continue whisking until very light and foamy.
- Soak the gelatin in the cold water, then melt over hot water.
- Add the melted gelatin and the liqueur to the egg mixture. Beat well.
- Whip the cream and fold into the egg mixture. Cool and let set slightly. Pour into the baked shell.
- To prepare the garnish, peel the grapes.
- Dip them in the egg whites and roll in the fruit sugar. Allow to dry before decorating the flan.

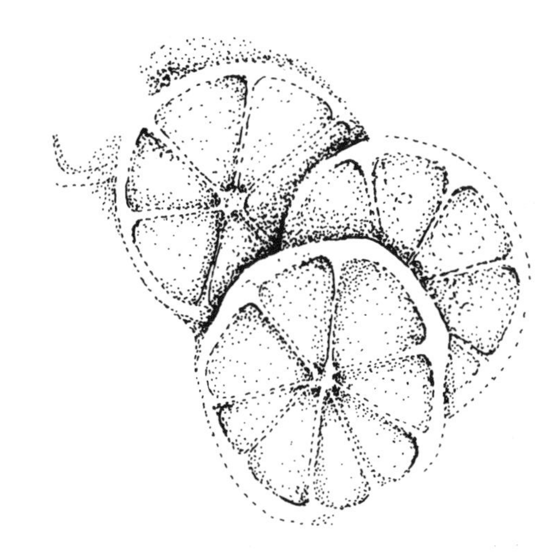

Wine serving suggestions:
National: Special Late Harvest Steen, Noble Late Harvest, Hanepoot
International: Coteaux-du-Layon, Ste-Croix-du-Mont, white Barsac, Beaumes-du-Venise, Piccolit, Asti Spumante

Tony Aspler's choice: Moulin Touchais
Jacques Marie's choice: Edelkeur
Chef's choice:________________________________

In its purest form, American cuisine is as simple and straightforward as the Mayflower colonists who first cleared the New England forests to build their settlements in the seventeenth century. Those hardy pioneers had little time for the niceties of the table; the primary duty of food was to nourish and sustain them in their labors.

But if preparation was plain, the raw materials were fine and abundant. The Puritans found the bays and coves of the New World alive with lobsters, clams, oysters and mussels. The fertile plains of the interior yielded enormous crops of corn, beans and barley. Endless ranges of pastureland could support herds of cattle, producing rich dairy products and succulent meat that had hitherto been enjoyed only by the very wealthy in the old country.

The lakes and rivers were home to wild geese, ducks, eels, salmon and bass. The forests sheltered deer and all manner of game birds. Berries, wild onions and nuts abounded. The outdoors was an enormous pantry for the earliest settlers, and the simplicity with which the food was prepared reflected the simplicity of their lives.

Gradually other influences made their mark on American cuisine, from the French and Spanish in Louisiana, the Mexican Indians in the southwest and the nomadic native tribes of the great plains. Succotash was the name of an old Indian dish prepared by the Mischquatash from Narragansett. Originally a rib-sticking mixture of corn, beans and fowl, it evolved into a more delicate concoction of corn, cream and lima beans. With each wave of immigration and the pushing of the frontier farther west, new culinary ideas were introduced from Europe. Perhaps the greatest single revolution in American dining habits occurred after the Second World War, when returning troops brought home with them a taste for European cuisine.

During the vibrant presidency of Thomas Jefferson, who had an intimate knowledge of Bordeaux wines, the austerity of the Virginian table was ameliorated by French culinary art. Creole cooking, a mixture of French, Spanish and Choctaw Indian influences, provided New Orleans with its own distinctive cuisine, highly flavored and spiced, but based on fresh local fish, shellfish and wild game, rice, tomatoes and capsicum peppers.

The eastern seaboard, the destination of so many immigrants who brought their own cultural heritages with them, can boast a mosaic of cooking styles from every part of the globe. Authentic ethnic restaurants of every nationality and region are available in cities like New York, Washington and Boston to service the growing numbers of sophisticated diners eager for new taste sensations.

But perhaps the most significant happening in American cuisine in the last twenty years—apart from the culinary innovations emanating from the kitchens of San Francisco—is the growth of the American wine scene and its effect on popular dining habits and food preparation. Wine, whether domestically grown or imported, is now a familiar beverage on the table. And Californian winemakers have begun to style their wines on European models for consumption with food—striving for a more elegant and subtle taste than the mouth-filling, oaky Cabernets and Chardonnays of the 1970s, which overpowered most dishes.

Manhattan Clam Chowder

(Serves 6)

The word "chowder" is a corruption of the French *chaudière*, which comes from *chaudron* (cauldron). A chaudière was a fish-based potluck stew to which the whole community added the ingredients they could afford.

There are two main varieties of clam chowder popular in the United States. Boston clam chowder has its roots in Normandy and Brittany, which accounts for the cream base, with lard and potatoes used as a thickening agent. Manhattan clam chowder is of Basque and Portuguese origin, hence the tomatoes and bacon and the use of crackers in the slurry as a thickener. Originally the crackers were the tough sea biscuits used as a survival ration on ships—they could only be consumed when soaked in liquid.

4	steak tomatoes	4
36	large clams, or a 15-oz/425-g can baby clams	36
2 tbsp	butter	30 mL
6	slices bacon, finely diced	6
1	medium onion, finely chopped	1
6	black peppercorns, crushed	6
1	large stick celery, without leaves, finely chopped	1
1	medium carrot, finely chopped	1
1	bouquet garni (1 large bay leaf, 1 sprig thyme, 3 sprigs Italian parsley)	1
3 cups	water	750 mL
3	medium potatoes, peeled and diced	3

10	soup crackers	10
2 tbsp	finely chopped celery leaves	30 mL
	Worcestershire sauce	

- Immerse the fresh tomatoes in boiling water for 15 seconds. Refresh and remove skins with a paring knife. Cut the tomatoes in half and squeeze to remove the seeds. Dice.
- Shuck the clams, drain and reserve the juice. Chop the clams if fresh and reserve.
- In a heavy saucepan, melt the butter and sauté the diced bacon until golden but not crisp.
- Add the finely chopped onion and cook until soft without coloring.
- Add the crushed peppercorns, celery and carrot and cook for 4 minutes, stirring frequently.
- Add the tomatoes, clam juice, bouquet garni and water. Bring to a boil, then lower the heat and simmer for 30 minutes.
- Add the diced potatoes and cook until the potatoes are soft.
- Add the clams and bring back to a boil. Remove from heat and let rest for 30 minutes in a warm place. Before serving remove the bouquet garni.
- To serve, crush the crackers in a bowl, add some liquid from the soup and make a slurry. Return to the soup and mix well. Taste and adjust seasonings. Add chopped celery leaves and Worcestershire sauce and serve hot.

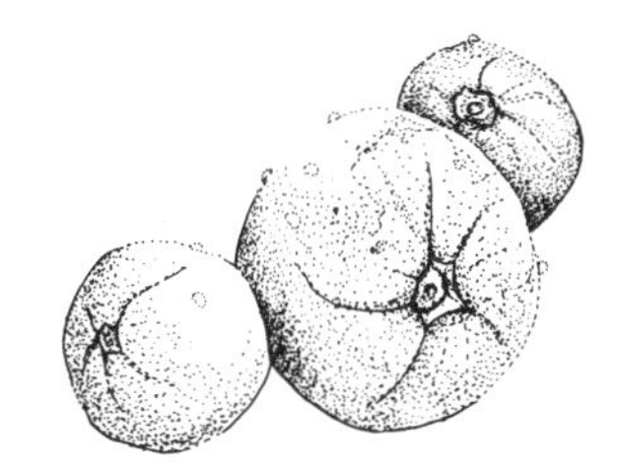

Wine serving suggestions:
In general, soup is not the best companion for wine—but you could accompany this with a young acidic white like a Loire Sauvignon Blanc (Sancerre, Pouilly-Fumé) or a chilled young Beaujolais or Bardolino.

Shrimp Creole

(Serves 6)

The word *creole* refers to the descendants of the original French and Spanish colonists of Louisiana. Louisiana was first settled by the French in 1799. Then came the Spanish who adapted their native dishes to the ingredients available in the new land. Creole cooking was later influenced by the arrival of different cultures from Africa, the West Indies, Mexico and by the local Indians. The result is a style of cooking celebrated today in dishes and restaurants all over the continent.

Adjust the amount of hot red pepper in this recipe to your own taste, but remember that the more spices you use, the less you will be able to appreciate the wine. If you like this dish very hot, drink beer instead.

12	medium, very ripe tomatoes (or 4 cups/1 L canned tomatoes, drained)	12
2 tbsp	coarse salt	30 mL
3 lb	raw green shrimps, peeled and deveined	1.5 kg
1/2 cup	peanut or good vegetable oil	125 mL
2	large onions, peeled and chopped	2
2	medium green peppers, seeded and chopped	2
1	medium pimento, chopped	1
2	stalks celery, without leaves, chopped	2
8	cloves garlic, pasted	8
2	large bay leaves	2
1 tbsp	paprika	15 mL
1/2 tsp	cayenne pepper	2 mL
	Salt	

1¼ cups	water	300 mL
2 tbsp	cornstarch	30 mL

- If using fresh tomatoes, place them in boiling water for 15 seconds. Refresh under cold water and peel off the skins with a paring knife. Cut the tomatoes in half and squeeze the halves to remove the seeds. Coarsely chop the tomatoes. (If you use canned tomatoes, chop them and reserve.)
- Melt the coarse salt in 6 cups/1.5 L water. Soak the shrimps for 5 minutes, then drain and pat dry.
- Heat the oil in a heavy skillet or saucepan until it gives off a haze. Add the onions, green peppers, pimento, celery and garlic. Stirring frequently, cook for 5 minutes, or until soft.
- Add the tomatoes, bay leaves, paprika, cayenne, salt and water. Bring to a boil, then lower heat and simmer for 30 minutes.
- Add the raw shrimps, stir and simmer, covered, for 3 to 5 minutes, depending on the size of the shrimps.
- Add cornstarch diluted with 2 tbsp/30 mL water and cook for a further 3 minutes. Remove the bay leaves, taste and adjust seasoning. Serve immediately with hot steamed rice.

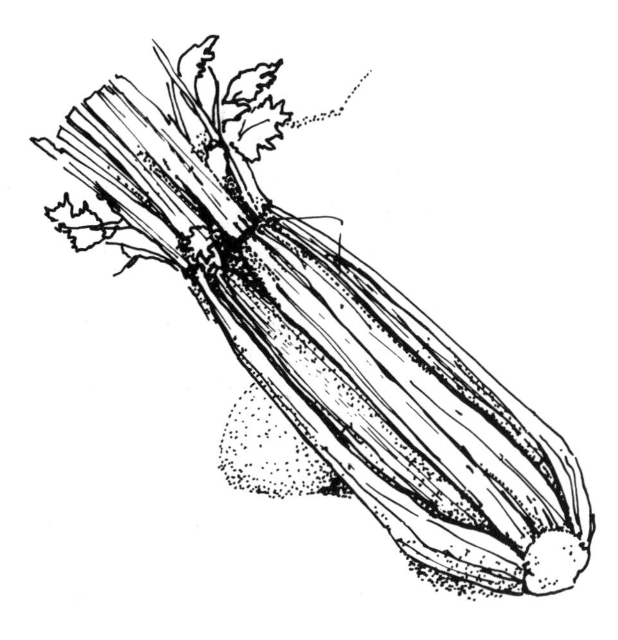

Wine serving suggestions:
National: Fumé Blanc, Sauvignon Blanc, heavy Chardonnay
International: Sancerre, Condrieu, Pomino, dry Muscat

Tony Aspler's choice: white Corvo from Sicily
Jacques Marie's choice: Gewürztraminer Vendange Tardive
Chef's choice: ______________________________

New England Boiled Dinner

(Serves 8)

This plain, substantial and nourishing dish reflects the no-frills Puritan roots of New England. The meal-in-one-dish recipe is reminiscent of the French pot-au-feu, the Italian bollito misto and Spanish olla podrida.

Do not be put off by the simplicity of this dish. It can be a refreshing change to have vegetables that taste like vegetables and unadorned meat, especially when fresh garden produce and top-quality fresh beef and chicken are used. Serve this dish accompanied by horseradish sauce, mustard pickles and rye bread.

4 lb	corned brisket of beef, mildly cured	2 kg
1 lb	salted pork belly	500 g
3	bay leaves	3
14	whole black peppercorns	14
1	boiling chicken, approx. 4 lb/2 kg	1
6	medium onions	6
6	large carrots, peeled	6
6	large potatoes, peeled	6
2	medium turnips, peeled and quartered	2
1	medium white cabbage, cored and quartered	1
6	medium beets	6
	Chopped fresh parsley	

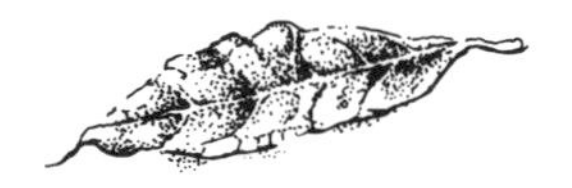

- Cover the brisket with cold water. (Make sure the corned beef is not oversalted or it must be parboiled first.) Add the pork belly, bay leaves and peppercorns. Simmer over low heat for 1 hour.
- Add the chicken. Cook for 1 to 1½ hours, or until tender but firm.
- Add the onions, carrots, potatoes and turnips. Cook for 15 minutes. Add the cabbage. Cook until tender.
- Meanwhile, wash the beets and trim the stems to 1 in/2.5 cm. Cook in salted water until tender. Cool slightly. Then rub peels away and trim stems.
- Serve the meat on a platter garnished with the vegetables. Sprinkle with parsley.

Wine serving suggestions:
Regional/National: ale, New York Baco Noir, Oregon Pinot Noir, New York Chelois
International: Dolcetto, Côtes-du-Ventoux, Riesling

Tony Aspler's choice: Beaujolais Villages
Jacques Marie's choice: dry Sauvignon
Chef's choice: ______________________

Southern-fried Chicken

(Serves 2 to 4)

The technique of deep-frying is closer to boiling than pan-frying, since the food is completely immersed in the fat. Fat reaches at least double the temperature of boiling water, so the food cooks more rapidly and the exterior is browned by caramelization. If the chicken is well covered with a batter or coating, the fat doesn't really touch the meat, which means the flesh cooks in its own steam—this dish should never be greasy!

This recipe uses a shallow-frying method, which is a cross between deep-frying and pan-frying, and commonly used in the South.

3 lb	chicken	1.5 kg
1 tbsp	salt	15 mL
1 tbsp	freshly ground black pepper	15 mL
	Flour	
2 lb	lard	1 kg
2 cups	cream	500 mL

- Cut the chicken into serving pieces. Pat dry if necessary. Season the chicken pieces with salt and pepper and dust generously with flour.
- Preheat the oven to 150°F/65°C.
- Heat the lard in a thick skillet over moderate heat. The lard should be 1 in/2 cm deep when melted (oil can be used instead of lard). When the lard reaches about 375°F/190°C, place the chicken, skin side down, in the lard and fry until evenly colored, turning the pieces as often as necessary.
- When the chicken pieces are cooked, with a crisp, golden skin, place them on a tray covered with paper towels and keep them warm in the oven.
- When all the chicken is cooked, discard all

the lard from the skillet except 2 tbsp/30 mL. Add 2 tbsp/30 mL flour and cook until golden in color and sandy in texture.

- Add the cream, mix well and cook for 3 to 5 minutes. Taste and adjust the seasoning with salt and pepper.
- Serve the sauce in a sauce boat and the chicken piping hot. (This dish is often garnished with corn fritters.)

Wine serving suggestions:
Regional/National: Finger Lakes Chardonnay, Ontario Riesling, Seyval Blanc
International: white Graves, Orvieto (secco), Macon Blanc, Australian Chardonnay

Tony Aspler's choice: Alsace Riesling
Jacques Marie's choice: Inniskillin Chardonnay (Seeger Vineyard)
Chef's choice:____________________

Roast Turkey with Oyster Stuffing

(Serves 6)

If Benjamin Franklin had had his way, the American national symbol would be a turkey instead of an eagle. Franklin considered the eagle to be of "bad moral character... generally poor and often very lousy," but he found the turkey "a much more respectable bird, and withal a true original native of America."

It's a shame that inflexible tradition has condemned this bird to be eaten only at Christmas and Thanksgiving. The firm, white flesh is very tasty, but must be basted with fat during cooking because of its leanness and tendency to dry out. Do not discard the carcass or leftovers—they make a marvelous stock for soup.

This oyster stuffing is so good that I can never decide if I like some stuffing with my turkey or some turkey with the stuffing. Both go wonderfully well with wine—this is a dish truly fit for a feast!

1	10- to 12-lb/5- to 6-kg young, fresh turkey with trimmings	1
	Salt and freshly ground black pepper	
1	medium carrot, scrubbed	1
1	medium onion, peeled	1
2	stalks celery	2
1	sprig thyme	1
1	bay leaf	1
1	clove garlic	1
8	whole black peppercorns	8
1/2 tsp	rock salt	2 mL
6 cups	cold water	1.5 L

STUFFING:

2 cups	finely chopped onions	500 mL
1 cup	butter	250 mL
2 cups	finely chopped celery	500 mL
2 tbsp	freshly grated lemon peel	30 mL
2 tbsp	finely chopped fresh sage (or 1 tbsp/15 mL dried sage)	30 mL
3 cups	shucked oysters	750 mL
1/2 tsp	freshly ground black pepper	2 mL
1 tsp	salt	2 mL
2 lb	white bread, trimmed and diced	1 kg
1	egg	1
1/2 cup	finely chopped fresh parsley	125 mL
3 tbsp	flour	45 mL

- Cut the neck, wings and winglets off the turkey. Remove the liver, heart and gizzard from the cavity.
- Rinse the bird with lukewarm water and pat dry with paper towels. Season the cavity with salt and pepper and set aside.
- Prepare a stock with the chopped neck, heart, gizzard, wings, winglets, carrot, onion, celery, thyme, bay leaf, garlic, peppercorns, rock salt and cold water. Simmer until the meat on the wings can be easily removed from the bones. Strain and reserve 2 cups/500 mL stock.
- Preheat the oven to 425°F/220°C.
- To make the stuffing, cook the onions in the butter until golden. Add the celery and cook for 2 minutes.
- Add the lemon peel, sage, oysters, pepper and salt and toss quickly for 1 minute. Then place in a bowl.
- Add the bread and egg mixed with 1/2 cup/125 mL stock and parsley. Mix well. Place the stuffing in the cavity of the turkey. Truss the turkey with kitchen twine.
- Grease the skin of the turkey with some oil and roast in the oven on a rack, breast side up, for 30 minutes. Reduce the oven temperature to 325°F/160°C, turn the turkey breast down and roast for 1 hour.
- Turn the breast up again and roast for another hour, basting every 15 minutes. When cooked, place the turkey on a serving dish.
- Skim 3 tbsp/45 mL fat from the roasting pan into a skillet. Add flour and cook until golden. Add 1 1/2 cups/375 mL turkey stock and bring to the boil. Add the liquid back to the roasting pan juice and stir well. Adjust seasoning, strain and serve the gravy in a warmed sauceboat.

Wine serving suggestions:
Regional: New York Maréchal Foch
National: Petite Sirah, white Zinfandel
International: Taurasi, Australian Cabernet, Bandol, St-Joseph, Côte-Rôtie

Tony Aspler's choice: Tavel rosé
Jacques Marie's choice: Oregon Cabernet Sauvignon
Chef's choice:______________________________

Old-Fashioned Pecan Pie

(Serves 6 to 8)

Pecans are a species of hickory (true hickory nuts are not edible as they contain too much tannin) believed to be native to the Mississippi River Valley. Georgia is the leading pecan-producing state today. The word is of Algonkian origin—natives prized the tree greatly for the nutritious oil extracted from the nuts. Today there are over three hundred varieties of pecans. Although tender, flavorful and nutritious (71 percent fat and 687 calories per 100 grams), pecans are one food that has never made it across to the Old World.

This pie is very rich and high in calories; serve it warm and offer small portions!

PASTRY:

1 cup	all-purpose flour	250 mL
1/3 cup	chilled butter or lard	75 mL
pinch	salt	pinch
4 tbsp	cold water	60 mL

FILLING:

4	eggs	4
1 1/2 cups	corn syrup	375 mL
1/4 cup	melted butter	50 mL
1 tsp	vanilla	5 mL
1/4 cup	Bourbon or brandy	50 mL
1 1/2 cups	pecans	375 mL

- Sift the flour into a mixing bowl. Add the butter and combine by rubbing the butter and flour between tips of the fingers until the mixture has a coarse, mealy texture.
- Dissolve the salt in the water. Add to the flour, combining lightly until it forms a ball. Cover and chill for 30 minutes.
- Preheat the oven to 400°F/200°C.
- Roll the dough on a floured surface and line a 10-in/1.5-L pie plate.
- Bake the shell for 15 minutes.
- In a mixing bowl, whisk the eggs for 30 seconds. Then continue whisking while adding the corn syrup, melted butter, vanilla and Bourbon.
- Place the pecans in the pie crust and pour the mixture over them. Shake the pie to allow the pecans to disperse evenly.
- Bake in the middle of the oven for 35 minutes, or until the filling is firm. Serve warm.

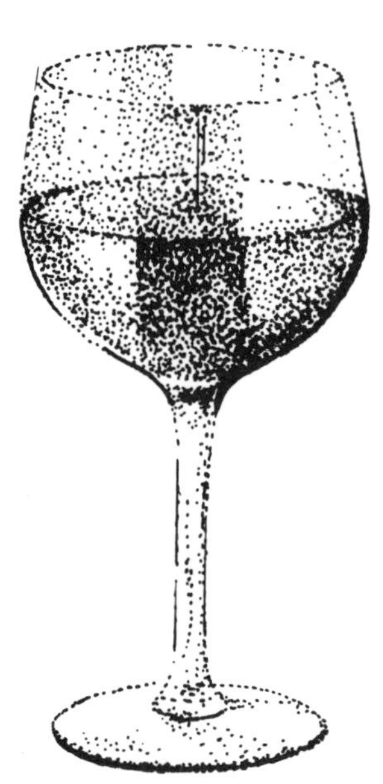

Wine serving suggestions:
National: sweet New York whites or Californian sparkling
International: Tokay Aszu (3 puttonyos), Oloroso sherry, dry Marsala

Tony Aspler's choice: Asti Spumante
Jacques Marie's choice: old Sercial
Chef's choice:______________________________

Canada

After the Soviet Union, Canada is the largest country in the world. But it is an empty giant: twenty-five million people are dispersed across its enormous area—the vast majority within easy reach of the American border.

Like its mighty neighbor to the south, Canada is a land of immigrants who brought with them particular tastes and culinary skills. The original British and French settlers have been joined this century by the Germans, Italians, Ukrainians, Dutch, Poles, Portuguese, Greeks, Asians and many other nationalities.

There is really no such thing as a recognizable Canadian cuisine. There are regional dishes like habitant pea soup and tourtière (Quebec), seal flipper pie (Newfoundland), wild rice (Manitoba) or steamed fiddleheads (tender shoots of the ostrich fern grown in New Brunswick); but these owe more to ethnic and provincial boundaries than to an autonomously Canadian taste in food.

The closest Canada comes to a national dish is, perhaps, pancakes and maple syrup served with peameal bacon—a hearty farmhouse breakfast for the working man in winter.

The Maritime provinces rely heavily on the fishing industry which yields a harvest of cod, Gaspé salmon, mackerel, herring, lobster and crab. The Malpeque and Buctouche oysters are first rate.

Specialties such as Arctic char and Winnipeg goldeye are worth crossing the border for, as are the sea trout and scallops of British Columbia and the lake trout of the Northwest Territories.

Ontario breeds delectable spring lamb and makes a variety of cheeses, especially Cheddar. The pride of Quebec is its Oka cheese and its succulent pork and bacon. The McIntosh apple and soft fruits of the Niagara

Peninsula and British Columbia's Okanagan Valley, the wheat and other grains of the prairie provinces and the wealth of game for hunters in the northern forests suggest an abundance of quality produce. But there is no tradition of turning this splendid raw material into haut cuisine dishes; the climate and the Canadian temperament have developed a country kitchen style—food means nourishment and energy.

Unknown to the world outside, Canada makes wine on a large commercial scale. There are some thirty wineries in Ontario and British Columbia, making a range of varietal products and blends. The best are the Rieslings and Chardonnays with some interesting hybrids like Seyval Blanc and late harvest Vidal. Nova Scotia and Quebec are currently developing their own domestic vineyards.

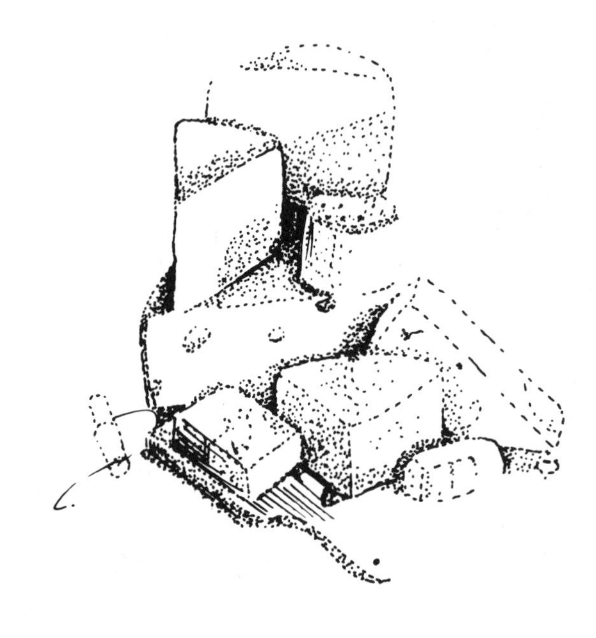

Tourtière Québécoise

Meat Pie Quebec Style
(Serves 6 to 8)

A tourtière is an earthenware pie dish—the word *tourte* comes from the Latin *tortus*, meaning making round.

Tourtière is one of the oldest Quebec dishes, dating back to the first French settlers. Originally game was used in the pie, depending on the success of the hunt. Later, as farms were established, pork became the traditional filling.

PASTRY:

3 cups	sifted all-purpose flour	750 mL
1 tsp	salt	5 mL
3/4 cup	shortening or lard, cold	175 mL
1	egg	1
4 tbsp	milk, cold	60 mL

FILLING:

1 lb	pork neck or shoulder	750 g
1 lb	veal neck or shoulder	750 g
2	slices bacon	2
1	large clove garlic, peeled	1
1	onion	1
1/4 cup	water	50 mL
1 tsp	salt	5 mL
1/2 tsp	freshly ground black pepper	2 mL

pinch each	thyme, sage, savory and allspice	pinch each
1	medium potato, peeled and grated	1
1/4 cup	grated carrot	50 mL
1/4 cup	chopped fresh parsley	50 mL

- To make the pastry, sift the flour and salt together.
- Cut the shortening into small pieces and work into the flour with the fingertips until you have a cornmeal consistency.
- Combine the egg with the milk and add to the flour mixture. Work lightly together until a ball of dough is formed. Cover and place in the refrigerator for at least 1 hour.
- To make the filling, grind together the pork, veal, bacon, garlic and onion. Combine well and cook in a large saucepan over medium heat for 10 minutes, or until the meat has lost its redness.
- Add the water, salt, pepper, thyme, sage, savoury and allspice. Cook, covered, for 25 minutes.
- Add the grated potatoes and carrots. Cook for another 5 minutes, then add the parsley.
- Preheat the oven to 400°F/200°C.
- Remove the dough from the refrigerator and divide into four pieces (two should be slightly larger). Roll each piece of dough in a circular shape on a floured surface.
- Line two 9-in/23-cm pie plates with the two large circles of dough. Fill the pie with the meat mixture. Cover each pie with the remaining dough and brush with a little salted water. Cut a few slits on the top to let the steam escape and bake for 15 minutes. Lower the heat to 325°F/160°C and bake for another 30 minutes.

Wine serving suggestions:
National: Chardonnay, Chelois, Gamay Beaujolais, Riesling
International: Rosé de Marsannay, Provence red or rosé, Alsatian white, Vouvray, Pinot Noir, Chiaretto, Valpolicella

Tony Aspler's choice: Castel Grifone (Lungarotti's rosé)
Jacques Marie's choice: Sauvignon Blanc Fumé
Chef's choice:______________________________

Glazed Canadian Ham

(Serves 6 to 8)

In Canada, a ham is traditionally served at Easter. This recipe is easy to prepare and is a good dish to offer for a buffet or garden party. Serve it with baked squash or roasted new potatoes sprinkled with fresh herbs. A light fruity rosé or white wine is a good accompaniment, but a good sparkling cider will go well, too.

1	ham, approx. 8-10 lb/4-5 kg	1
	Whole cloves	
3/4 cup	maple syrup	175 mL
2 tsp	dry mustard	10 mL
1/3 cup	breadcrumbs	75 mL
1/4 cup	cider vinegar or apple juice	50 mL
1 cup	dry white wine	250 mL
1 cup	unsweetened applesauce	250 mL
	Salt and freshly ground black pepper	

- Preheat the oven to 325°F/160°C.
- Bake the ham for 30 minutes per pound/500 g. Take the ham out of the oven and remove the skin. Turn up the oven temperature to 425°F/220°C.
- In a criss-cross pattern, score the fat of the ham about 1/2 in/1 cm deep and insert a clove into each section of fat.
- Combine the maple syrup, mustard, breadcrumbs and vinegar. Spread the mixture over the ham.
- Bake the ham until the crust is golden brown, basting the meat from time to time.
- Transfer the ham to a serving dish. Degrease the roasting juices and deglaze the pan with the wine. Add the applesauce. Combine well and season with salt and pepper. Serve the sauce in a sauce boat alongside the ham.

Wine serving suggestions:
National: Chardonnay, Ontario rosé or blush, white sparkling
International: Kabinett Riesling or Sylvaner, Bardolino, Anjou white or rosé, Dôle, Valpolicella, Beaujolais, Macon, Bairrada, blush Zinfandel

Tony Aspler's choice: Vouvray (preferably Poniatowsky's Clos Baudoin)
Jacques Marie's choice: Grüner Veltliner
Chef's choice: ______________________________

Crab Legs in Patty Shells

(Serves 6)

If crabs come close to being the ugliest maritime creatures, their soft flaky texture and sweet taste makes them one of the most popular seafoods in North America, ranked second only to shrimp.

Crab meat has been praised as an aphrodisiac, as well as a rich source of minerals, vitamins and protein. Alaska King crab can reach a span of nine feet. They can be bought freshly cooked, or frozen, shelled and cooked. If crab seems expensive, remember that there is no waste when it is bought shelled; one pound of crab meat should yield approximately two cups, or enough for four servings.

6	large frozen patty shells	6
5 tbsp	butter	75 mL
2 tbsp	finely chopped onion	30 mL
1 lb	frozen King crab legs, thawed and cut in 1-in/2.5-cm pieces	500 g
3/4 cup	dry white wine	175 mL
	Salt and freshly ground black pepper	
3 tbsp	all-purpose flour	45 mL
2 cups	whole milk or light cream	500 mL
3	egg yolks	3
1 tbsp	minced fresh chives	15 mL
2 tbsp	grated white Cheddar cheese	30 mL

- Bake the patty shells according to package directions and keep warm.
- Melt 2 tbsp/30 mL butter over medium heat until foaming and sauté the onions until slightly golden.
- Add the crab legs and toss for 1 minute.
- Add the white wine and bring to a boil. Season with salt and pepper. Remove from the heat and keep warm.

- To make the sauce, melt 3 tbsp/45 mL butter over medium heat. Add the flour and cook for 1 minute without coloring.
- Gradually add the milk or the cream, stirring constantly until the sauce thickens.
- Mix the egg yolks in a bowl with 3 tbsp/45 mL sauce. Return the mixture to the sauce, stirring well. Season with salt and pepper and cook over very low heat for 5 to 8 minutes. Do not boil.
- Add the sauce to the crab legs. Mix gently and taste for seasoning.
- Add the chives and spoon the mixture into the patty shells.
- Sprinkle the Cheddar cheese on top and glaze under a broiler.

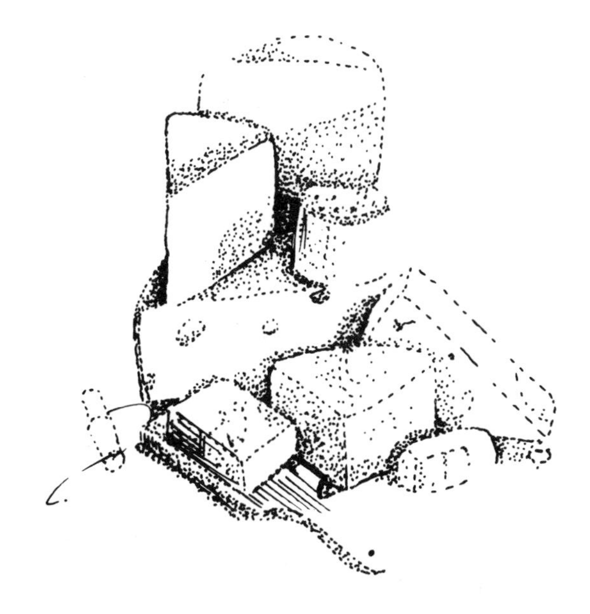

Wine serving suggestions:
National: Riesling, Chardonnay, Chenin Blanc
International: Sylvaner, Pinot Blanc, Muscadet, Blanc fumé, Aligoté, dry Sauvignon, dry or medium rosé, Orvieto (secco), white Corvo, Verdicchio, Alella, Steen, Viña Sol, Tierra del Viño.

Tony Aspler's choice: Wiemer Vineyard Chardonnay (New York State)
Jacques Marie's choice: Château des Charmes Chardonnay 1985 (Ontario)
Chef's choice:______________________________

Marinated Roast Haunch of Venison

(Serves 4)

More massacres have been perpetrated in the kitchen than in the bush. Being both a hunter and a conservationist, I hate to see the life of a wild animal wasted by poor cooking. One of my greatest joys and honors is to share with friends the rare sensation of a well-prepared game dish perfectly matched with the right wine—which is why I created this recipe. It's delicious served with roasted potatoes or baked yams.

Venison meat is only as good as the hunter who killed the animal. The kill should be swift and the carcass skilfully dressed. The meat should be hung according to the season and the age of the animal to permit the natural enzymes to tenderize the meat. The older the animal and the cooler the temperature, the longer the hanging time.

MARINADE:

1 tsp	Worcestershire sauce	5 mL
2 cups	dry strong red wine	500 mL
1/2 cup	cider vinegar	125 mL
2 tsp	black peppercorns, lightly crushed	10 mL
2 tsp	juniper berries, lightly crushed	10 mL
6	cloves	6
2	large bay leaves	2
4	large cloves garlic, crushed	4
1	large onion, sliced	1
1	large carrot, sliced	1
1 tsp	dried thyme	5 mL
1 tsp	dried rosemary	5 mL

6 tbsp	vegetable oil	90 mL
3 tbsp	maple syrup	45 mL
1/4 tsp	cayenne pepper	1 mL

ROAST:

4-6 lb	saddle, shoulder or leg of deer, moose or wild boar, with bones in	2-3 kg
8 oz	bacon or fresh pork belly, diced	250 g
3 tbsp	flour	45 mL
1 cup	water	250 mL
1/2 cup	dry sherry	125 mL
2 tbsp	red currant jelly	30 mL
1/2 cup	sour cream	125 mL
	Salt and freshly ground black pepper	
1/3 cup	Dutch gin	75 mL

- Place all marinade ingredients in a large earthenware or stainless steel bowl. Mix well and leave standing to reach room temperature before soaking the venison.
- Place the meat in the marinade and turn until all sides are coated. Cover and let stand at room temperature for 2 to 4 days, turning at least four times a day. (Marinate young deer for about 2 days; older, tougher deer require longer. The purpose of a marinade is to tenderize and flavor the meat. Marinating the meat too long may alter the natural flavor of the game.)
- Preheat the oven to 350°F/180°C.
- Remove the haunch of game from the marinade, scraping off all solid particles. Pat the meat dry. Strain the marinade, reserving the liquid and the solids in two separate containers.
- Sprinkle the flour all over the roast. Cook the roast in the hot bacon fat on all sides, to form a golden crust all over. Remove the meat without puncturing the crust and reserve.
- Fry the solids from the marinade in the same bacon fat for 3 minutes.
- Place the meat back on the bed of spices and vegetables. Roast in the oven for about 45 minutes, roughly to the medium stage.
- Add the liquid from the marinade and the water and cook for another 40 minutes, basting every 10 minutes.
- Remove the roast and keep warm. Strain the juices, degrease and place back in the Dutch oven over medium heat.
- Add the sherry, red currant jelly and sour cream. Bring to a gentle boil, reduce slightly and season with salt and pepper to taste. The sauce should be sweet, rich and spicy. Place in a hot sauce boat.

- In a Dutch oven, cook the diced bacon over medium heat until golden.
- To serve, place the roast on a tray for carving. Warm up the gin, ignite and pour over the roast. Carve and serve immediately.

Wine serving suggestions:
National: wood-aged Maréchal Foch, Baco Noir
International: Shiraz, Barolo, Côte-de-Nuits, Pomerol, Châteauneuf-du-Pape, Coronas, strong Cabernet, Tinta Barocca, Bucaco red, Garrafeira, Sfursat, Zinfandel, Petite Sirah

Tony Aspler's choice: Ridge Zinfandel
Jacques Marie's choice: mature Hermitage
Chef's choice:____________________

Maple Bread Pudding

(Serves 4)

Today pure maple syrup is considered a luxury, but in colonial times it was the most common sweetener available. If you have trouble finding maple sugar, you can use maple syrup that has been reduced on low heat until it is thick enough to coat the pudding mold.

1 cup	milk	250 mL
1 cup	light cream	250 mL
2 tsp	vanilla	10 mL
8 oz	maple sugar, grated	250 g
1/2 cup	slivered almonds	125 mL
4	eggs	4
3 tbsp	soft butter	45 mL
6	slices white bread	6
1 tbsp	pure maple syrup	15 mL

- Preheat the oven to 275°F/130°C.
- In a bowl combine the milk, cream, vanilla and 1 oz/30 g grated maple sugar. Stir together until the sugar is completely dissolved.
- Add the slivered almonds and soak for 15 minutes.
- Drain the almonds and reserve. Add the eggs to the milk and cream. Mix well.
- Coat a 6-cup/1.5 L-pudding mold with 1 tbsp/15 mL butter. Coat the buttered mold with the remaining grated maple sugar, pressing the sugar into the sides of the mold to cover it evenly.
- Cut the crusts from the bread and butter each slice with the remaining butter. Cut each slice into cubes.
- Warm the maple syrup in a casserole and toss in the slivered almonds. Add the bread cubes and the milk and egg mixture.
- Pour the mixture into the prepared mold and cover with aluminum foil. Place the mold in a pan filled with enough boiling water to reach halfway up the sides of the mold. Bake for 1 1/2 hours, or until the pudding is set.
- Unmold the pudding while it is still hot by loosening the sides with a thin-bladed knife. Place a circular dish on top and then turn quickly upside down. Serve hot or cold with whipped cream.

Wine serving suggestions:
National: Eiswein or sparkling white, Riesling or Vidal Beerenauslese
International: Tokay Aszu, Eiswein, Monbazillac, Barsac, sweet Muscat, Beerenauslese, Oloroso sherry or Marsala, Asti Spumante, sweet Champagne

Tony Aspler's choice: Rivesaltes
Jacques Marie's choice: sweet sparkling Vouvray
Chef's choice:____

Mexico

Mexican cooking is as exotic as the country's history, music and art—a cuisine of contrasts, where color and texture are as important as flavor and aroma.

Beyond the supermarket image of spicy tacos, enchiladas, tortillas and guacamole is a culinary tradition that stretches back to a civilization older than that of the Greeks. The sixteenth-century Spanish conquistadores had little to teach the Aztecs and Mayans when it came to preparing game birds, rabbit, hare and chicken.

In Mexico, Cortes' men saw for the first time wild turkeys, the vanilla pod, potatoes, green tomatoes, peanuts, squash and chocolate. The basic Mexican staples were then—as they are now—corn and a variety of beans.

From the European pantry, the Spanish introduced to Mexico onions, garlic, rice, cinnamon and the hog. As a conquered people the Indians accepted the culture of Spain whose own cuisine had been tempered by six hundred years of Moorish occupation. The spices of the East combined with the indigenous sweet and hot peppers to form the basis of a new style of cooking.

The Spaniards taught the local inhabitants how to fry instead of roast, and lard became an essential ingredient in Mexican recipes. Most of the sauces for meats still involve frying a paste of beans and peppers with spices.

Perhaps the most original dish and one that can claim national status is Mole Poblano—turkey or chicken with a hot sauce made with chili peppers, almonds, onions, green tomato, raisins, a variety of spices and bitter chocolate.

The Mexicans make good use of everything that grows, including the leaves and fruit of the cactus, the fruit of the tamarind tree, and a bitter herb called epazote, an essential ingredient for frijoles—fried mashed black beans.

Wine is made in the northern regions of Mexico, close to the Californian border, but the industry has yet to produce reds or whites to rival its northern neighbor. Ninety percent of grape production goes for distillation. Mexico does produce a unique eau-de-vie—tequila—from the root of a cactus-like plant, as well as some exceptionally good beer.

Mole Poblano de Guajolote

Turkey in Chocolate and Chili Sauce
(Serves 8)

Mole sauces (from the Nahuatl Indian word *molli*, meaning a sauce made with chili) are very hot and spicy, but can be adjusted to one's individual taste. There are more than fifty varieties of peppers in Mexico, ranging from the mild to unbearably hot. Ancho chilies are the dried poblano chilies—they are dark-red in color, mildly hot and about 4 inches/10 cm long. Pasilla chilies, which are hotter and darker, can also be used in this dish or, as a last resort, 2 tablespoons/30 mL chili powder plus a touch of cayenne.

6-8 lb	turkey, cut into serving pieces	3-4 kg
2 tsp	salt	10 mL
14	dried ancho chilies	14
1/2 cup	salted peanuts or peanut butter	125 mL
3	green peppers, seeded and coarsely chopped	3
1 cup	coarsely chopped onions	250 mL
6	cloves garlic, peeled	6
8	tomatoes	8
1/2 cup	seedless raisins	125 mL
1/4 tsp	cumin	1 mL
1/2 tsp	cinnamon	2 mL
1/2 tsp	freshly ground black pepper	2 mL
1/4 tsp	coriander	1 mL
3 tbsp	chili powder	45 mL
1/2 tsp	anise seeds	2 mL

1	tortilla or piece of dry white toast	1
3 oz	unsweetened chocolate, grated	85 g
1/2 cup	olive oil	125 mL
2 tbsp	sesame seeds	30 mL

- Place the turkey pieces in a large casserole and add enough water to cover, with 1 tsp/5 mL salt. Bring to a boil and simmer, covered, for about 1 hour, or until almost tender.
- Drain the turkey, reserving 2 cups/500 mL of the cooking liquid.
- Preheat the oven to 350°F/180°C.
- To prepare the sauce, cut the dried chilies in half and remove the seeds and stems under cold running water. Place the chilies in a bowl and pour in the boiling turkey stock. Let the chilies soak for 30 minutes.
- In a blender or food processor, blend together the peanuts, chilies with stock, green peppers, onions, garlic, tomatoes, remaining salt, raisins, cumin, cinnamon, pepper, coriander, chili powder, anise seeds, tortilla and chocolate.
- Heat half the olive oil in a frying pan. Add the turkey pieces and brown well on all sides. Place the turkey pieces on an ovenproof casserole in one layer.
- Heat the remaining oil in the frying pan and add the mixture from the blender. Cook over low heat for about 5 minutes, stirring continuously. Ladle the sauce over the turkey pieces and bake, covered, for 1½ hours. Sprinkle with sesame seeds and serve hot with boiled rice.

Wine serving suggestions:
National: Mexican Zinfandel or Petite Sirah
International: Châteauneuf-du-Pape, Amarone, Zinfandel, Riesling Spätlese, Primitivo, Shiraz

Tony Aspler's choice: Serego Aligheri Recioto di Amarone
Jacques Marie's choice: Paarl Roodeberg
Chef's choice:____

3

WINE AND FOOD AFFINITY CHARTS

"It is the part of a wise man to feed himself with pleasant food and wine."

—**Spinoza**

Wine and Food Charts

As a quick and ready reference guide for choosing wines to match different foods (or selecting a specific dish for that bottle of wine you want to try) we offer a series of wine and food affinity charts. These charts cover every imaginable fish, seafood, poultry, meat and game dish you will want to serve, with specific reference to the method of preparation—whether the dish in question is made by braising, frying, baking or served with a light or heavy sauce.

In addition, we have recommended wines for soups, desserts, cheeses and nuts.

Rather than listing hundreds of individual brands and proprietary names, we have indicated wine styles. To simplify matters we have categorized some four hundred of the world's most readily accessible wines by their flavor characteristics. The whites range through nine styles from dry light-bodied (WDL) to sweet full-bodied (WSB). The reds cover four styles, from light (RL) to heavyweight (RH), and rosés three, from light-bodied (RoL) to full-bodied (RoB). These initials are each color-coded on the charts for easy identification. When you have chosen your dish and the way you want to prepare it simply follow the axes to the suggested wine style and then turn to the Wines of the World section on page 207, where you will find an entire range of wines listed by country which will complement the dish. (Where there are blanks in the chart, this signifies that we suggest wine be avoided with this particular dish.) For example, if you happen to fancy lake trout in a cream sauce, you will find the initials WDB (white dry full-bodied) on the fish chart. Under the dry full-bodied category of white wines on page 208 you can make your choice from some thirty different full-bodied white wines from around the world.

If you are not sure of the style of wine from the varietal description of the wine (i.e., Chardonnay, Gamay, Trebbiano, etc.), we have included profiles on all the major wine grapes used around the world. You'll find these entries on pages 215 to 222.

These wine recommendations are merely guideposts for you in your enjoyment of fine dining. You should not feel constrained to the suggested categories if you want to experiment. In the final analysis there are no hard and fast rules. The best advice we can give is for you to follow your own preferences. The charts will help you to avoid initial disappointments.

Wine and Nuts

Nuts, like other foods, have their own particular character and taste which can be enhanced by your wine selection. Rich in protein, carbohydrates and vitamins, nuts can be a meal in themselves, especially when accompanied by a glass of wine. One general principle: because of their fatty nature, nuts require a substantial wine, either fortified (Oloroso sherry, Bual, tawny or vintage port), sweet or powerful. If the kernels are salty the perfect companion is a chilled Fino sherry or Manzanilla.

NUTS	RECOMMENDED WINES
Almonds	Reds: Chianti Classico Reserva or Amarone (to complement the bitter finish) Whites: Orvieto Aboccato or Entre-Deux-Mers
Brazil Nuts	Pineau des Charentes or aged Barolo
Cashews	Alsatian Sylvaner or German Müller-Thurgau
Chestnuts	(Roasted) Recioto di Valpolicella Amarone, late harvest Zinfandel, port; (Pureed) Sauternes, sweet Champagne
Hazelnuts	white Burgundy, vintage port or cider
Macadamia Nuts	Tokay Aszu, Setubal
Mixed Nuts	medium sherry, Bual
Nuts and Raisins	Amarone, dry Muscat
Pecans	Madeira, port, Pineau des Charentes, sparkling Vouvray
Pistachio Nuts	Asti Spumante, Piccolit
Spiced Nuts	Traminer, red Rhône
Walnuts	chilled Beaujolais Nouveau, port, sweet sherry, Bual or Malmsey Madeira

Wine and Soup

There really is no need to serve wine with soup. Cold and hot liquids don't do much for each other. Cold soups are easier to marry, especially in summer. The most versatile wines for this purpose are dry sherry, dry port or dry Madeira—particularly if a spoonful of these wines is added to the soup just prior to serving.

Where the soup is hearty enough and contains meat, sausage, potato or beans—in fact, a meal on a spoon—you can opt for a robust, youthful red wine with good fruit and acidity.

In the recipe section we chose only three soups from around the world which, perhaps, expresses our own bias when it comes to matching food and wine. But for the dedicated oenophile who likes a glass with each course, we offer the following suggested wine styles.

SOUP	RECOMMENDED WINES
Vegetable	
Beans and pasta	red light-bodied
Borscht	red medium-bodied
Caldo verde	white fruity medium-bodied
Cream of vegetable	white fruity medium-bodied
Gazpacho	white dry full-bodied; fino sherry
Minestrone	red medium-bodied
Onion	red light-bodied; dry rosé
Tomato (and tomato-based)	red light-bodied
Vichyssoise	white fruity medium-bodied
Fish	
Bouillabaisse	white dry medium-bodied; dry rosé
Clam chowder	white dry medium-bodied; dry sherry
Lobster/shrimp bisque	white dry full-bodied
Meat	
Chicken	white dry light-bodied
Consomme	port; Amontillado sherry; Madeira
Game	port; sherry; Madeira
Mulligatawny	Gewürztraminer; Marsala
Turtle	white dry full-bodied; sherry; Madeira
Fruit	German Spätlese; Monbazillac; dry sparkling

Crustaceans and Mollusks

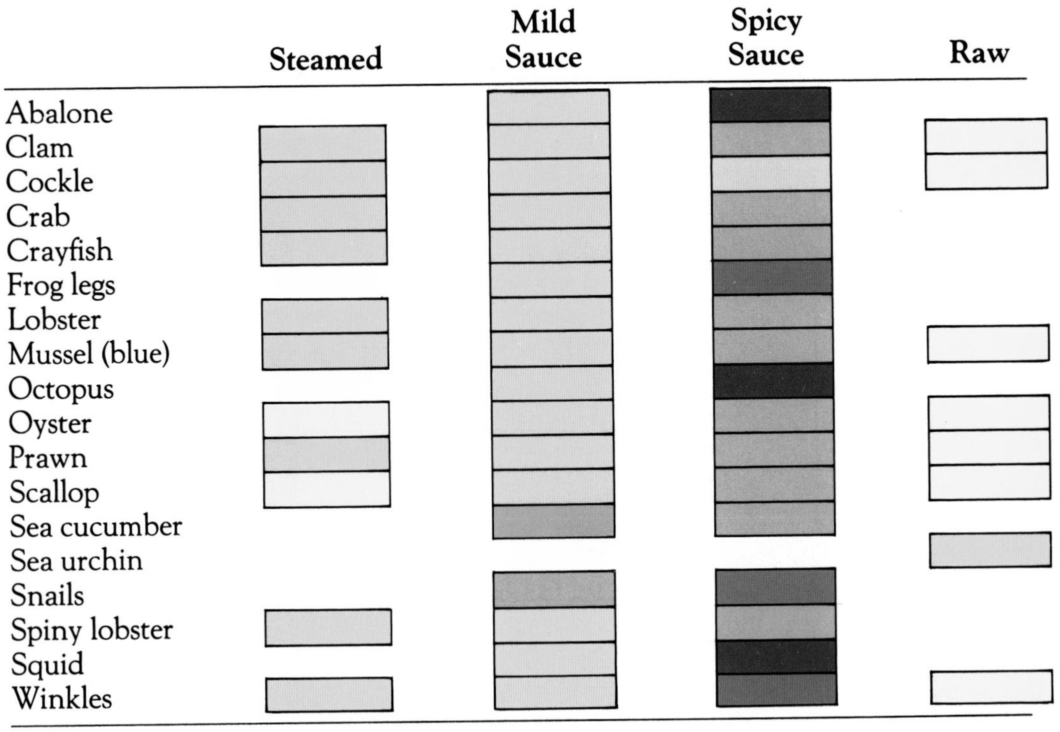

	Steamed	Mild Sauce	Spicy Sauce	Raw
Abalone				
Clam				
Cockle				
Crab				
Crayfish				
Frog legs				
Lobster				
Mussel (blue)				
Octopus				
Oyster				
Prawn				
Scallop				
Sea cucumber				
Sea urchin				
Snails				
Spiny lobster				
Squid				
Winkles				

KEY*

WDL	white dry light-bodied
WDM	white dry medium-bodied
WDB	white dry full-bodied
WML	white medium-dry light-bodied
WFM	white fruity medium-bodied
WMB	white medium-dry full-bodied
WSL	white sweet light-bodied
WSM	white sweet medium-bodied
WSB	white sweet full-bodied
RL	red light-bodied
RFL	red fruity light-bodied
RM	red medium-bodied
RFB	red fruity full-bodied
RH	red heavyweight
RoL	rosé light-bodied
RoM	rosé medium-bodied
RoB	rosé full-bodied

*Wine styles are discussed in the section *Wines of the World*, pages 207–213.

Salt and Freshwater Fish

Grilled/ Broiled/ Pan-fried | Braised | Deep-fried | Poached | Mild Sauce | Spicy Sauce | Smoked | Raw

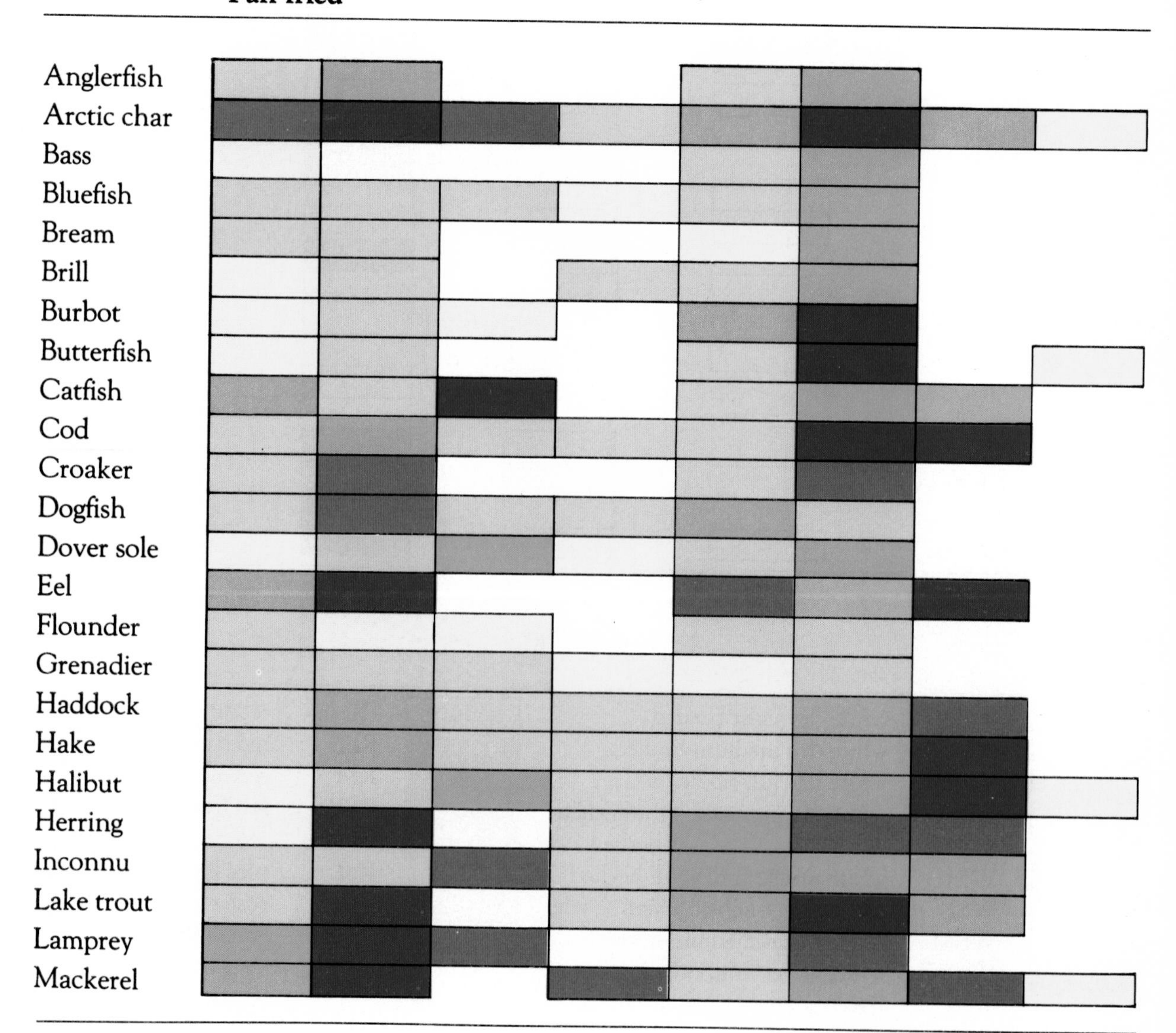

Salt and Freshwater Fish

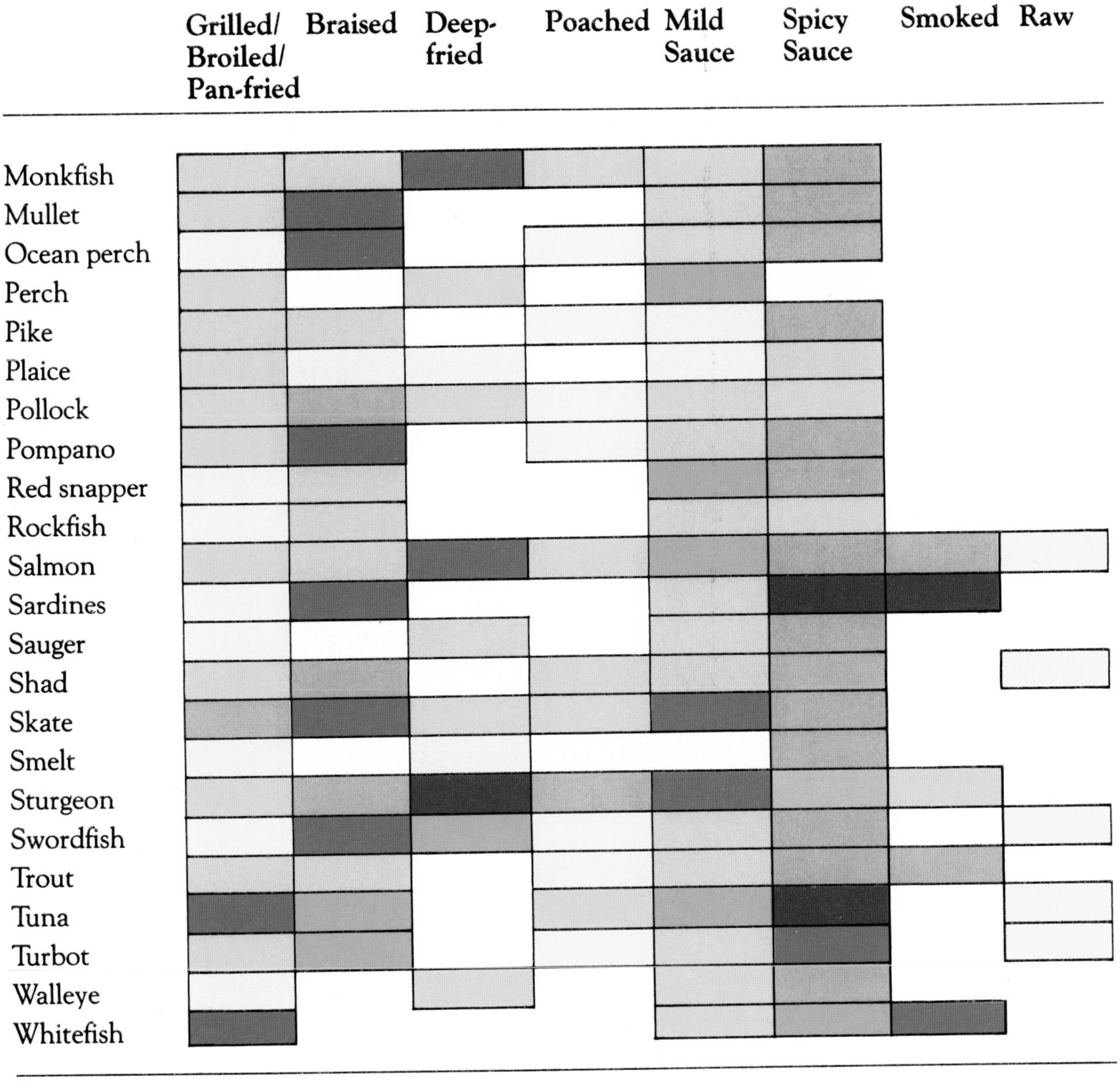

	Grilled/ Broiled/ Pan-fried	Braised	Deep-fried	Poached	Mild Sauce	Spicy Sauce	Smoked	Raw
Monkfish								
Mullet								
Ocean perch								
Perch								
Pike								
Plaice								
Pollock								
Pompano								
Red snapper								
Rockfish								
Salmon								
Sardines								
Sauger								
Shad								
Skate								
Smelt								
Sturgeon								
Swordfish								
Trout								
Tuna								
Turbot								
Walleye								
Whitefish								

Poultry and Game Birds

Grilled/ Broiled | Roasted | Braised | Mild Sauce | Spicy Sauce | Pâtés/ Terrines | Cold

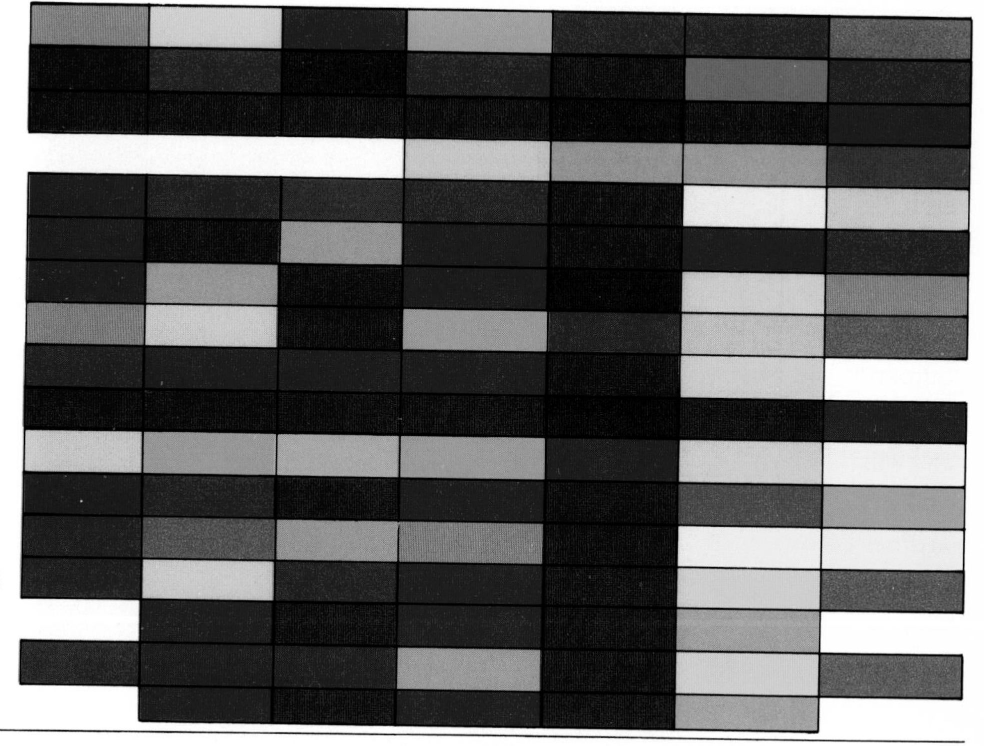

Chicken
Duck, domestic
Duck, wild
Foie gras
Fowl
Goose
Grouse
Guinea fowl
Partridge
Pheasant
Pigeon, domestic
Pigeon, wild
Quail
Rock Cornish hen
Snipe
Turkey
Woodcock

Meat, Game and Venison

Grilled/ Broiled | Roasted | Mild Sauce | Spicy Sauce | Pâté/ Terrine | Cold

Antelope
Bear
Beef
Brains
Buffalo
Deer
Elk
Goat
Ham
Hare
Kidneys
Lamb
Liver
Moose
Mutton
Oxtail
Pork
Rabbit
Sausage, fresh
Sausage, smoked
Squirrel
Suckling pig
Sweetbreads
Tongue
Tripe
Veal
Wild boar

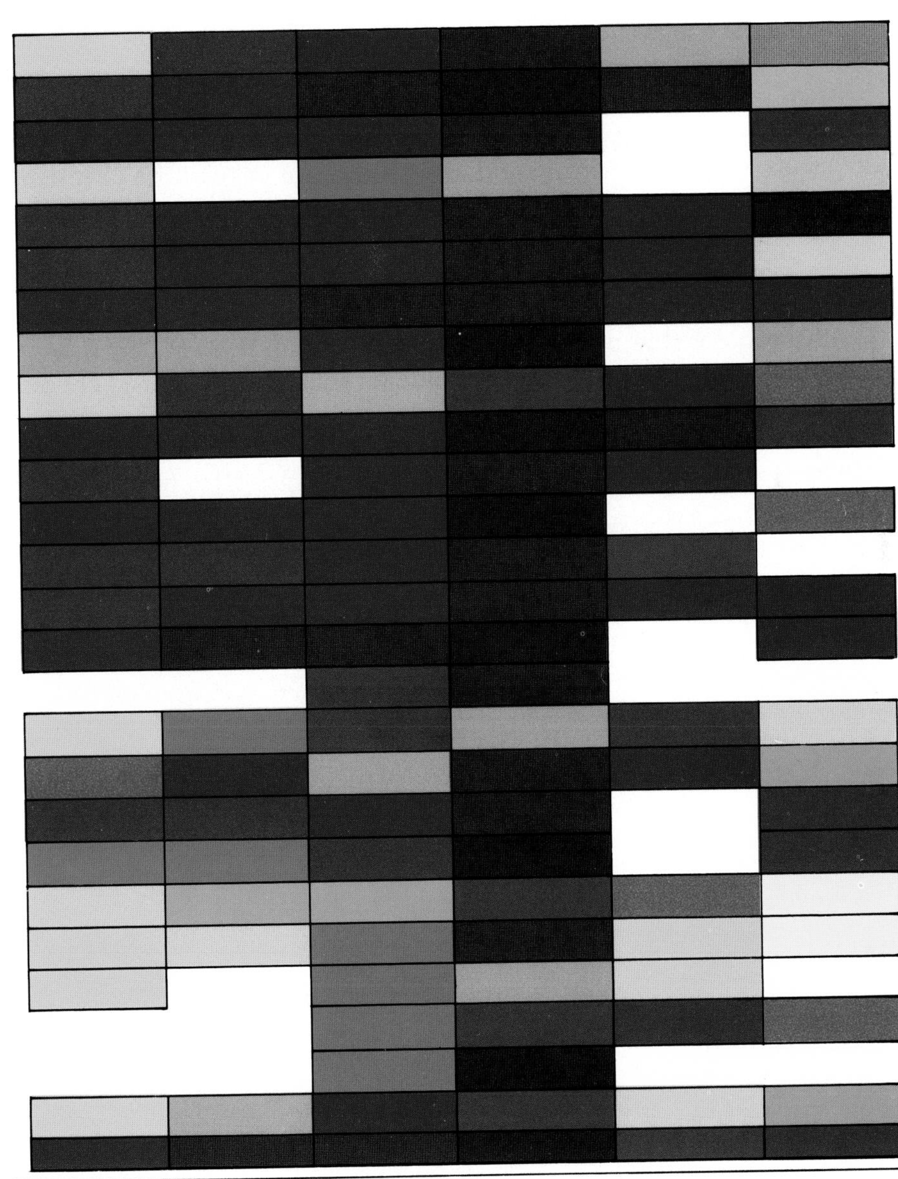

Wine and Cheese

Cheese can actually improve the flavor of a wine. There is an old adage in the wine trade: "Buy on apples and sell on cheese." The acidity in apples works against the taste of the wine, while the alkaline component of cheese brings out the flavor of the wine.

There are as many tastes and different styles of cheese as there are wines—ranging from the very mild to the aggressively pungent. Strong cheeses can overpower many wines; the match-up has to take into account the consistency, texture and assertiveness of taste of the cheese in question and the body and acidity of the wine. The happiest marriages can often be found between the cheese and wine of the same region. If you have ever had a glass of Sancerre with a slice of chèvre on French bread outdoors, overlooking the Loire River, you'll know what we mean. Or port and Stilton, for that matter.

Here is an easy reference guide for matching wine and cheese, followed by a more specific list.

CHEESE	RECOMMENDED WINES
Soft cheese	
Cow's milk (Brie, Camembert)	red fruity full-bodied; white dry full-bodied
Goat's milk (Chèvre)	white dry medium-bodied or off dry; chillable red, such as Beaujolais or Valpolicella
Firm cheese (Brick, Gruyère, Port Salut)	white dry medium-bodied; red medium-bodied; rosé medium-bodied
Hard cheese (Cheddar, Parmesan)	red fruity full-bodied of character
Blue cheese (Roquefort, Gorgonzola)	robust dry red or sweet dessert white; port; Madeira
Smoked cheese	red fruity full-bodied from a hot climate, such as Châteauneuf-du-Pape, or Castel del Monte
Processed cheese	white dry full-bodied; red fruity full- bodied; dry rosé

Appenzell (Swiss) Beaujolais-style red

Asiago (Piedmont) Barolo, Barbaresco

Banon (Provence) Bandol or Cassis, white, red or rosé

Beaumont (Savoy) light fruity red, Pinot Noir, Gamay

Bel Paese (Lombardy) Valpolicella, Barbera or light red

Bleu d'Auvergne robust Rhône red

Bleu de Bresse (France) Cru Beaujolais

Bondon (Normandy) Sauvignon Blanc, Sancerre

Boursin (Normandy) dry rosé, Beaujolais

Brick (N. America) Cabernet Sauvignon, Zinfandel

Brie (France) good red Bordeaux, Cabernet Sauvignon or Sancerre

Caciotta (Italy) Dolcetto, Chianti

Caerphilly (Wales) Manzanilla sherry or Mosel Riesling

Camembert (Normandy) good red Bordeaux, red or white Burgundy

Cantal (Auvergne) Cahors, Fronton red, Barbera

Chaource (Champagne) Bouzy rouge, chillable red

Cheddar (England) mature Rhône red, Barolo, Zinfandel, Dâo, port

Cheshire (England) chillable reds, Valpolicella, Chinon

Cheshire, blue (England) Australian Shiraz or Chilean Cabernet, Zinfandel

Chèvre (goat's cheese) Sancerre or fruity red

Colby (Canada) Médoc red, Barbaresco (regional alternative: Maréchal Foch, Baco Noir)

Cottage cheese Soave, sparkling Vouvray

Coulommiers (France) Beaune red, Pinot Noir, Rioja

Cream cheese crisp fruity white, Verdicchio, Chenin Blanc

Danish Blue red Burgundy, Rhône, Barolo or sweet white (Barsac)

Edam (Holland) Rhine Riesling, light fruity red, Barbera

Emmenthal (Swiss) Fendant, light Chardonnay, Rheinpfalz Riesling

Esrom (Denmark) young Loire red, mature Gaillac, Bordeaux, Californian Cabernet

Feta (Greece) Retsina, Demestica, Chablis, Chasselas

Fontina (Italian Alps) Carema, Donnaz, Veneto red

Fourme d'Ambert (Auvergne) Châteauneuf-du-Pape, Hermitage, Barbaresco or sweet white Monbazillac

Gammelost (Norway) southern Italian red, Zinfandel, Cornas

Gaperon (Auvergne) Corbières red, Côtes-du-Rhône

Gloucester (England) Barolo, Rioja, Rhône red, Taurasi

Gorgonzola (Lombardy) Valtellina, Nebbiolo from Piedmont, Rhône, Zinfandel

Gouda (Holland) Beaujolais, Bourgueil, Italian Cabernet, Catalan red

Gruyère (Switzerland) Dôle, Pinot Noir, Californian or Australian Chardonnay

Havarti (Denmark) Soave, Sylvaner, Graves white

Herve (Belgium) Shiraz, Rhône red, port

Lancashire (England) tawny port, dry sherry

Leiden (Holland) Cru Beaujolais, Rhône white

Liederkranz (USA) Rioja, Australian Cabernet, beer

Limburger (Belgium) robust red such as Rhône, Zinfandel, Shiraz or Traminer Auslese

Livarot (Normandy) Burgundy red, Bordeaux, red Catalan

Manchego (Spain) Valdepeñas red, Rioja, Rhône

Mascarpone (Lombardy) Monbazillac, Müller-Thurgau Spätlese

Monterey Jack (USA) Cabernet, Petite Sirah, Rhône

Mozzarella (Italy) Chianti, Valpolicella, Barbera

Munster (Alsace) Gewürztraminer, dry Muscat

Oka (Quebec) white Côtes-de-Duras, Mâcon, Sylvaner, Verdicchio

Olivet (France) red Beaune, Pinot Noir, Rioja

Parmesan (Emilia-Romagna) Bonarda, Lambrusco, Chianti

Pecorino (Italy) Primitivo, Zinfandel, Rhône

Piora (Switzerland) Dôle, Beaujolais-Villages

Pont l'Evêque (Normandy) red Bordeaux, Burgundy, Rioja

Port-Salut (France) Chardonnay, white Châteauneuf-du-Pape, red St-Julien

Provolone (Italy) Taurasi, red San Severo, Gigondas

Raclette (Switzerland) Valais Johannesburger, Chasselas, Pouilly-Fumé

Reblochon (Haute-Savoie) Gamay, light Chardonnay, young red Rioja

Rollot (Normandy) Pomerol, Italian Merlot

Romano (Italy) Chianti Classico, Barbaresco

Roquefort (France) Sauternes, Tokay, late-harvest Riesling or red Rhône, Zinfandel, Shiraz

Saint André (France) Pouilly-Fuissé, Graves, Orvieto or red Bordeaux, Dão, Rioja

Saint Paulin (France) red Médoc, Beaune, wood-aged Chardonnay

Samsoe (Denmark) light rosé, Trebbiano, Frascati

Serra (Portugal) Vinho Verde, Galestro

Stilton (England) Sauternes or old tawny port, vintage port

Tilsit (Germany) Sylvaner or Spätburgunder, Beaujolais, Valpolicella, fino sherry

Vacherin (France) Cabernet d'Anjou, Beaujolais or dry Vouvray, Sancerre

Wensleydale (England) red Garrafeira, Rhône or white Burgundy

Wine and Dessert

As with soups and bisques, if a dessert has been prepared with a particular wine or liqueur or flambéd in alcohol, that particular beverage should be your choice to accompany it.

In general, the sweetness of the dessert will dictate the sweetness of the wine. Unless the wine has sufficient residual sugar to match the dish, it will taste sharp and disagreeable. The texture of the dish will suggest the weight of the wine needed: a rich dessert made with butter, eggs and cream, for instance, requires a luscious, full-bodied wine to stand up to it.

Having said that, the most versatile dessert wine is a sweet or off-dry sparkler—Champagne or Asti Spumante—which can hold its own against creams and custards. Sugar tends to dull the palate. Sparkling wines (as long as they have good acidity) will cleanse and enliven it once more.

Most wine-producing regions make a sparkling wine, and although the best comes from Champagne, there are less-expensive products of good quality from Italy, Germany (Sekt), Spain (Cava), Portugal, California, New York and Ontario, as well as Australia and the southern hemisphere countries. They will range in style from brut (very dry) to medium-dry. Nowadays it is hard to get a sweet Champagne; most of those exported are dry or semi-dry, but even a Champagne labeled extra-dry will have sufficient residual sugar to accompany strawberries and cream, for example.

The sweetest sparklers generally available come from Italy, specifically from around the town of Asti where the Muscat grape flourishes. The Muscat makes an ideal dessert wine because of its perfumed sweetness. At its most concentrated it produces the luscious Beaumes-de-Venise in the Rhône and Setubal in Portugal—both lightly fortified products.

There are, however, various pitfalls in choosing a wine for dessert. Chocolate is Public Enemy Number One. The only wines we have found that stand up to chocolate are old Amarone, Primitivo from southern Italy and Zinfandel essence.

Certain fruits, especially those high in acidity (oranges, lemons, limes, grapefruit, pineapple, gooseberries and uncooked apples) work against many sweet wines. These fruits will only harmonize with dessert wines of high acidity, such as Mosell and Rheingau Auslesen, Beerenauslesen and Trockenbeerenauslesen. Eiswein would be perfect with gooseberry fool, for example, since the cream softens the acidity of the berries.

Ice cream, however, is also unfriendly toward wine, especially coffee or chocolate flavors. Sherbets are difficult to match as well; liqueurs of the same flavor base would be best, although the acidity in sweet German wines can tolerate fruit sherbets.

The most rewarding match-ups are the simplest—a fresh peach or pear with a Sauternes; Champagne and strawberries; Vin Santo with almond torte for the adventurous; Madeira and plain cake.

DESSERT	RECOMMENDED WINES
Apple pie/ Apfel Strüdel	white sweet light-bodied e.g. late-harvest Riesling
Apricots	white sweet medium-bodied
Baked Alaska	white sweet sparkling
Baked apple	white sweet medium-bodied
Bread pudding	white sweet light-bodied
Cake	sweet Madeira (Malmsey); cream sherry; citrus-flavored sweet German wines
Cheesecake	white sweet medium-bodied
Christmas pudding	white sweet sparkling
Creme brûlé	white sweet full-bodied
Crêpes	white sweet medium-bodied; white sweet sparkling
Fresh fruit (soft)	white sweet full-bodied
Fruit compot	sweet red (Pineau des Charentes, Muscat Beaumes-de-Venise)
Fruit fritters	white sweet medium-bodied (German acidic)
Fruit preserved in alcohol	white sweet full-bodied; robust reds (Amarone, Zinfandel)
Fruit tart	white sweet medium or full-bodied depending on the sweetness of the fruit
Lemon meringue pie	Eiswein
Mont Blanc	white sweet full-bodied
Pastries	off-dry sparkling
Peaches/pears in red wine	red light-bodied
Pumpkin pie	cream sherry; sweet Madeira
Rum Baba	rum; Hungarian Tokay
Strawberries and cream	white sweet full-bodied; off-dry sparkling
Strawberry shortcake	white sweet full-bodied
Summer pudding	white sweet medium-bodied
Sweet soufflés	white sweet light-bodied; off-dry sparkling
Syllabub	cream sherry; Madeira; Marsala

Wines of the World

Wines have a specific taste depending on the grape variety or blend, the soil in which they were grown, the ripeness at the time of picking and the method of vinification. In order to express the affinity of wines with different foods, we have categorized the wines of the world in terms of their taste and weight in the mouth. When consulting the food charts you will see cross-references to the wine styles listed here. If a specific dish calls for a white dry light-bodied wine (WDL), for example, you will find a range of alternatives by country.

WHITE WINES

white dry light-bodied

France Alsatian Sylvaner and Riesling, Muscadet, Quincy, Saumur, Touraine, Petit Chablis, Aligoté, Savoie, Crépy, Cassis

Germany/Austria Sylvaner, Mosel and Rheingau Riesling trocken style, Franconian whites, some Grüner Veltliner

Italy Galestro, Cortese di Gavi, Frascati, Friuli Tocai, some Pinot Grigio, Riesling

Spain/Portugal Vinho Verde, Valdepeñas, Azeitao

Europe Swiss Riesling, Fendant; Luxembourg Auxerrois; Hungarian and Bulgarian Riesling

America Washington Riesling, Aligoté, dry Seyval Blanc

Southern Hemisphere Australian and New Zealand Riesling, Sauvignon

white dry medium-bodied

France Sancerre, Pouilly-Fumé, Montlouis, Ménétou-Salon, Graves, Chablis, Pinot Blanc, Coteaux Champenois

Germany/Austria Müller-Thurgau, Sylvaner, Rheinpfalz and Rheinhessen Riesling (QbA)

Italy Soave, Orvieto, Lacrima Christi, Trebbiano, Müller-Thurgau, Sauvignon, dry Verduzzo, Gambellara, Torgiano, Corvo, Pinot Bianco, Chardonnay, Traminer

Spain/Portugal Rioja and Penedès whites, Dão

Europe Hungarian and Bulgarian Chardonnay and Sylvaner, Yugoslavian Traminer, Furmint

America some Chardonnay, Sauvignon Blanc, Fumé Blanc, Seyval Blanc, Vidal

Southern Hemisphere New Zealand Riesling, South African dry Steen and Colombar, Chilean Riesling and Sauvignon Blanc (new style)

white dry full-bodied

France white Burgundy, white Rhône, Condrieu, estate Pouilly-Fumé and Sancerre, Alsatian Gewürztraminer, Pinot Gris

Germany/Austria Austrian Traminer, Muscat

Italy Torbato, estate Chardonnay, Greco di Tufo, Friuli Malvasia, Südtiroler Weissburgunder, Clastidium, Pomino, Regaleali, Locorotondo

Spain/Portugal wood-aged Rioja (Murrieta, Tondonia), Penedès Chardonnay, Colares, Garrafeira, Dão

Europe Retsina

America white Zinfandel, estate Chardonnay and Chenin Blanc

Southern Hemisphere South African Blanc Fumé, Argentinian Chardonnay, Australian Chardonnay, Chilean Sauvignon and Sémillon

white medium-dry light-bodied

France Anjou, Jurançon, Roussillon, Gaillac, Alsatian Edelzwicker and Pinot Blanc

Germany/Austria Mosel Spätlesen, Rulander, Scheurebe, Austrian Pinot Blanc

Italy Frascati Superiore, Orvieto Classico, Soave Riserva

Europe English estate wines

America some Riesling, Vidal

Southern Hemisphere some Riesling, Sauvignon

white fruity medium-bodied

France Entre-Deux-Mers, Côtes-de-Bergerac, Alsatian Muscat

Germany German Spätlese Riesling, Gewürztraminer, Liebfraumilch

Italy Tocai, Malvasia, Südtiroler Müller-Thurgau

Spain/Portugal some Rioja (Siglo, Yago), white Mateus

Europe East European Traminer and Riesling, Israeli whites

America Chablis, jug wines, Chenin Blanc, some Rieslings, Gewürztraminer, late-harvest Vidal

Southern Hemisphere Australian Riesling, South African Steen, Chenin Blanc

white medium-dry full-bodied

France Savennières, Gewürztraminer (Vendange Tardive), estate Vouvray, dry Barsac and Sauternes, Vin jaune, Château-Chalon

Germany/Austria Austrian Spätlese

Spain/Portugal Masia Bach Extrissimo secco, Bucelas

Europe dry Tokay, Hungarian Pinot Gris (Badasconyi Szurkebarat), Debroï Harslevelü

America French Colombard, some Chenin Blanc

Southern Hemisphere Australian Sauvignon Blanc, South African Fonternel, Muscat d'Alexandrie

white sweet light-bodied

France Monbazillac, Côteaux du Layon, Cerons

Germany/Austria Rheingau and Mosel Auslese

Italy Moscato, Albana di Romagna Amabile, Orvieto Abbocato

Europe Tokay (3 puttonyos), Morio-Muskat

America Sauternes

Southern Hemisphere South African late-harvest Steen

white sweet medium-bodied

France Vouvray, Loupiac, Gaillac liquoreux wines, Ste-Croix-du-Mont

Germany/Austria Beerenauslesen and Eiswein

Italy Picolit, Passito, Aleatico, Verduzzo di Ramandolo

Spain/Portugal Spanish Malvasia and Muscatel, Portuguese Setubal, Granjo

Europe Tokay (5 puttonyos)

America late-harvest Riesling and Californian Chenin Blanc

Southern Hemisphere Australian late-harvest Sémilon, South African late-harvest Steen

white sweet full-bodied

France Barsac, Sauternes, Beaumes-de-Venise, Jura Vin de paille, Rivesaltes, Banyuls, Pineau des Charentes

Germany/Austria Trockenbeerenauslese, Austrian Beerenauslese and Eiswein

Italy Vin Santo, Recioto di Soave, Malvasia di Lipari

Europe Tokay Escenzia, Samos Muscat

America some late-harvest Rieslings

Southern Hemisphere South African Edelkeur, Muscadel, Australian late-harvest Sauvignon Blanc, Muscat

RED WINES

Most white wines are made to be consumed within eighteen months of the vintage, while they are still fresh and young. Red wines, on the other hand, develop in the bottle and require some age to round out the tannins extracted from the skins during fermentation and from the cask if aged in wood.

Depending on the quality of soil, climate and grape variety, red wines exhibit a vast range of color intensity, depth, flavor and weight. While white wines can happily be consumed on their own as aperitifs or digestifs, red wines are best drunk with a meal. Flavor and weight—as well as aesthetic considerations of color co-ordination—should be kept in mind when matching food and wine. Hot country reds, high in alcohol and flavor, can overpower many recipes, so a judicious choice of an accompanying wine is called for.

As with the white wines, we have broken the reds of the world down into categories by style. The first characteristic we are looking at is the weight of the wine on the palate—is it light, medium or full-bodied? Then we look at extract—how much fruit is in the wine.

red light (mainly from northerly vineyards)

France Alsatian Pinot Noir, Clairette, Bouzy Rouge, Savoie, Anjou-Gamay, red Cassis

Germany/Austria most red wines

Italy Bardolino, Santa Maddalena, Casteller, Lago di Caldaro

Spain/Portugal Somontano, Galician reds, red Vinho Verde

America Californian Claret, de Chaunac, Chelois

red fruity light-bodied

France Beaujolais, Chinon, Touraine, Côtes d'Auvergne, Fronsac, Jura, Haut-Poitou

Germany/Austria Spätlese reds

Italy Grignolino, Valpolicella, Chianti, Freisa, Lambrusco, Marzemino

Spain/Portugal some Rioja, Navarra

Europe Swiss Valais reds, Hungarian Kekfrankos, Yugoslavian Cabernet and Cviicek, Bulgarian Pamid

America east coast Merlot, Chelois, Gamay, Chambourcin

red medium-bodied

France Beaujolais Cru, Loire Cabernet, Bourgueil, non-vintage Bordeaux, village wines of Burgundy, Côtes-de-Bergerac, Gaillac, Corbières

Austria Auslese reds, St-Laurent

Italy Chianti Riserva, Barbera, Bonarda, Cabernet, Merlot, Nebbiolo, Ghemme, Lessona, Carema, Valtellina, Pinot Nero, SangiDolcetto, Regaleali

Spain/Portugal Rioja, Penedes, Valdepeñas, Bairrada, Bucelas

Europe Hungarian Cabernet and Pinot Noir, Swiss Dole, Yugoslavian Prokupac, Kraski Teran, Greek Demestica

America Californian Pinot Noir, Barbera, some Zinfandel, Washington and Oregon reds, east coast reds, Maréchal Foch, Baco Noir, Castel

Southern Hemisphere Australian Burgundy, Cabernet Sauvignon, Merlot, Pinot Noir, Argentinian Cabernet

red fruity full-bodied

France châteaux-bottled Bordeaux, domaine-bottled Burgundy, Côtes-du-Rhône, Châteauneuf-du-Pape, Vacqueyras, Lirac, Provence, Fitou, Bandol, Pecharmant, Cahors

Germany/Austria Beerenauslese

Italy Barolo, Barbaresco, Vino Nobile di Montepulciano, Sassicaia, Tignanello, Chianti Classico Riserva, Gattinara, Spanna, Brusco di Barbi, Rubesco, Taurasi, Cannonau, Sfursat

Spain/Portugal the better Riojas, Gran Coronas, Dão, Colares

Europe Hungarian Szekszardi, Yugoslavian Cabernet, Merlot, Vranac, Bulgarian Mavrud, Romanian Cabernet, Greek Mavroudi, Nemea, Turkish Buzbag, Adakarasi Karasakiz, Israeli Cabernets, Château Musar (Lebanon)

America Californian Cabernet, Petite Sirah, Zinfandel

Southern Hemisphere Australian Cabernet, Shiraz (Hermitage), South African Cabernet, Roodeberg, Pinotage, Cinsaut, Chilean Cabernet, Argentinian Varietals

red heavyweight

France Hermitage, Côte Rotie

Italy Amarone, Brunello di Montalcino, Primitivo, Castel del Monte

Spain/Portugal Garrafeiras

Europe Egri Bikaver (Bull's Blood), Kastelet, Postup (Dalmatia)

America high alcohol Zinfandel, Petite Sirah, some Cabernets

Southern Hemisphere Australian Hermitage (Shiraz), some Cabernet/Shiraz blends

red sweet

France Banyuls, Rasteau

Italy Recioto di Valpolicella, Giro

ROSÉ WINES

Rosé wines are made by leaving the grape juice in contact with the skins of red grapes just long enough to give it color. Usually this process lasts only a matter of hours, according to the depth of hue desired by the wine maker. Or he can blend a red and a white wine (as in pink Champagne) for the same effect, but generally not the same quality.

Rosé wines can vary in color from the palest of blush wines ("eye of the partridge") to light ruby. They can run the gamut in style from light in alcohol and effervescent and sweet to full-bodied, high in alcohol, dry and rich in flavor, depending on the region and how they are made. Rosé wines from hot climates like southern France and southern Italy tend to be of the latter style. The current fashion for blush wines is merely a change in nomenclature. Don't be fooled by marketing jargon—blush is a rosé, and a rosé is a rosé is a rosé...

Because of their color, rosé wines can add aesthetic appeal to a meal. But ultimately it is their taste that should dictate what style of wine is served with a given dish. When there is a dilemma as to what to serve when both meat and fish are ordered, a dry rosé can be an admirable compromise. And it will blend well with an al fresco meal of cold cuts, or at a picnic.

Rosés can be sweet or dry. We have divided them into three categories—light, medium and full-bodied. Assume that they are all dry or off-dry, unless marked with an asterisk (*), in which case they will be sweet. Sparkling wines are also noted (sp).

Rosés should be drunk young; unlike red and white wines, they do not exhibit a great variety of styles.

rosé light-bodied

France Marsannay, Chinon, Jura Vin gris, Foussy (*sp)

Italy Chiaretto, Lagrein Rosato, Marzemino d'Isera

Spain/Portugal Perelada, Mateus (*sp), Lancers (*sp), Faisca (*sp), Casal Mendes (*sp)

California Korbell (*sp)

rosé medium-bodied

France rosé Champagnes, Cabernet d'Anjou, Côte Chalonnais, Arbois, Jura, Savoie, Alsatian Pinot Noir

Italy Lacrimosa, Castel Grifone, Rosato di Montegabbione

Germany/Austria Baden Rotgold, Weissherbst, Schillerwein, Austrian Süssdruck

Europe Yugoslavian Ruzica, Bulgarian Pamid

California most blush wines, Cabernet Blanc, Korbell (*sp), Simi Rosé of Cabernet, Charles LeFranc (*sp)

rosé full-bodied

France Tavel, Côtes-du-Rhône, Provence, Bandol, Lirac, Marlenheim

Italy Apulian and Sicilian rosatos such as Castel del Monte and Regaleali, Etna and Cannonau from Sardinia

Spain/Portugal rosés of Rioja such as Murrietta and Caceres

California Zinfandel rosés, Petite Sirah (Mirassou)

FORTIFIED WINES

Fortified wines (sherry, port, Madeira, Marsala, Malaga, etc.) are those to which grape spirits or neutral alcohol has been added to stop the fermentation of the wine in order to retain residual sugar. Spirits can also be added to freshly pressed grape juice to create such aperitif wines as Pineau des Charentes and Muscat Beaumes-de-Venise.

As a group, these beverages range from 15 percent alcohol by volume (fino sherry) to a maximum of 22 percent (cream sherry or Malmsey). In virtually all cases they are used either as an accompaniment to a starting course or to the dessert or cheese course. They can also be offered as aperitifs at the start of a meal (especially if accompanied by nuts) or as digestifs after it. Rarely are they served with the main course.

Fortified wines run the gamut from dry (fino or Manzanilla sherry, some white ports and the driest of the Madeiras) to sweet (Oloroso sherry, vintage port, Bual). There are four styles of Madeira, named after the grape variety from which they are made—Sercial, as dry as a fino sherry, Verdelho, soft and sweet, Bual, rich and golden, and Malmsey, deep golden and very sweet.

When choosing a menu that involves starting with a fortified wine, i.e., a fino sherry with gazpacho or avocado, or melon with port, ensure that the following wine is of sufficient weight not to be overpowered by the lingering taste of the starting wine. The same rule stands for using fortified wines in cooking. Even though the alcohol will be burned off, the richness of taste will interfere with delicate wines you may wish to serve.

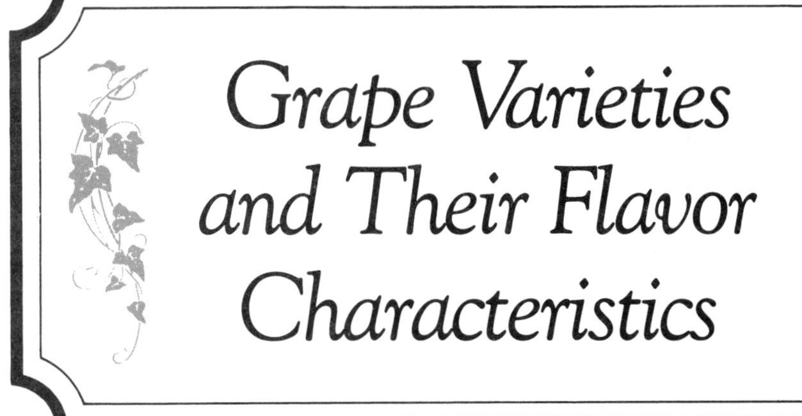

Many wines in the shops are labeled by grape variety. This means that they have been made entirely or predominantly (depending on the local wine regulations) of a single grape type. They are, to use the jargon of the trade, varietals. You can get a good idea what the wine will taste like and what style it will be by knowing the characteristics of the grapes from which it is made. Some are noble varieties which make the great wines of the world, such as Pinot Noir, Cabernet Sauvignon, Chardonnay and Riesling. Others are excellent wine grapes (Sauvignon Blanc and Barbera) while a third group are the hybrids—crossings of two varieties to get a clone which is earlier-ripening, disease- and winter-resistant or heavy-bearing. We offer here short profiles on the most widely used wine grapes around the world.

WHITE WINES

Aligoté French origin. Old Burgundian variety producing a light crisp, pale white wine with good acidity. Fast maturing, drink young.
Alias: Blanc de Troyes, Chaudenet gras.

Bacchus German origin. The fifth most planted grape in Germany. A crossing of three grapes (Sylvaner, Riesling and Müller-Thurgau), producing a wine with a light Muscat bouquet and low acidity. Used as a blend mainly in Rheinhessen.

Blanc-fumé See Sauvignon Blanc.

Bual On the island of Madeira, this grape produces a sweet, full-bodied fortified wine, burnt topaz in color and aromatic on the nose.

Chardonnay French origin (though some say the Bekaa Valley in Lebanon). This noble grape produces the best white wines of the Côte-de-Beaune (Montrachet, Meursault, Corton-Charlemagne) as well as

Chablis, Mâcon and Champagne. It is sometimes erroneously called Pinot Chardonnay, although it is not a member of the Pinot family. Produces a rich, buttery, well-balanced wine with a toasty or nutty bouquet and flavor. Produces excellent wines in California and Australia. Ages very well.
Alias: Pinot Chardonnay, Melon blanc, Beaunois, Epinette blanche, Petite Saint-Marie, Weisser Klevner (Germany).

Chasselas Eastern European origin. This fine table grape produces light wines of delicate bouquet and crisp taste. Particularly good in Switzerland, Pouilly-sur-Loire, Savoie (Crépy) and Baden. Drink young and fresh, does not age.
Alias: Fendant (Switzerland), Gutedel (Germany), Golden Chasselas (California), Royal Muscadine (England).

Chenin Blanc French origin. Noble old variety of the Loire Valley where it produces dry to medium-dry still and sparkling Vouvray. Very fruity, fresh, attractive wines with apple and pineapple bouquets and good acidity. Quick to medium aging, though some sweet wines can live for decades.
Alias: Steen (South Africa), Pineau de la Loire, white Pinot, Blanc d'Anjou.

Emerald Riesling Californian origin. A new high-yielding Riesling clone developed in the 1940s to grow in warm climates. Produces a crisp wine with fruity fragrance.

Furmint Hungarian origin. Main grape for the famous Hungarian Tokay wines. Ranging from dry to sweet with apple or apricot honeyed aromas depending on style. Also used as a blending wine in Germany. Quick to mature, can age well, especially in the sweet style.
Alias: Sipon (Yugoslavia).

Gewürztraminer German origin. Originally from Rheinpfalz, this grape was introduced to Alsace in the second half of the nineteenth century. Also performs well in the Alto Adige, Germany and South Africa. Distinctively aromatic with a spicy bouquet of lychees or incense, producing high alcohol and suitable for late harvesting. When well produced, it can age well.
Alias: Savagnin rosé, Traminer Musque, Gentil Aromatique, red Traminer (California).
The Traminer, a much earlier variety, is of Hungarian origin, and was brought to France in the tenth century. Used in the magnificent Vins jaune of Château Chalon in the Jura. This grape is seldom used in the Alsace today where it is confused with the Gewürztraminer of German origin. Vin jaune develops flor (like sherry) during fermentation. The nose

with age becomes nutty. The wine is dry and lingers on the palate. One of the longest-aging and longest-living white wines.
Alias: Tramin (Alsace), Savagnin, Formentin (Hungary), Edeltraube (Germany), Savagnin blanc.

Grüner Veltliner Austrian origin. Grows best around Vienna, Wachau and Weinviertel districts. Produces a fresh, lively, fruity wine exemplified by Gumpoldskirchner. Must be drunk young (even in its infancy as Heurige).

Johannisberg Riesling See Riesling.

Kerner German origin. A crossing of Riesling and the red Trollinger. The fourth most planted grape in Germany. Produces a fruity wine with a hint of Muscat on the nose. Mild flavor with good acidity.

Malvasia Greek origin. An ancient grape that produces lusciously sweet dessert wines, fortified or natural, around the Mediterranean basin and dry wines in northern Italy (formerly one of the four grapes used in Chianti). Best known as the grape for the dark, sweet Madeira known in England as Malmsey. Ages very well.
Alias: Malvoise (France), Malvagia (Italy).

Morio-Muscat German origin. A high yielding cross of Sylvaner and Pinot Blanc, used mainly in blends. The wine is full-bodied and unctuously fruity. Medium aging.

Müller-Thurgau German origin. The most widely planted variety in Germany, thought originally to be a cross between Riesling and Sylvaner. Now believed to be a crossing of two Riesling clones. The backbone of the less expensive German blended wines. Low acidity, round, fruity with a light Muscat nose. Also grown in Austria. Does not age well.
Alias: Rivaner (Luxembourg), Riesling Sylvaner.

Muscadelle Grown principally in the Bordeaux region where winemakers use it to give a Muscat-like aroma to blends of Sauvignon and Semillon.
Alias: Guillan, Muscat fou, Muscadet, Douzanelle.

Muscadet French origin. Originally called Melon de Bourgogne. Makes light fruity wines with crisp acidity suitable for shellfish. Very dry and pale in color. Should be consumed young.
Alias: Lyonnaise blanche, Gros Auxerrois.

Muscat Greek origin. This perfumed table grape is best suited for the production of lusciously sweet dessert wines with the characteristic spicy Muscat nose—except in Alsace where it is produced in dry style. When left on the vine to over-ripen it makes a wine of high alcohol and powerful bouquet. Best examples are Beaumes-de-Venise, Frontignan and Lunel

from southern France, Samos from Greece, Setubal from Portugal and Italian Moscatos. Ages very well.
Alias: Weisse Muskateller (Germany), Muskuti (Greece), Muscatel branco (Portugal), white Frontignan (England).

Pinot Blanc French origin. Fine quality grape originally native to Burgundy now producing well in Alsace. Dry, soft fruity wine with a crisp finish. Easy drinking. Planted in California, Germany, Italy and Eastern Europe. Quick maturing, medium aging.
Alias: Weissburgunder (Germany), Pinot Bianco (Italy).

Pinot Gris Eastern European origin. Called Tokay in Alsace and Tocai in northeast Italy, this grape has nothing to do with Hungarian Tokay. Produces a full-flavored wine with a strongly scented bouquet and a faintly bitter finish. Ages well.
Alias: Rulander (Germany), Pinot Grigio (Italy), Tocai (Italy, Yugoslavia), Tokay (Alsace), Pinot Beurot, Auxerrois gris, Gris Cordelier.

Riesling German origin. Finest German wine grape, number two in acreage. Produces very well in Alsace, Austria, California, Australia, South Africa and Chile. Under the right microclimate and soil it produces wines of extraordinary finesse with subtle fruit flavors and a floral bouquet. Good acid balance permits wines of great sweetness that do not cloy. Ages very well.
Alias: Johannisberg Riesling, Rheingauer, Welschriesling (Germany, Austria), Riesling Italico (Italy), Olasz Rizling (Hungary), Laski Rizling (Yugoslavia).

Sauvignon Blanc French origin. Blended with Sémillon and Muscadelle to make the famous dessert wines of Sauternes and Barsac, in Bordeaux the dry whites of Graves and Entre-Deux-Mers. Successful as a varietal in the Loire as Pouilly-Fumé and Sancerre, characterized by their flinty, grassy bouquets and taste of gooseberries. Very dry with lingering aftertastes. This variety produces well in California (Fumé Blanc), Australia, Chile and South Africa. Ages well.
Alias: Blanc Fumé, Fie, Muskat Sylvaner (Germany), Surin.

Scheurebe German origin. A Riesling-Sylvaner cross, this grape exhibits a pronounced bouquet of blackcurrants. High in acid, it is best when ripe enough to provide dessert wines of Auslese quality and higher. Does well in the Rheingau and Rheinhessen. Can age well.

Sémillon French origin. Susceptible to noble rot (botrytis cinerea), this grape is ideally suited for the production of dessert wines, especially in Barsac and Sauternes. The botrytized grapes take on a honeyed character. Lacking acidity and bouquet this variety is blended with Sauvignon Blanc to create the finest dessert wines of Sauternes and Barsac. Ages well.

Alias: Riesling (Australia), Colomier, Malaga, Blanc doux.

Sercial German origin (thought to have been a clone of Riesling grape). Produces the driest of the fortified wines of Madeira. Grown on the uppermost vineyard slopes. Ages very well.

Sylvaner Austrian origin. High-yielding producer of simple but pleasant wines with light bouquets, moderate acidity but rather short in the mouth. Third most planted grape in Germany. Does well in Alsace, Franconia, Rheinhessen, Rheinpfalz, Austria and the Italian Tyrol. Drink it young.
Alias: Riesling (California), Franken Riesling, Silvaner (Germany), Oesterricher, Schwabler, Gruber, Szilvani zöld (Hungary).

Traminer See Gewürztraminer.

Trebbiano The most important Italian white grape and currently the most widely planted white variety in France. Known there as Ugni Blanc or St-Emilion, it is responsible for virtually all the Cognac produced. In the Midi it makes a pale yellow acidic wine.

RED WINES

Barbera Italian origin, producing best in the Piedmont region. Also doing well in California. Medium color, fruity, light bodied with good acidity and some sharpness.

Cabernet Franc French origin, usually blended with Cabernet Sauvignon. Particularly fine in Bordeaux. Produces good red and rosé wines in the Loire Valley. Medium depth of color and aromatic bouquet. Good character, ages well.
Alias: Breton, Gros Cabernet, Gros Bouchet.

Cabernet Sauvignon French origin. Main grape for red Bordeaux. Produces well in California, Australia, Italy, Chile, South Africa and Eastern Europe. Deep-red color, astringent and short when young, developing great finesse and elaborate bouquet (characteristically of violets) when well aged. Slow to mature.
Alias: Petit Cabernet, Bouchet, Vidure.

Carignan Spanish origin. Prolific grape which produces well in hot climates like the south of France, Spain and California. Robust wine with good color and character. Harsh and astringent when young but softens with age. A good blending wine. Best results in Aragon, Catalonia, Rhône Valley, Midi.
Alias: Carignane (U.S.), Catalan, Roussillonen, Mataro, Carinena, Tinta Mazuela (Spain).

Cinsaut French origin. Vigorous wine adding softness and bouquet when blended with Grenache and Carignan. Mainly used in Rhône and Midi wines as a blend, and in Australia and South Africa.
Alias: Cinsault, Cinq-saou, Black Malvoisie, Picardan Noir, Malaga, Hermitage (South Africa).

Gamay French origin. The grape of Beaujolais. Produces a zesty, fruity, light-bodied, bright red wine. Blended with Pinot Noir in Burgundy to produce Passe-tout-Grains. Also produces a very agreeable, fruity rosé. Fast maturing. Californian Gamay Beaujolais is a Pinot Noir clone.
Alias: Bourguignon Noir, Gamay Noir, Gamay Beaujolais, Petit Gamay, Kekfrankos (Hungary), Valdiguie.

Grenache Spanish origin. Sweet pink grape used in the Rhône Valley as the major constituent of Châteauneuf-du-Pape. Main grape for Tavel rosé and Lirac. Also used in Rioja, Catalonia and California. Attractive, high alcohol, soft red wine. Produces the naturally sweet wines of Banyuls in Roussillon and the finest pale rosés of California. Very fast maturing.
Alias: Granache, Garnacha (Spain), Alicante, Carignane Rousse, Tinto (Portugal).

Grignolino Italian origin. Grown in northern Italy and California. Produces wines with a fragrant strawberry bouquet, austerely dry with a light orange-red color. Used for rosé wines in California. Drink young.

Merlot French origin. Dark-blue, thick-skinned grape used in the Medoc as the main blending wine for Cabernet Sauvignon. Imparts softness and roundness. Major grape of St-Emilion and Pomerol. Produces well in Italy, Chile, Switzerland and California. Supple wines of good quality and deep color. Somewhat rich. Petrus is a good example. Quick to mature, medium aging.
Alias: Petit Merle, Vitraille, Crabutet Noir, Bigney, Sémillon rouge (Medoc).

Mourvedre Spanish origin. Produces alcoholic, highly colored, strong wine which requires aging. Grown in Côte-de-Provence, Bandol and Spain.
Alias: Mataro, Trinchiera, Negron, Espar, Beni-Carlo, Estrangle-chien, Damas Noir, Maneschaou, Balzac Noir.

Nebbiolo Italian origin. One of the best Italian grapes. Deep, powerful, aromatic and firm wines. Best in Barolo, Barbaresco, Gattinara and Spanná. Raisiny flavor when aged, austere, dry finish.
Alias: Picotener, Pugnet, Spanna, Chiavennasca.

Petite Sirah Californian name for French Durif. Used in California to make a hearty wine of good color and a "black pepper nose" but lacking in finesse and character. Generally blended into generic "Californian

Burgundy" for its deep color. Not to be confused with the Syrah of the Rhône. Slow to age.
Alias: Sirane fauchure, Pinot de l'Ermitage.

Pinot Noir French origin. One of the great red grapes of France that yields the famous Burgundy and the blanc de noir juice (white juice from black grapes) for Champagne. This dark-purple grape is a late ripener, which in Burgundy produces a velvety, perfumed, unctuous red wine with great length. (This distinctive character is lost in hot climates.) Also grown in Switzerland, the Italian Tyrol, Germany and Alsace where it gives light-colored wines. California and Oregon have come closest to achieving the finesse of Burgundy reds. Medium to long aging.
Alias: Spätburgunder (Germany, Austria), Cortaillod (Switzerland), Klevner (Alsace), Pineau, Savagnin, Morillon, Auvernat Noir, Vert dore.

Pinot Meunier French origin. Hardy and productive grape used mainly in Champagne to add strength to the blend. A lacklustre red wine on its own, but makes an interesting rosé in the Loire Valley. Also planted in Germany and New Zealand.
Alias: Schwarzriesling or Müller Rebe (Germany), Auvernat Gris, Plant de Brie, Blanche Feuille.

Pinotage South African origin. Cross between Pinot Noir and Cinsaut, formerly called Hermitage in South Africa. A useful, hardy hybrid produces supple red wine with a characteristic "acetone" nose and a gamey quality when young. They develop into robust wines with good length and aging potential. Fast maturing.

Ruby Cabernet Californian origin. A high-producing cross between Cabernet Sauvignon and Carignan. Developed to produce in warm climates, it yields a wine deep in color with good flavor but somewhat short and less distinguished than Cabernet Sauvignon. Quick to mature, medium aging.
Alias: Cabernet, red Bordeaux.

Sangiovese Italian origin. One of the noble grapes of Italy particularly in Chianti, Brunello di Montalcino and Vino Nobile di Montepulciano. Makes a ruby-red wine which changes to tawny red or brick with age. Firm, dry taste, sometimes tannic with a bitter aftertaste. Medium weight. Taste characteristics change with place of production. Moderate aging.
Alias: Sangioveto, S. Zoveto.

Syrah Origin unknown. An excellent wine grape, native to the Rhône Valley, originally planted by the Romans. Main grape of the Rhône for wines such as Cornas, St-Joseph, Côte Rotie, Hermitage, Châteauneuf-du-Pape. Deep colored, robust with a spicy aroma, richly textured. Needs age to develop its full character. Also grown in Switzerland, California,

Australia and South Africa. Ages well.
Alias: Sirah, Serine, Sirac, Shiraz (Australia and South Africa), Hignin Noir.

Zinfandel European origin, probably the Primitivo grape of Apulia. Now indigenous to California where this versatile grape produces a wide range of wines from white to light reds, medium up to port-like reds. Characteristically raspberry or bramble nose. Can age very well.

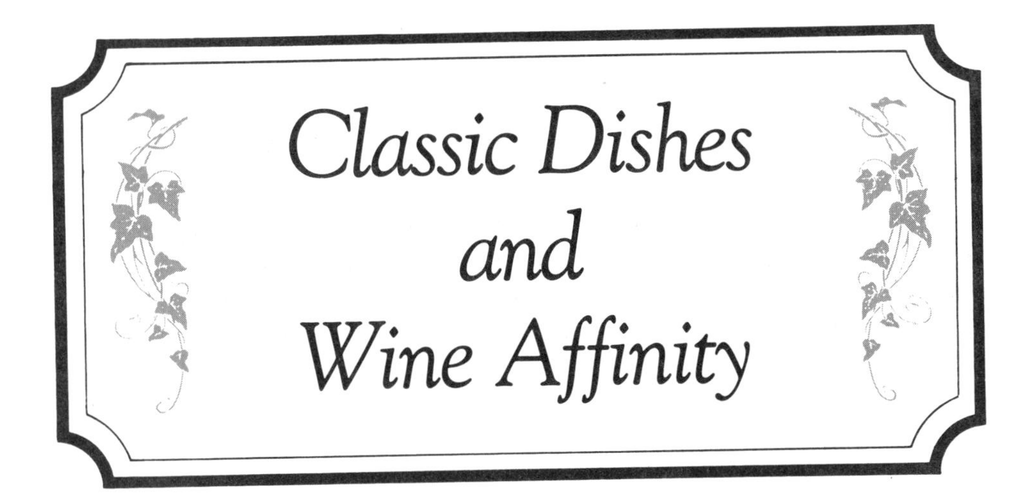

In addition to the international recipes and their wine affinities in Part II of *The Wine Lover Dines*, we offer this ready wine reference guide to some classic dishes (and some not so classic!) that you may order in a restaurant or prepare yourself in your own kitchen.

For each dish we give our own personal choice of wine style (never the same!), generally listing a particular region or product. Since these wines may not be readily available at your local wine store, we begin by listing the grape variety which would produce a wine complementary to this dish. For more information on these varietals, turn to page 215 (Grape Varieties and Their Flavor Characteristics) where you will find descriptions and taste profiles of all the major wine grapes.

This chart is merely a point of reference. As we have stressed throughout this book, ultimately it is your palate that dictates what goes with what in terms of food and wine. Our own choices are highly personal and, at times, idiosyncratic. The fun is in experimenting to find the perfect marriage.

Classic Dishes and Wine Affinity

POULTRY

Dish	Grape Variety	Tony Aspler's Choice	Jacques Marie's Choice
Cassoulet Toulousain	Grenache	Cahors	red Corvo
Chicken cacciatore	Sangiovese	St-Joseph	red Rioja
Chicken Kiev	Chardonnay	Pomino	white Rioja
Chicken à la king	Chardonnay	Riesling Kabinett	dry rosé
Chicken and pineapple	Sémillon	Monbazillac	Riesling Spätlese
Chicken pot pie	Riesling	Californian Chenin Blanc	Orvieto
Chicken Tandoori	Riesling	Taurasi	Shiraz
Chopped chicken liver	Riesling	dry rosé	Bergerac
Confit d'oie (potted goose)	Cinsaut	Zinfandel	Australian Cabernet/Shiraz
Coq au vin	Pinot Noir	Côte-de-Beaune	Barbaresco
Curried chicken	Gewürztraminer	Zinfandel	Châteauneuf-du-Pape
Duck with olives	Syrah	Italian Merlot	Californian Cabernet
Duck à l'orange	Grenache	Châteauneuf-du-Pape	Zinfandel
Duck terrine	Riesling	dry Muscat	Fronsac
Pâté de foie	Sémillon	Sauternes	Riesling Auslese
Peking duck	Riesling Spätlese	Greco di Tufo	Australian Semillon
Pheasant roasted with bread sauce	Merlot	Chianti Riserva	Chilean Cabernet
Pigeon pie	Pinot Noir	Bourgueil	red Sancerre
Quail in wine sauce	Cabernet	Venegazzu	Coronas
Southern-fried chicken	Sylvaner	Entre-Deux-Mers	Trebbiano
Turkey	Cabernet	St-Julien	Californian Chardonnay

Classic Dishes and Wine Affinity

SEAFOOD

Dish	Grape Variety	Tony Aspler's Choice	Jacques Marie's Choice
Anguille au vert (eel)	Grüner Veltliner	Vinho Verde	Galestro
Bouillabaisse	Grenache	Bandol rosé	Entre-Deux-Mers
Brandade de morue (creamed salt cod)	Pinot Gris	white Graves	Côtes-de-Provence
Coquilles St. Jacques	Riesling	Montrachet	Californian Chenin Blanc
Coulibiac de saumon (salmon pie)	Chardonnay	Alsatian Riesling	white Graves
Crab quiche	Riesling	Alsace whites	Austrian whites
Fish and chips	Pinot Blanc	Soave	Emerald Riesling
Fritto misto mare (deep-fried seafood)	Chardonnay	dry Vouvray	Australian Chardonnay
Frogs' legs	Chardonnay	Condrieu	Sauvignon Blanc
Gefilte fish	Pinot Blanc	white Hermitage	Sylvaner
Gravadlax	Gewürztraminer	Traminer Italico	white Hermitage
Herring, pickled	Muscadet	Franconian white	Tocai de Lison
Kedgeree	Traminer	dry Muscat	Pinot Grigio
Kippers	Sauvignon Fumé	Coteaux Champenois	Napa Sauvignon
Lampreys à la bordelaise	Sauvignon	Sancerre	Côtes-de-Bourg
Lobster Newburg	Riesling	Rheingau	Californian Chardonnay
Moules marinières	Muscadet	Vinho Verde	Alsatian Sylvaner
Octopus in garlic and tomato sauce	Trebbiano	Soave	Tavel rosé

Classic Dishes and Wine Affinity

SEAFOOD

Dish	Grape Variety	Tony Aspler's Choice	Jacques Marie's Choice
Oysters Rockefeller	Sauvignon	Pouilly-Fumé	Californian Sauvignon
Paella Valencia	Viognier	fino sherry	Tavel rosé
Pike baked in sour cream sauce	Morio-Muskat	Pouilly-Fumé	Californian Chardonnay
Prawn cocktail	Riesling	white Graves	Lachryma Christi
Quenelles de brochette	Chardonnay	dry Vouvray	Rhine Riesling
Salmon, grilled, with Hollandaise sauce	Sauvignon	Meursault	Napa Chardonnay
Salmon, poached	Chardonnay	Mâcon white	Californian Sauvignon
Salmon, smoked	Gewürztraminer	Alsatian Pinot Gris	Chablis Grand Cru
Sardines, grilled	Trebbiano	Vinho Verde	Aligoté
Sashimi	Riesling	Mosel whites	Friuli whites
Scampi meunière	Verdicchio	Castelli dei Jesi	Sancerre
Sea urchins	Sylvaner	Muscadet	Sancerre
Shrimp curry	Scheurebe	Rheinpfalz white	Gewürztraminer
Sole bonne femme/ véronique/grilled, etc.	Chardonnay	Rhine Riesling	Orvieto secco
Spaghetti vongole	Verdicchio	white Graves	Chenin Blanc
Tempura	Sylvaner	white Rioja	Fendant
Trout in almonds	Chardonnay	Côte-de-Beaune	white Graves
Truite au bleu	Riesling	Rheingau	San Gimignano
Whitebait	Sylvaner	Vinho Verde	Muscadet

Classic Dishes and Wine Affinity

BEEF

Dish	Grape Variety	Tony Aspler's Choice	Jacques Marie's Choice
Beef goulash	Zinfandel	Taurasi	Dâo Garrafeira
Beef Stroganoff	Sangiovese	Gattinara	Châteauneuf-du-Pape
Beef Wellington	Cabernet	St-Emilion	Côte-de-Beaune
Blanquette de veau	Chardonnay	Côte-de-Beaune	Riesling Kabinett
Boeuf à la mode (braised beef in wine)	Cinsaut	Pinotage	dry rosé
Boeuf Bourguignon	Pinot Noir	Chambertin	Oregon Pinot Noir
Boiled beef and carrots	Chardonnay	Lirac	Pinot Blanc
Braised tongue	Pinot Noir	red Sancerre	Jurançon
Brisket	Sauvignon	Rosé d'Anjou	Valpolicella
Carbonnade à la flamande (beef casserole in beer)	Grenache	Côtes-du-Rhône	Barbera
Chateaubriand with Béarnaise sauce	Merlot	Pomerol	Beaujolais Cru
Chili con carne	Zinfandel	Primitivo	Amarone
Curried beef	Primitivo	Gewürztraminer	Zinfandel
Daube de boeuf Provençal	Grenache	Bandol red	Sangre de Torro
Dolmas	Viognier	Traminer	St-Péray
Escalope of veal	Chardonnay	Chablis	Chenin Blanc
Fegato alla Veneziana (calf's liver and onions)	Sangiovese	red Mâcon	Haut Poitou Sauvignon
Fondue Bourguignonne	Pinot Noir	Nuits-St-Georges	Tignanello
Greek meat balls	Scheurebe	Nemea	Castel del Monte
Hamburger	Gamay	Beaujolais	Valpolicella
Liver and bacon	Gamay	Chiaretto	Alsatian Pinot Noir

Classic Dishes and Wine Affinity

BEEF

Dish	Grape Variety	Tony Aspler's Choice	Jacques Marie's Choice
Osso bucco	Sangiovese	Chianti	Côtes-du-Rhône
Pepper steak	Syrah	Barolo	Hermitage
Piccata Marsala (veal medallions in Marsala)	Barbera	St-Emilion	Rhine Riesling
Pot au feu	Gamay	Santa Maddalena	Dâo
Roast beef and Yorkshire pudding	Cabernet	Médoc	Australian Cabernet
Roast stuffed loin of veal	Sauvignon	Riesling Kabinett	white Graves
Shepherd's pie	Sangiovese	Beaujolais	Anjou
Spaghetti Bolognese	Nebbiolo	Barbaresco	Beaujolais-Villages
Steak Diane	Merlot	St-Emilion	red Rioja
Steak and kidney pie	Merlot	Australian Cabernet	red Graves
Steak tartare	Sangiovese	Brolio Chianti	Bairrada
Sukiyaki	Traminer	Californian Fumé Blanc	dry Muscat
Sweetbreads	Chardonnay	Manzanilla	Riesling Spätlese
Tournedos Rossini (steak with foie gras and truffles)	Merlot	St-Estèphe	Californian Cabernet
Tripe à la mode	Grenache	Tavel	Chinon
Veal cordon bleu	Chardonnay	Montrachet	Alsatian Pinot Gris
Veal cutlets Milanese	Nebbiolo	Ghemme	red Loire
Vitello tonnato (veal in tuna sauce)	Trebbiano	Traminer	Trentino Alto Adige

Classic Dishes and Wine Affinity

LAMB

Dish	Grape Variety	Tony Aspler's Choice	Jacques Marie's Choice
Cervelles d'agneau	Pinot Blanc	Sancerre (red)	Chinon
Couscous	Zinfandel	Châteauneuf-du-Pape	North African reds
Curried lamb	Syrah	Primitivo	Zinfandel
Deviled kidneys	Nebbiolo	Barolo	Hermitage
Noisette d'agneau	Sangiovese	red Graves	Australian Cabernet
Irish stew	Sauvignon	Puilly-Fumé	Entre-Deux-Mers
Lamb chops	Cabernet	Chianti	red Rioja
Lamb polo	Zinfandel	Shiraz	Pomerol
Lancashire hotpot	Chardonnay	Rhine Riesling Spätlese	Californian rosé
Leg of lamb	Cabernet	Margaux commune	Chilean Cabernet
Mixed grill	Pinot Noir	Beaujolais Cru	Valpolicella
Moussaka	Grenache	Côte-Rotie	Retsina
Rack of lamb	Cabernet	St-Estephe	Mercurey
Roast mutton	Merlot	Hermitage	Australian Shiraz
Saddle of lamb	Cabernet	Pauillac	red Macon
Shishkabab	Merlot	Hungarian red	light Zinfandel
Stuffed shoulder of lamb	Merlot	St-Emilion	Spanna

Classic Dishes and Wine Affinity

PORK

Dish	Grape Variety	Tony Aspler's Choice	Jacques Marie's Choice
Bacon and eggs	Grenache rosé	Beaujolais	Pinot Blanc
Baked ham	Pinot Noir	Californian Cabernet	Côte-de-Beaune
Barbecued spareribs	Grenache	Châteauneuf-du-Pape	Barbera
Boiled ham	Gamay	Beaujolais Cru	Alsatian Pinot Noir
Braised pork and sauerkraut	Riesling	Gewürztraminer	Pinot Grigio
Curried pork	Gewürztraminer	Muscat dry	Riesling Spätlese
Frankfurters and beans	Sangiovese	Shiraz	Côtes-du-Rhône red
Gammon steak and pineapple	Riesling	Anjou rosé	Orvieto abboccato
Glazed ham	Riesling	Sauvignon Blanc	Monbazillac
Ham omelet	Chardonnay	Cabernet d'Anjou	Rioja white
Ham soufflé	Aligoté	Alsatian Riesling	St-Croix-du-Mont
Head cheese	Sylvaner	red Loire	Bardolino
Hot dog	Gamay	Beaujolais	German Sylvaner
Pig's trotters	Gamay	Jura red	Sancerre red
Pork with prunes	dry Muscat	Riesling	Sauvignon Blanc
Pork rillettes	Sauvignon	Chinon	Californian Riesling
Pork sausages	Riesling	Beaujolais	Valtellina
Prosciutto and melon	Muscat	ruby port	Pineau des Charentes
Roast pork and apple sauce	Chenin Blanc	Vouvray	Riesling Spätlese
Salami	Grenache	Côtes-du-Rhône	Valpolicella
Sweet and sour pork	Sylvaner	Verbesco	Verdicchio
Veal and ham pie	Pinot Gris	Beaujolais	Brunello

Classic Dishes and Wine Affinity

GAME

Dish	Grape Variety	Tony Aspler's Choice	Jacques Marie's Choice
Bear	Zinfandel	Taurasi	Shiraz
Game pâté	Nebbiolo	Côte-Rotie	Californian Cabernet
Grouse	Cabernet	St-Julien	Chianti Classico
Hare	Merlot	Pomerol	Dâo Garrafeira
Moose	Pinot Noir	Côte-de-Beaune	Barolo
Partridge	Cabernet Sauvignon	Médoc	Petite Sirah
Pheasant	Pinot Noir	Côte-de-Beaune	Cornas
Pigeon	Chardonnay	Montrachet	Lirac
Rabbit	Gamay	Beaujolais Cru	Rioja red
Snipe	Cabernet	St. Estèphe	Barbaresco
Venison	Pinot Noir	Côte-de-Nuits	Brunello
Wild boar	Syrah	Hermitage	Riesling Spätlese
Wild duck	Pinot Noir	Côte-de-Nuits	Californian Cabernet
Wild goose	Chardonnay	Corton	Riesling Spätlese
Woodcock	Merlot	St-Emilion	Rioja red

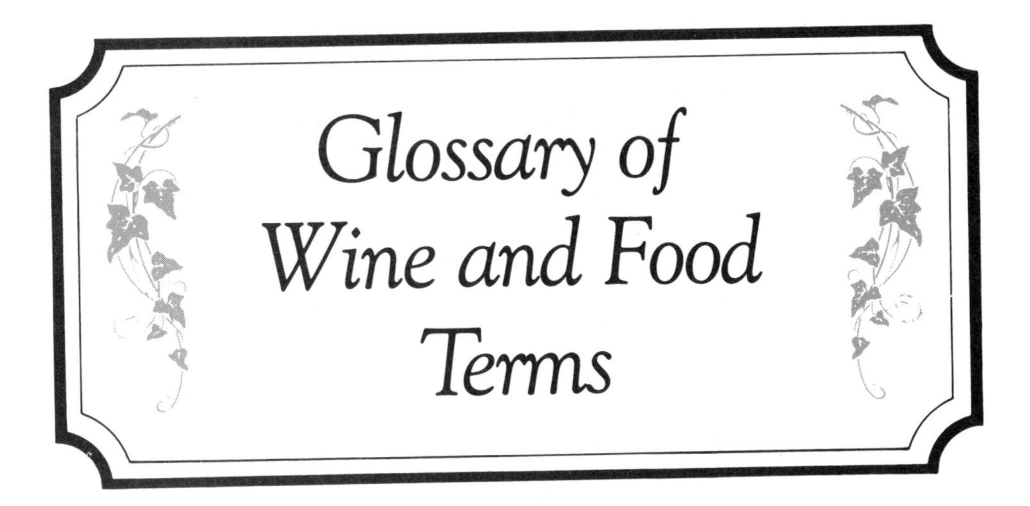

Glossary of Wine and Food Terms

Acidity, fixed The term denoting the constituent acids in a wine—tartaric, malic, citric, lactic, succinic, etc. Total acidity refers to a combination of fixed acids and volatile acids.

Acidity, volatile In a word, vinegar. Sharp and sour to the nose, volatile acidity is present in all wines, but in a sound product it is undetectable.

Aftertaste The final taste of a wine once it has been swallowed.

Aldehyde When alcohol oxidizes, it gives off components called aldehydes, which carry the bouquet of the wine.

Appellation contrôlée The French body of wine laws which defines regions and districts for specific grape production and viticultural practices. A guarantee of quality on the label.

Aroma The smell of the grapes in new wines (as opposed to **bouquet**—see below).

Aspic From the Greek *aspis*, which means a shield or to protect. A flavored jelly, or food arranged in a flavored, molded jelly.

Auslese A German term referring to the quality of the grapes at harvest; late-picked, selected grapes.

Bain Marie Literally a double boiler used to cook food at a low temperature or to keep food or liquid hot.

Balance A wine is well balanced if its acidity, fruit, tannin and alcohol are harmonious, without one or the other predominating on the palate.

Beerenauslese A German term referring to the selected berries from bunches affected by **Botrytis cinerea** (see below).

Beurre manié Literally, a kneaded butter. A thickening agent composed of half butter and half flour, mixed to a smooth paste and used to bind a small amount of sauce at the last minute.

Blind baking Baking a pie shell or crust without garnish or filling. Often a layer of dried peas or weights is placed on top of the dough to prevent blistering or lifting. This method is used for flans, quiches or tarts when the garnish or filling is already cooked or takes less time to cook than the pie shell.

Body The sensation of the wine's weight on the palate according to its alcohol and fruit glycerin content. It can range from light, medium or full to heavyweight. Hot growing regions that produce high-sugar grapes will make full-bodied wines.

Botrytis cinerea Known as "noble rot." A fungus that attacks grapes in certain warm, damp climates. The rotting process concentrates the berries' sugars and acids which when pressed and fermented produce lusciously sweet dessert wines such as Sauternes, Tokay and Trockenbeerenauslese wines.

Bouquet The perfume of wine carried by its evaporating esters.

Bouquet garni A flavoring agent composed of aromatic herbs or plants tied together. The composition varies according to the nature of the dish.

Braising To cook in a relatively airtight container with a small amount of liquid.

Chaptalization The process whereby sugar is added to the **must** (see below) before fermentation to build up the alcohol content of a wine. When practiced in northerly growing areas, particularly Burgundy, it is strictly controlled. Named after Jean-Antoine Chaptal, Napoleon's minister of agriculture.

Claret The British term for the red wines of Bordeaux. Originated from the Old French word *clairet*, meaning wines made from red and white grapes.

Corked/corky A wine that has been spoiled either by a diseased cork or a faulty cork, which lets air into the bottle.

Court bouillon A flavored liquid mainly used to poach fish or meat. The aim is to transfer the tastes of the flavoring agents (vegetables, spices, herbs, etc.) to the liquid, where they can be more easily absorbed by the food.

Decanting The act of separating the wine from its sediment to preserve its brilliance in the glass or to allow the wine to breathe.

Deglaze To dilute with a liquid the concentrated juices in a pan in which food has been cooked.

Degrease To remove the excess fat that forms on the surface of a liquid.

Eau-de-vie Grape or fruit brandy; a colorless dry distillate.

Eiswein (Ice wine) An expansive and rare white wine, originating in Germany and produced in northerly vineyards by pressing frozen grapes that have been left on the vine until the first frost. High in sugar and acid, these wines are mostly sold in half bottles.

Ester The action of alcohol and acids in wine produces esters, which carry the bouquet.

Fats and oils:

Butter One of the best cooking fats because of its flavor, body, texture and color. It is easily digested and contains large amounts of vitamins A and D. It is, however, very sensitive to odors, light, air and heat, and should be kept well wrapped. It has a low smoking temperature and is a saturated fat. Stored in the freezer, butter will keep almost indefinitely. *Dairy butter* is made on a farm from cream that comes from one herd of cattle. *Creamery butter* is factory made from cream that comes from many herds. *Sweet cream butter* is made from sweet cream with a pure culture of lactic acid added before churning. *Sour cream butter*, the most common butter, is made from cream that has been allowed to sour naturally. *Sweet* or *unsalted butter* is made with sweet or sour cream with no salt added. *Salted butter* has salt added as a preservative.

Margarine Margarine consists of vegetable and/or animal oils and fats blended with cultured or sweet fat-free milk and partially crystallized. It is a poor cooking fat, since it smokes at low temperatures.

Oils Oils are derived from plants, and unlike fats are liquid at room temperature. The most popular are olive, cottonseed, corn, peanut, soybean and walnut.

Olive oil is probably the oldest vegetable oil used as food. The best oil is produced immediately when the olives are crushed without the pits, after ten days of drying. The first cold pressing will produce extra-virgin oil and is the highest in quality. It has a distinctive flavor with a greenish or golden color, depending on whether it has been filtered (the color is not an indication of quality). It will keep fresh the longest. Virgin oil is second quality and not necessarily from the first pressing or extracted by the cold mechanical method. Other olive oils may be extracted by boiling or by the use of solvent and are treated with sulfate of carbon. A good olive oil is never cheap! Each brand will have a distinctive flavor due to the nature of the oil, type of olive and method of extraction.

Cottonseed oil has a high smoking temperature and should be amber in color (never brown). It is practically odorless.

Corn oil also has a high smoking temperature; it is suitable for cooking and salads. It should have a light golden color and a distinctive cornmeal taste when fresh. However, it does develop a stronger flavor at high temperatures.

Peanut or **groundnut oil** has a very high smoking temperature of 450°F/230°C. It is golden in color but is often bleached to produce a colorless oil. It has no flavor and little odor.

Soybean oil is used in the production of compounded fat or margarine. It develops an unpleasant odor and taste when heated, unless it has been stabilized. It is very yellow in color and is inexpensive.

Walnut oil is rarely used in cooking because of its strong flavor, high price and poor shelf life. When fresh, it is particularly good in salads.

Fortified wine A wine to which grape spirits have been added—usually for the purpose of stopping the fermentation, as in port and sherry. Fortified wines generally have an alcoholic content of 15 to 20 percent alcohol by volume.

Frying:

Pan frying is a dry method of cooking reserved for thin cuts or small items. The amount of fat or oil used is very small—it prevents the food from sticking to the pan and brings the food's uneven surface into a uniform contact with the source of heat. It also develops the flavor by caramelizing and browning the surface of the food, and by giving the food some of the flavor of the oil or fat. The temperature used in pan-frying is relatively high to seal in the moisture and natural flavor.

Deep-frying is a dry method of cooking in which the food is completely immersed in oil. The food colors and cooks quickly at a high temperature. The food should be coated with a batter or breading to minimize the absorption of fat and seal in moisture. Technically, the food cooks in its own steam; properly deep-fried food should never be greasy or oily!

Garlic Garlic is a relative of the onion family and like its cousins (leeks, shallots, chives) it releases a pungent taste and smell when the cells are disturbed by being cut or bruised. To obtain a strong garlic flavor, the cloves are pasted with a little salt, which facilitates the grinding process and releases the maximum flavor by disturbing all the cells. If the garlic is sliced, fewer cells are opened and the flavor is not as strong. If the garlic is cooked whole in the skin, the strong garlic compounds are converted to a very complex molecule that is sixty times sweeter than a molecule of sucrose or table sugar!

Glycerin An alcohol formed from the conversion of grape sugar, which gives the wine roundness. It shows as a slow-moving colorless liquid on the side of the glass.

Grilling/broiling/griddling A dry method of cooking with intense heat, where oil is used just to prevent sticking. In grilling, the source of heat comes from under the rack. In broiling the heat comes from above. Griddling is the same as grilling, except the food is cooked on a flat metal surface instead of an open grill.

Hock The British term for the white wines of the Rhine Valley.

Hybrids Grape varieties that are crossings between two other varieties to produce a higher-yielding, disease-resistant and winter-hardy strain. Müller-Thurgau, for instance, is the offspring of Riesling and Sylvaner. Maréchal Foch is a cross between Pinot Noir and Gamay.

Julienne A finely shredded cut used mainly for garnish.

Kabinett A German wine term originally meaning a reserve wine. Now a designation of grape sugar. Dry but has more body than a QbA wine.

Lees The by-product of fermentation—grape particles, tartrates, tannins and dead yeast cells which form a sediment left at the bottom of a wine cask.

Legs The tears that form on the side of the glass after the wine has been swirled. The thickness and speed of falling denote the amount of glycerin, alcohols and all sugars in a wine. The sweeter the wine, the more full and slow are its legs.

Length A measure of time rather than distance—how long the aftertaste of a wine remains in the mouth.

Maderized A tasting term referring mostly to white and rosé wines that have altered their character through a combination of oxidation and overly warm storage. The wines take on a brownish hue and taste of Madeira.

Mirror That portion of the cork in contact with the wine when the bottle is laid down.

Mousse The bubbling activity in sparkling wines. The best mousse is a persistent stream of hundreds of tiny bubbles, evident in good Champagne.

Must Unfermented freshly pressed juice.

Organoleptic evaluation A fancy name for the pleasurable pursuit of wine tasting. Judging the color, bouquet, taste and overall quality of a wine.

Oxidized A prematurely aged wine that has been exposed to air. An oxidized red wine will taste flat and pruny. Oxidized white wines will take on a metallic quality and a darker color than a fresh wine of the same vintage, and will taste like dry sherry.

Pasteurization A method of killing the harmful bacteria in wine by heating it to between 130° and 180°F (54° to 82°C). Usually only performed on wines for immediate consumption to give them better shelf life. A pasteurized wine does not improve with aging.

Pâté/terrine A *terrine* is an earthenware dish in which a meat or fish mixture is cooked. Technically, a terrine is never unmolded but is served cold from the dish in which it was cooked. A *pâté* is a mixture baked in a molded dough and served unmolded, hot or cold. The name pâté may also refer to an unmolded filling encased in bacon strips or pork fat, though technically this is an unmolded terrine. A *galantine* is a poached pâté that uses the skin of the animal as casing and is pressed in a symmetrical shape.

Petillant The French term for a wine that prickles on the tongue. The Italian equivalent is *frizzante*; the German, *spritzig*.

Poaching To cook in a liquid at or just below the boiling point.

Phylloxera A plant louse that destroys vines. Introduced to Europe from the eastern United States in the 1860s, it laid to waste the vineyards over the next three decades. Now virtually all European vines are grafted onto the phylloxera-resistant North American root stock.

Punt The conical indentation in the bottom of Champagne bottles and some older French wine bottles, to catch the sediment and reinforce the glass.

Residual sugar The amount of grape sugar left in a wine when it is fully fermented or when the winemaker halts fermentation. Generally measured in grams per litre. Dry wines average under 5 grams per lite.

Sauté To cook quickly over brisk heat with a small amount of fat, shaking the pan continuously to prevent sticking and color evenly. Literally, to jump.

Sediment Solid matter composed of tannins, precipitated in a wine aging in the bottle, mainly red.

Spätlese A German wine term referring to late-picked grapes, generally gathered two weeks or more after the harvest begins.

Sommelier Wine waiter in charge of stocking and serving wines in a restaurant.

Spice bag A mixture of spices placed in cheesecloth and tied with string. Used as a flavoring agent.

Stock Flavored liquid used as a base to make soups and sauces.

Sugar A water-soluble crystal that varies in sweetness according to the plant or substance from which it was extracted—sucrose (cane or beet sugar), levulose (fruit sugar), maltose (malt sugar) or lactose (milk sugar).

> **Powdered, icing** or **confectioner's sugars** are sugars ground to a very fine powder and are used in uncooked foods where a non-grainy texture is desired, such as frostings. They absorb moisture rapidly and should be stored in an airtight container. Approximately 3 percent cornstarch is added to prevent lumping, but the sugar should be sifted before using.
>
> **Granulated sugars** consist of sugar (sucrose) crystals and can be ultra-fine (used for dusting or coating), very fine (used for meringues, gelatins, etc.), fine (all-purpose sugar used in cakes, etc.), medium-coarse (used for syrups and decorating) and coarse (used mainly in decorating and seldom as a sweetener).
>
> **Yellow or brown sugar** is unrefined cane sugar (sucrose) that contains a small amount of molasses. It has a distinctive flavor, is sometimes referred to as "soft" sugar and melts at a low temperature. It should be stored in a cool place in an airtight container (a slice of apple or bread placed in the container may prevent drying and hardening).
>
> **Molasses** is the liquid left after the sugar crystals have been removed.
>
> **Fruit sugar** (also called breakfast sugar) is extracted from fruits such as grapes, dates, figs, etc. It is very fine, has a low melting point and dissolves easily in liquid, but is expensive due to the cost of extraction and refinement.

Tartrates Known as "wine diamonds," potassium bitartrate crystals can form in white wine that has been overchilled. These crystals are harmless and do not affect the taste of the wine.

Tastevin The flat silver cup that looks like a tiny ashtray, used in Burgundy to sample wine in the cellars. Also a decoration for wine waiters (who invariably don't know how to use them!)

Trockenbeerenauslese A German term referring to the sweetest of wines made from individually selected grapes affected by **Botrytis cinerea** (see above), which are left to dry on the vine.

Vin de paille Literally "straw wine." Grapes in the Jura region are left to dry on straw mats to concentrate their sugars before pressing.

Vin jaune A late-picked wine made in the Jura region of France, which is allowed to develop floor, like sherry, which it resembles on the nose.

Vinifera The thirty or so vines such as Cabernet Sauvignon, Pinot Noir, Chardonnay, Riesling, Gwewürztraminer, etc., responsible for the world's great wines.

Yeast The catalyst that turns grape juice into wine. Yeast attacks the grape sugars and converts them to alcohol and carbon dioxide. Grapes have a natural yeast on the bloom of their skins, but most winemakers prefer to control the fermentation by injecting their own yeast culture into the must.

Index of Recipes